Contents

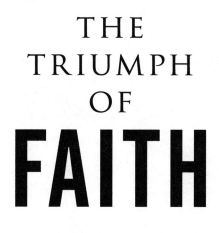

THE
TRIUMPH
OF
FAITH

Introduction

CONFOUNDING THE
SECULARIZATION FAITHFUL

The world is more religious than it has ever been. Around the globe, four out of every five people claim to belong to an organized faith, and many of the rest say they attend worship services. In Latin America, Pentecostal Protestant churches have converted tens of millions, and Catholics are going to Mass in unprecedented numbers. There are more churchgoing Christians in Sub-Saharan Africa than anywhere else on earth, and China may soon become home of the most Christians. Meanwhile, although not growing as rapidly as Christianity, Islam enjoys far higher levels of member commitment than it has for many centuries, and the same is true for Hinduism. In fact, of all the great world religions, only Buddhism may not be growing.

Furthermore, in every nook and cranny left by organized faiths, all manner of unconventional and unchurched supernaturalisms are booming: there are more occult healers than medical doctors in Russia; 38 percent of the French believe in astrology; 35 percent of the Swiss agree that "some fortune tellers really can foresee the future"; and nearly everyone in Japan is careful to have a new car blessed by a Shinto priest.[1]

Despite all this, the media regularly report new "proofs" of the rapid decline of religion in America and abroad. A high-profile example came as I was writing this book. In May 2015 the Pew Research Center

1

released its latest Religious Landscape Survey. Commenting on the findings, Pew's director of religion, Alan Cooperman, declared, "The country is becoming less religious as a whole, and it's happening across the board."[2] Fewer Americans identified as Christian, Pew said, and the percentage of people who gave their religious affiliation as "none" had increased substantially in recent years. The media rushed to report the story. The Reuters headline on May 12 was typical: "Poll Shows Those in U.S. Drifting Away from Religion."

But, despite these confident proclamations about the decline of religion, Pew's findings were certainly misleading and probably wrong. Consider only one fact: the overwhelming majority of Americans who say they have no religious affiliation pray and believe in angels![3] How irreligious is that? As for the decline of religion elsewhere in the world, this, too, is merely wishful thinking and entirely at odds with reliable data. And it is data that make this book different.

Every important claim that I make is based on carefully reported solid evidence. For example, the enormous increase in the number of Muslims making a pilgrimage to Mecca is verified by the annual figures published by the Saudi Arabian immigration office. Or the number of Christians in Singapore is based on official census data. I often make use of reliable survey data, too. The empirical backbone of the whole book is provided by the truly remarkable Gallup World Polls, which began in 2005 and consist of annual, national surveys conducted in 163 nations that by now add up to more than a million interviews. Never before has a scholar had access to such a body of data, and I am very grateful to the Gallup Organization for its generosity.

And what do the data tell us? Quite simply, that a massive religious awakening is taking place around the world. Unfortunately, I do not expect even these solid facts to have any impact on the group of Western intellectuals who proclaim the inevitability of a worldwide triumph of *secularization*—the demise of beliefs in the supernatural, these being replaced by entirely material or secular beliefs. For them, secularization is an unshakable matter of faith.

THE SECULARIZATION FAITHFUL

A bedrock of faith in the eventual triumph of secularization is the lack of church attendance in modern Europe. It is assumed that this represents a huge decline from earlier times and reflects the rejection of religious beliefs. False! As chapter 2 will demonstrate, there has been no decline because hardly any Europeans attended church in the Middle Ages, and medieval Christian theologians condemned the popular religion of the day as mere superstition and magic, or even as witchcraft. Still, no one would suggest that medieval Europe was highly secularized. Rather, because nearly everyone in medieval Europe believed in the ubiquity of supernatural forces and appealed to them for benefits, it is rightly regarded as an Age of Faith. There may have been a shortage of good Catholics, but there were very few atheists—then or now.

Although popular books by the likes of Richard Dawkins, Sam Harris, Daniel Dennett, and Christopher Hitchens have led commentators to proclaim the "New Atheism," there is nothing new about atheism. Given that the distinguished anthropologist Clifford Geertz observed atheists in preliterate, "primitive" societies, it seems likely that there were atheists even among the Neanderthal.[4] But even today atheists make up only tiny percentages of populations in most of the world: usually fewer than 5 percent of people report being atheists.

Faith in secularization began during the "Enlightenment," that falsely celebrated time when Voltaire and his friends claimed that they had brought Europe out of the "Dark Ages" and were about to liberate humanity from the grip of religion. Of course, these *philosophes* played no role in the recent scientific achievements they cited as proof for their pretensions, and they ignored the fact that many prominent figures in this glorious scientific era were members of the clergy and most others were unusually devout. Isaac Newton wrote far more theology than he did physics, and Johannes Kepler spent a good deal of his time working out the date of the Creation, finally settling for 3992 BC.[5] As for the age the *philosophes* condemned as dark, it has long since been revealed as an era of great technical and cultural achievements—even the encyclopedias now admit that the "Dark Ages" never existed. Still, none of these revelations has discredited the *philosophes'* equally silly predictions that religion was in its last days.

True to form, it was an Anglican clergyman who first proposed that religion was going to disappear. Writing in about 1710, Thomas Woolston predicted that all traces of religion would be gone from Europe by 1900.[6] Many of Woolston's contemporaries thought he must be mad, and after he published denials of miracles and the resurrection of Christ, they had him shut away.

Fifty years later, Frederick the Great concluded that Woolston was not mad, only too pessimistic. Writing to his friend Voltaire, Frederick noted that "the Englishman Woolston...could not calculate what has happened quite recently." He concluded that religion "is crumbling of itself, and its fall will be the more rapid."[7] In response, Voltaire proposed that religion would be gone within the next fifty years—by about 1810.

Although religion was still vigorous in his day, Thomas Jefferson, who rejected the Christian doctrine of the Trinity (God as Father, Son, and Holy Spirit), predicted in 1822 that "there is not a young man now living in the United States who will not die a Unitarian."[8] Although Unitarians soon took control of the Harvard Divinity School, they remained as scarce as ever, while the Methodists (a very conservative group in those days) and Baptists continued their spectacular rate of growth.[9] Now, nearly two centuries after Jefferson wrote, and subsequent to a merger with the Universalists, Unitarians number about 160,000. In 2014 they put their Boston headquarters on the market because they were short of funds.[10]

Following Jefferson, the secularization faithful have been no less confident, but they have become reluctant to set specific dates. Writing in the 1840s, Auguste Comte announced that the "theological stage" of social evolution was ending and the "positive stage" was dawning, wherein the new science he was pioneering, sociology, would replace religion as the basis for moral judgments. But he didn't say just when. Not long after that, Friedrich Engels gloated that the socialist revolution would cause religion to evaporate. When? Soon. Then, in the 1878 Hibbert Lectures, the Oxford orientalist Max Müller complained, "Every day, every week, every month, every quarter, the most widely read journals seem just now to vie with each other in telling us that the time for religion is past, that faith is an illusion or an infantile disease, that the gods have been found out and exploded."[11]

At the start of the twentieth century, religion seemed as robust as ever, but self-styled unbelievers held firm to the "faith" of secularization. The English anthropologist A. E. Crawley explained, "The opinion is everywhere gaining ground that religion is a mere survival from a primitive...age, and its extinction is only a matter of time."[12] His views were ratified by the famous German sociologist Max Weber, who acknowledged that modernization was rapidly causing the "disenchantment" of the world, and then by Sigmund Freud, who assured his disciples that this greatest of all neurotic illusions would soon be cured by psychoanalysis.

By the end of World War II, faith in secularization had become nearly universal among social scientists. Writing from Columbia University in 1959, C. Wright Mills (taking time off from defending the Soviet Union) expressed the common view: "Once the world was filled with the sacred—in thought, practice, and institutional form. After the Reformation and the Renaissance, the forces of modernization swept across the globe and secularization, a corollary historical process, loosened the dominance of the sacred. In due course, the sacred shall disappear altogether except, possibly, in the private realm."[13] Seven years later, the distinguished anthropologist Anthony F. C. Wallace explained to tens of thousands of undergraduate students assigned his introductory textbook that "the evolutionary future of religion is extinction.... Belief in supernatural powers is doomed to die out all over the world as a result of the increasing adequacy and diffusion of scientific knowledge.... The process is inevitable."[14]

No one described the demise of religion more colorfully than did Peter Berger, the Boston University sociologist, who told the *New York Times* in 1968 that by "the 21st century, religious believers are likely to be found only in small sects, huddled together to resist a worldwide secular culture.... The predicament of the believer is increasingly like that of a Tibetan astrologer on a prolonged visit to an American university."[15] In light of the subsequent lionization of the Dalai Lama by the American media and his warm welcome on various campuses, Berger's simile now admits of a rather different interpretation. In any event, when his prediction had only three years left to run, Berger gracefully recanted his belief in secularization.[16]

The growing evidence that religion not only wasn't fading away but actually was growing stronger may have led Berger to recant, but it did not faze most of the secularization faithful. In response to my objections to the secularization thesis, Oxford's Bryan Wilson smugly claimed that nearly all scholars "take secularization for granted" and regard those still interested in the subject with "some amusement."[17] Steve Bruce at the University of Aberdeen has pounded out books ridiculing every-one who fails to agree with him that religion has nearly disappeared already.[18] Pippa Norris and Ronald Inglehart won a prize for a book that appeared to demonstrate statistically that "the publics of virtually all advanced industrial societies have been moving toward more secu-lar orientations."[19] Norris and Inglehart are reputable scholars, but their analysis was faulty, as will be demonstrated in chapter 2.

In addition, Norris and Inglehart made a mistake that is typical of the secularization faithful, which is to limit the focus to major, well-organized faiths such as Christianity and Hinduism. Thus, five people who have ceased attending church and say they no longer believe in Jesus are counted in favor of the demise of faith, despite the fact that they now are devoted spiritualists. Let me demonstrate.

On the basis of its lack of church attendance, most sociologists of religion classify Iceland as among the most secularized nations. But to do so, they must ignore the fact that 34 percent of Icelanders believe in reincarnation and another 16 percent aren't sure about it.[20] Moreover, a national survey found that 55 percent of Icelanders believe in the exis-tence of *huldufolk*, or hidden people, such as elves, trolls, gnomes, and fairies.[21] Consequently, planned highways are sometimes rerouted so as not to disturb various hills and large rocks wherein *huldufolk* may dwell, and Icelanders planning to build a new house often hire "elf spotters" to ensure that their site does not encroach on *huldufolk* settlements.[22] In addition, half of Icelanders have visited a fortune teller,[23] and spiri-tualism is very widely practiced; it is popular even among intellectuals and academics.[24] According to a Reuters dispatch (February 2, 2015), a rapidly growing group of Icelandic neopagans broke ground for a temple dedicated to worship of the old Norse gods. And only 3.5 percent of Icelanders claim to be atheists, as chapter 1 will show. But they don't go to church, so Iceland must be a secularized nation.

Of course, some will claim that Iceland is truly secularized because much of what remains is mere superstition, unworthy of the name *religion*, as only organized faiths with elaborate theologies qualify as religions. That certainly would fit the Chinese view of such things. Seventy-seven percent of people in China claim to have no religion. But nearly all of these same "irreligious" Chinese frequently flock to folk temples, where they offer prayers and gifts to various gods in pursuit of particular requests.[25] If this is not religion, then most of the world has always been irreligious and secularity is the normal state of affairs. Since that is obviously nonsense, what is needed here is first to distinguish between religion and mere supernaturalism. It also will be useful to distinguish between churched and unchurched religions and supernaturalisms.

Supernatural refers to *forces or entities beyond or outside nature and having the capacity to suspend, alter, or ignore physical forces.*[26] Astrology, spiritualism, and fortune telling are common forms of supernaturalism. *Religion* is a form of supernaturalism that postulates the existence of *gods*, conceived of as *supernatural beings having consciousness and desires.*

Churched religions consist of relatively stable, organized congregations of lay members who acknowledge a specific religious *creed*. A creed is *a set of beliefs to which all members of a religious group are expected to assent*, and those who participate in churched religions are expected to do so *regularly and exclusively*. The major world faiths all sustain churched religions, although many forms of Buddhism are unchurched. Some forms of pure supernaturalism also sustain churches—for example, many groups devoted to spiritualism, to contact with the dead, though they do not postulate the existence of a god or gods.

Both *unchurched religions* and *unchurched supernaturalism* lack organized congregations and usually lack a creed. Although in many instances people involved in unchurched religions may regularly gather to worship in a sacred building such as a temple, they are patrons, not members, and it is not unusual for them to patronize a number of different temples, worshipping many different gods. More often, followers of an unchurched religion rarely or never gather but instead pursue their faith in an entirely personal way (as did medieval villagers) or do so as "spiritual consumers" via the mass media. Unchurched religious "suppliers" do sustain belief systems, but these are not creeds, because little or no effort is made to limit participants to those who assent to the beliefs. Rather, participants typically hold a self-selected jumble of belief systems.

The same points apply to unchurched spiritualisms, which, significantly, also lack gods. The following quotations come from an Internet "New Age" dating site. Each registrant was asked to include her or his "spiritual interests."

> Female, 42: "Self-awareness, Astrology, Tarot, UFOs, Reiki, Channeling, Meditation."
> Male 47: "health food, yoga, astrology, Ascended Masters, meditation."
> Female, 30: "Astrology, past lives, crystals, tarot, dreams, angels, Egyptology, spirit guides, fairies, mermaids."[27]

Whatever else one may say about such individuals, they cannot be called unbelievers, and the secularization faithful can take no comfort in the remarkable strength of unchurched religions in Asia or of unchurched supernaturalism in Europe (see chapter 2).

In addition, for all their constant chatter, the secularization faithful have been amazingly silent about the most powerful test ever made of their thesis that modernity and science render religion implausible. For generations, the Soviet Union closed churches and persecuted believers, and it mandated that all students at all levels of education receive classes every year in "scientific atheism."[28] As my late friend Andrew Greeley explained, the Soviet government "thought of itself as pushing forward the inevitable process of secularization in which religion would disappear from the face of the earth—a process which, in perhaps milder form, is an article of faith for many dogmatic social scientists."[29] This Soviet effort constituted a remarkable natural experiment. And what was the result? A national survey conducted in 1990, as the Soviet Union was collapsing, found that more than sixty years of this intense instruction had resulted in 6.6 percent of Russians saying they were atheists—only slightly more than in the United States![30]

EXPLODING THE CONVENTIONAL WISDOM

Despite ample evidence of the persistence of religious faith in our modern, scientific world, Peter Berger is the only prominent member of the secularization faithful to have recanted. As he put it, "I think what I and most other sociologists of religion wrote in the 1960s about secularization was a mistake.... Most of the world today is certainly not secular. It's very religious."[31]

And that is precisely what this book is about. The world is not merely as religious as it used to be. In important ways, it is much *more* intensely religious than ever before; indeed, it is far more churched. The chapters that follow present for the first time reliable statistics on the global religious awakening, giving close attention to major geographical regions. Although the details often differ from place to place, the story remains much the same: the temples, mosques, pagodas, chapels, and churches are full, and even most people who do not attend say they are religious.

What effect is this religious awakening having? The bright side is quite obvious and will be examined at length in the concluding chapter. But along the way I will not shrink from reporting on the dark side—on how religious enthusiasm too often generates religious hatred and terrorism. Indeed, in combination with globalization, the worldwide intensification of religiousness is causing what Samuel Huntington called the "Clash of Civilizations."[32]

But above all this book exposes the conventional wisdom about secularization as unfounded nonsense. The secularization faithful applaud whatever is interpreted as a sign of religious decline, for it seems to confirm their belief that faith is doomed by modernity. Religious believers, meanwhile, lament these same signs. The crucial point is that *both sides* accept the premise that the world is becoming more secular.

Well, they are both wrong. In these pages I will show you why.

1

A GLOBAL PORTRAIT OF FAITH

We live in a very religious world. Surveys of more than a million people living in 163 nations show that:

- 81 percent claim to belong to an organized religious faith, and many of the rest report attending worship services or taking part in other religious activities.
- 74 percent say that religion is an important part of their daily lives.
- 50 percent report that they have attended a place of worship or religious service in the past seven days.
- 56 percent believe that "God is directly involved in things that happen in the world."
- In very few nations do as many as 5 percent claim to be atheists, and only in Vietnam, China, and South Korea do atheists exceed 20 percent.

These statistics alone are enough to upend the common narrative that faith is on the wane. But the data go far deeper than that, and they allow us to examine religion around the world from many different angles. These statistics, previously unavailable, paint a fascinating portrait of worldwide faith. The deeper one digs into the data, the clearer it becomes: the popular notion of an increasingly secularizing world is not merely wrong but actually the *opposite* of what has been taking place.

COUNTING WORLD RELIGIONS

Until now, worldwide religious statistics have been based on substantial guesswork.[1] Many nations do not have reliable counts of their religious makeup, and therefore all previously available statistics on worldwide religious affiliation have been rough estimates, which accounts for the huge differences among them. Thus, the *CIA World Factbook* reports that there are 2.1 billion Christians on earth, whereas the *World Christian Database* places the Christian total at 3.2 billion.

Far more reliable statistics on religious affiliation now can be calculated based on data from the Gallup Organization's remarkable World Poll. In 2005 Gallup began conducting annual national surveys in 119 nations; now 163 nations are included, making up about 97 percent of the world's population. In each nation, a sample of 1,000 respondents or larger is drawn, and weights are assigned so the data properly reflect the population in terms of gender, age, education, household size, and socioeconomic status. The statistics reported in this chapter are based on merging the samples for all years, which yields very large numbers of cases, thus greatly increasing the accuracy of results—the average number of cases for all 163 nations now equals 7,567.

There are, however, several unavoidable shortcomings even to these statistics. In many nations, respondents were given the choice of affirming that they were Roman Catholics, Protestants, or Orthodox Christians. But in other nations it was necessary to settle for "Christian," without further specification. Hence, to create worldwide statistics, even those who reported being Protestant, Catholic, or Orthodox must be placed in the undifferentiated category "Christian." The same applies to Muslim respondents. For many nations there is no breakdown for Sunnis and Shi'a, and hence everyone is simply identified as a "Muslim."

A second deficiency is that even though by now there are about a million respondents to the World Polls, there still are too few cases to allow reliable statistics to be computed for some smaller religions, including Shinto, Zoroastrianism, Taoism, and Confucianism. This made it necessary to combine these, and all other small religions, into a hodgepodge category called "Other." (Jews could be treated separately because they are so highly concentrated in Israel and the United States that an accurate estimate is possible.) In the next several years, as the size of the world sample increases, it will be possible to break down the "Other" category.

In addition, some people said that they had no religion, or that they were secular, or atheists, or agnostics. All these respondents were collapsed into the category "Secular." This category is quite falsely inflated, however: millions of these "secular" people said they had attended religious services in the past week!

A final difficulty arises because the Chinese government does not allow Gallup, or any other foreign polling agency, to ask questions about religious membership. Consequently, the statistics for China are based on a national sample of 7,021 respondents interviewed in their homes in 2007 by Horizon Ltd., China's largest and most respected polling firm. The data were purchased from Horizon by the Institute for Studies of Religion at Baylor (where I serve as codirector) with a grant from the John Templeton Foundation.

As we will see in chapter 7, the Chinese data needed to be corrected because of a severe bias introduced by the greater unwillingness of Chinese Christians to take part in a survey and an additional tendency for those who did take part to deny that they were Christians. Even with this correction, adding the Chinese data results in a serious distortion because 75 percent of Chinese claimed to have no religion and must, therefore, be placed in the "Secular" category. But the fact is that most of them frequently visit temples where they pray to various statues of gods and offer them gifts of food, and 72 percent of those who said they had no religion said they had engaged in ancestor worship during the past year. This muddle stems from the fact that the Chinese have a rather narrow definition of religion—that it only involves participation in an *organized religious body*. Keep in mind that adding the Chinese doubled the size of the "Secular" category.

NOMINAL MEMBERS

Table 1–1 shows the membership of the major religions. Clearly, the CIA estimate is very close, and the Christian Database estimate is far too high. Around the world, a total of 2.2 billion people (33 percent) give their religion as Christian, far outnumbering Muslims, who total 1.5 billion (22 percent). Hindus are the third-largest religious group, with 1 billion affiliates (16 percent), followed by Buddhists with 500 million (8 percent). Jews make up only 13 million (less than 0.2 percent), and the Other faiths number 127 million (2 percent). Secularists make up 1.3 billion (19 percent).

Table 1–1: Worldwide Nominal Religious Affiliations

	Number	Percentage
Christians	2,243,570,000	33
Muslims	1,480,575,000	22
Hindus	1,046,389,000	16
Buddhists	507,132,000	8
Jews	13,106,000	0.2
Others	127,351,000	2
Secular	1,278,657,000	19
Total	6,696,780,000	100.2*

Total percentage more than 100 due to rounding error

Of course, some who claim a religious label are inactive. For example, some European "Christians" have never been inside a church and many others have only been there once, when they were baptized as infants, and some who say they are Muslims never visit a mosque. As will be seen, inactivity does not necessarily equate with irreligiousness. Still, it is quite enlightening to examine the worldwide distribution of just active members of the various faiths—reported here for the first time. As we will explore in this book, active membership provides a more meaningful view of world religions than that based on nominal members.

ACTIVE MEMBERS

The only available measure of active membership is stringent—"Have you attended a place of worship or religious service within the past 7 days?" Table 1–2 is limited to those who attended in the past week. Comparable data on attendance are not available for China, so the table eliminates Chinese Christians; this has only a minor effect on Christians but greatly reduces the number of Buddhists.

Table 1–2: Worldwide Active Religious Affiliations (China excluded)

	Number	Percentage
Christians	1,166,751,000	39
Muslims	941,394,000	31
Hindus	686,351,000	23
Buddhists	143,042,000	5
Jews	3,153,000	<0.1
Others	63,799,000	2
Secular	29,188,000	1
Total	3,033,678,000	101*

Total percentage more than 100 due to rounding error

Contrary to stereotypes of Muslims as ardent worshippers, their numbers have been reduced almost as greatly as those for Christians when the data are limited to weekly attenders. The table also reveals that more than 29 million of those classified as Secular have attended a religious service in the past seven days!

Overall, nothing much changes when only active members are examined: Christianity is still by far the largest religion (39 percent), followed by Islam (31 percent).

But as we will see, to gain a full understanding of religion in the world today, we must examine active membership even more closely than nominal membership.

REGIONALISM

Christianity is not only the largest religion in the world; it also is the least regionalized, as can be seen in Table 1–3. There are only trivial numbers of Muslims in the Western Hemisphere and in East Asia, but there is no region without significant numbers of Christians. Even in the Arab region of the Middle East and North Africa, Christians account for 2 percent of the population—although this is probably only half as many as lived there a decade ago.[2]

Table 1–3: Nominal Religious Affiliations by Regions

	Christians	Muslims	Hindus	Buddhists	Jews	Other	Secular
North America	81%	*	*	*	2%	6%	10%
Latin America	93%	*	*	*	*	2%	4%
Europe	82%	5%	*	*	*	1%	12%
Middle East and North Africa	2%	96%	*	*	1%	*	*
Sub-Saharan Africa	66%	30%	*	*	*	3%	1%
South Central Asia	9%	31%	57%	2%	*	2%	1%
Southeast Asia	21%	40%	1%	30%	*	2%	6%
East Asia	6%	*	*	20%	*	2%	72%
Oceania	71%	2%	1%	1%	*	2%	21%

Less than 0.5 percent

CHRISTIAN REGIONALISM

A more interesting way to examine Christian regionalism can be seen in Table 1–4, which underscores how widely distributed Christianity is, and shows how the picture changes when active membership is considered.

Christians are concentrated in Latin America (23 percent), Sub-Saharan Africa (23 percent), and Europe (22 percent). But when the statistics are based on weekly church attenders, Europe (16 percent) falls to a distant third and Sub-Saharan Africa rises to the top (33 percent), with Latin America second (25 percent). Despite the prominence of African bishops in the squabbles going on within the Anglican Communion, few know how highly Christianized is Africa, south of the Sahara. This is further disguised by the common tendency to treat Africa as a whole rather than to divide it into the overwhelmingly Arab North and the black South. When treated as a united continent, Africa has a Muslim majority. But that is very misleading, since Christians make up 66 percent of Sub-Saharan Africans, compared with 30 percent who are Muslims. We shall examine Sub-Saharan Christianity at length in chapter 5.

Table 1–4: The Regional Distribution of Christians

	Nominal	Active
North America	13%	12%
Latin America	25%	25%
Europe	23%	16%
Middle East and North Africa	*	*
Sub-Saharan Africa	24%	33%
South Central Asia	7%	4%
Southeast Asia	6%	7%
East Asia	1%	2%
Oceania	1%	*
Total	100%	99%**

Less than 0.5 percent
*** Total percentage less than 100 due to rounding error*

ISLAMIC REGIONALISM

Muslims are bitterly opposed to Christian growth in Sub-Saharan Africa, and where Muslim and Christian areas abut, as in Nigeria, anti-Christian terrorism is rife. Thus, it may be fortunate that Muslims are more geographically concentrated than are Christians, as Table 1–5 shows.

Interestingly enough, the Arab nations of the Middle East and North Africa do not sustain the largest share of the Muslim population.

More than a third of the world's Muslims live in the nations of South Central Asia, among them Afghanistan, Pakistan, Bangladesh, and India (more than 150 million Muslims live in India). The substantial proportion of Muslims living in Southeast Asia mainly reflects that Indonesia is the largest Islamic nation in the world. There are trivial numbers of Muslims in the Western Hemisphere, and not many in Europe, despite the conflicts that have arisen there from recent Muslim immigration.

Table 1–5: The Regional Distribution of Muslims

	Nominal	Active
North America	*	*
Latin America	*	*
Europe	2%	1%
Middle East and North Africa	28%	24%
Sub-Saharan Africa	16%	19%
South Central Asia	38%	36%
Southeast Asia	16%	20%
East Asia	*	*
Oceania	*	*
Total	100%	100%

Less than 0.5 percent

GROWTH

Beginning in the late twentieth century, many experts predicted that Islam would soon pass Christianity to become the largest religious group in the world.[3] These projections were based on the fact that Muslims had much higher fertility rates than did Christians, and this was not expected to change. But then Muslim fertility began to decline rapidly. It already is well below replacement levels in Iran, Syria, and Jordan, and the fertility rate for the world's Muslim population in general is expected to fall to replacement level or below within the next several years.[4] Yet "this sea change remains curiously unrecognized," as the scholars Nicholas Eberstadt and Apoorva Shah point out in their important analysis of the Muslim world's fertility decline.[5] As recently as April 2015, the Pew Research Center declared that Muslims will soon overtake Christians by way of superior fertility.[6] They won't.

Moreover, Islam generates very little growth through conversions, while Christianity enjoys a substantial conversion rate, especially in nations located in what my colleague Philip Jenkins describes as the "global south"—Asia, Sub-Saharan Africa, and Latin America.[7] And these conversions do not include the millions of converts being gained in China. Thus, current growth trends project an increasingly Christian world.

RELIGIOUSNESS

Thus far, the Gallup World Poll has asked only three questions about religiousness in addition to one's denominational preference. One question, as noted, asks about religious attendance in the past seven days; the second asks, "Is religion an important part of your daily life?"; and the third asks, "Do you believe God is directly involved in things that happen in the world, or not?"

I would much prefer that Gallup had asked the standard religious attendance item, which offers six answer categories ranging from "more than once a week" to "never." When we compare Gallup's results with standard survey results in nations where both are available, it becomes clear that the Gallup respondents didn't stick to the seven-day limit. Instead, it appears that respondents sensibly interpreted the "past seven days" question to really be asking whether they were regular attenders; they said yes if they did go regularly, even if they hadn't actually attended that particular week. Of course, this is merely a matter of how best to interpret these responses and does not in any way reduce the accuracy of nation-to-nation comparisons. Indeed, because the Gallup data are based on such large numbers of cases, they are more reliable than other international attendance figures, such as those reported by the World

Values Surveys or the International Social Survey Program, because they are subject to far less random variation.

Table 1–6 (beginning on the next page) shows worldwide response to the questions on attendance and on the importance placed on religion in one's daily life.

Despite constant references to the high levels of religiousness in the United States, that is true only by comparison with most European nations and the five nations classified as "Other." Church attendance is far higher in many Latin American nations than in the United States, and much higher in most Muslim and Sub-Saharan nations.

Few will be surprised at the very high levels of religiousness in the Islamic nations. But many will find it surprising that people in Sub-Saharan Africa, most of them Christians, attend worship services even more often than do Muslims, and are equally likely to say that religion is important in their daily lives. Most Latin American nations also have high rates of church attendance, the only marked exceptions being Uruguay, which is, in many ways, more of a European than a Latin American nation in that most of its population is of direct European descent, and Cuba, where religion has long been persecuted, and where the Communist state was officially atheistic until 1992 and remains officially secular today. Within Islam, the "stans" are noticeably less religious (with the exception of Pakistan). This is probably due to the fact that in Azerbaijan, Kazakhstan, Kyrgyzstan, Tajikistan, Turkmenistan, and Uzbekistan, the majority of the population consists of formerly nomadic, Turkic peoples.

Although it is certainly no surprise, perhaps the major feature of Table 1–6 is the low level of religiousness in Europe, especially in western Europe. Religiousness is especially low in Scandinavian nations, where Lutheran state churches prevail. Notice, too, a clear Catholic effect in western Europe. Roman Catholics make up 70 percent or more of the populations of Austria, Belgium, France, Ireland, Italy, Malta, Portugal, and Spain. With the exception of France, these nations display substantially higher levels of religiousness than do the other western European nations. Chapter 2 will be devoted to exploring religion in Europe.

Table 1–6: Worldwide Religiousness

	Percentage Who Attended in Past Week	Percentage Who Say Religion Important in My Daily Life
United States	46	66
Western Europe		
Austria	35	51
Belgium	23	37
Cyprus	48	75
Denmark	16	18
Finland	13	29
France	19	27
Germany	30	40
Great Britain	20	29
Greece	33	72
Ireland	56	54
Italy	48	70
Luxembourg	27	35
Malta	75	88
Netherlands	23	32
Norway	15	23
Portugal	39	67
Spain	31	44
Sweden	13	16
Switzerland	28	41
Average	**31**	**45**
Eastern Europe		
Albania	22	42
Armenia	32	72
Belarus	18	37
Bosnia-Herzegovina	43	72

Bulgaria	16	41
Croatia	35	66
Czech Republic	14	25
Estonia	11	18
Georgia	28	81
Hungary	20	39
Latvia	17	36
Lithuania	24	43
Macedonia	45	79
Montenegro	29	62
Poland	64	73
Romania	35	83
Serbia	27	55
Slovakia	44	50
Slovenia	35	43
Ukraine	24	47
Average	**29**	**53**
Latin America		
Argentina	29	63
Belize	62	65
Bolivia	57	88
Brazil	49	89
Chile	33	69
Colombia	63	86
Costa Rica	59	84
Cuba	20	35
Dominican Republic	51	88
Ecuador	59	84
El Salvador	65	88
Guatemala	70	89
Guyana	56	89

Haiti	75	83
Honduras	64	86
Jamaica	37	79
Mexico	58	66
Nicaragua	59	85
Panama	52	84
Paraguay	57	92
Peru	52	84
Puerto Rico	48	86
Trinidad & Tobago	48	87
Uruguay	16	40
Venezuela	41	78
Average	**51**	**79**
Islamic Nations*	** Nations in which the population is more than 50 percent Muslim*	
Afghanistan	70	97
Algeria	59	93
Azerbaijan	22	50
Bahrain	71	97
Bangladesh	82	99
Burkina Faso	72	92
Chad	82	93
Comoros	68	98
Djibouti	84	97
Egypt	63	95
Guinea	76	97
Indonesia	80	99
Iran	47	83
Iraq	51	86
Jordan	46	95
Kazakhstan	22	51

Kosovo	33	83
Kuwait	81	93
Kyrgyzstan	20	69
Lebanon	48	88
Libya	69	85
Malaysia	67	92
Mali	63	95
Mauritania	55	98
Morocco	55	95
Niger	74	98
Pakistan	56	96
Palestinian Terr.	52	93
Qatar	75	96
Saudi Arabia	70	97
Senegal	66	97
Sierra Leone	88	97
Somalia	89	99
Sudan	67	95
Syria	59	87
Tajikistan	27	84
Tunisia	36	95
Turkey	49	85
Turkmenistan	21	82
United Arab Emirates	72	95
Uzbekistan	14	62
Yemen	54	97
Average	**58**	**90**

Sub-Saharan Africa		
Angola	72	89
Benin	64	87
Botswana	49	82
Burundi	88	95
Cameroon	69	95
Central African Republic	75	98
Congo (Kinshasa)	73	96
Congo Brazzaville	76	91
Ghana	78	94
Ivory Coast	67	88
Kenya	74	94
Liberia	82	93
Madagascar	60	91
Malawi	73	98
Mozambique	65	88
Nambia	62	92
Nigeria	90	97
Rwanda	76	93
South Africa	58	85
Swaziland	—	94
Tanzania	76	95
Togo	65	87
Uganda	75	94
Zambia	75	95
Zimbabwe	61	86
Average	**71**	**92**

Asia		
Cambodia	41	93
Hong Kong	19	25
India	67	85
Japan	29	26
Laos	55	98
Mongolia	11	46
Myanmar (Burma)	65	97
Nepal	46	94
Philippines	65	95
Singapore	44	59
South Korea	35	43
Sri Lanka	75	99
Taiwan	24	48
Thailand	69	97
Vietnam	21	35
Average	**44**	**69**
Other		
Australia	21	32
Canada	27	43
Iceland	20	37
Israel	35	48
New Zealand	26	33
Average	**26**	**37**

AN ACTIVE GOD

The Gallup poll's item about God is subject to some ambiguity. Although it does not ask whether God is involved in *all* things that happen in the world, I suspect that many respondents understood it that way and therefore as a statement of belief in fatalism—that God makes our history. If the item was meant to ask whether God *ever* is involved in things that happen in this world—and thus to gauge belief in the possibility of miracles—it should have been worded that way. Even so, belief runs relatively high, even in many western European nations. Moreover, orthodox Muslims accept the idea that God is very active in this world—the traditional Muslim objection to science is that scientific "laws" presume to limit Allah's power.

In any event, Gallup asked the question in 105 nations, and the results are shown in Table 1–7.

Keep in mind that to respond no to this question is not necessarily to reject the idea of an active God. Were that the case, there ought to be a lot of atheists around the world.

Table 1–7: "Do you believe God is directly involved in things that happen in the world, or not?"

	Percentage Who Say Yes
United States	74
Western Europe	
Austria	29
Cyprus	56
Denmark	17
France	12
Germany	34
Great Britain	35
Greece	49
Ireland	54
Italy	43
Portugal	58
Spain	19
Sweden	14
Switzerland	28
Average	**35**

Eastern Europe	
Albania	38
Armenia	78
Belarus	48
Bosnia-Herzegovina	45
Bulgaria	36
Croatia	41
Czech Republic	18
Estonia	27
Georgia	66
Latvia	40
Lithuania	41
Macedonia	62
Montenegro	41
Poland	54
Romania	64
Russia	41
Serbia	28
Slovenia	26
Ukraine	51
Average	**45**
Latin America	
Argentina	31
Bolivia	46
Brazil	61
Chile	39
Colombia	39
Costa Rica	48
Dominican Republic	45
Ecuador	40
El Salvador	67

Guatemala	42
Honduras	44
Mexico	32
Nicaragua	47
Panama	47
Paraguay	46
Peru	42
Uruguay	37
Venezuela	33
Average	**44**
Islamic Nations*	** Nations in which the population is more than 50 percent Muslim*
Afghanistan	94
Algeria	79
Azerbaijan	86
Bangladesh	95
Chad	36
Djibouti	66
Indonesia	96
Iraq	87
Kazakhstan	52
Kosovo	69
Kyrgyzstan	73
Lebanon	76
Malaysia	84
Mali	54
Mauritania	75
Niger	82
Pakistan	71
Palestinian Terr.	90
Qatar	91

Senegal	61
Somalia	98
Sudan	90
Syria	78
Tajikistan	92
Tunisia	94
Turkey	73
Uzbekistan	83
Average	**79**
Sub-Saharan Africa	
Burundi	90
Cameroon	54
Congo (Kinshasa)	63
Ghana	78
Ivory Coast	56
Kenya	85
Malawi	90
Nigeria	74
Rwanda	89
South Africa	76
Tanzania	89
Uganda	79
Zambia	59
Zimbabwe	86
Average	**76**
Asia	
Cambodia	46
Hong Kong	30
India	65
Japan	14
Nepal	77

Philippines	82
Singapore	64
South Korea	32
Sri Lanka	38
Thailand	67
Vietnam	17
Average	**48**
Other	
Canada	47
Israel	71

ATHEISM

If one were to believe many popular writers, one would conclude that a rising tide of atheism is sweeping over the "modern" nations, as the long-predicted secularization finally comes to pass. Several years ago the sociologist Phil Zuckerman won a prize for his book *Society without God*, in which he reports how happy the Swedes and the Danes are even though they don't worship any gods. Zuckerman based his book on interviews with 150 Danes and Swedes. He might better have consulted the World Values Surveys, which are based on large, properly drawn samples and are the basis for Table 1–8, shown on the next page. Had he done so, he would have discovered that in "godless" Denmark, only 5 percent say they are atheists. In "godless" Sweden, only 16.8 percent claim to be atheists.

In most of the world, atheists make up only tiny percentages of the population. In only eleven nations do atheists account for more than 10 percent of the population, and in no nation do they exceed 30 percent. Meanwhile, atheists are extremely scarce in the Islamic nations, in Sub-Saharan Africa, and in Latin America. Even in the United States, which has made massive bestsellers of books by "New Atheists" like Richard Dawkins, Sam Harris, Daniel Dennett, and Christopher Hitchens, only 4.4 percent of the population identifies as atheist.

The only reasonable conclusion that can be drawn from Table 1–8 is that the vast majority of people all around the world believe in God.

Table 1–8: Percentage Who Say They Are Atheists

United States	4.4
Latin America	
Argentina	2.3
Brazil	1.2
Chile	4.2
Colombia	1.1
Ecuador	1.1
Guatemala	0.8
Mexico	2.4
Peru	1.8
Trinidad	0.3
Uruguay	11.3
Venezuela	1.2
Average	**2.5**
Western Europe	
Austria	1.8
Belgium	7.2
Cyprus	1.2
Finland	3.1
France	17.1
Germany	9.6
Great Britain	9.4
Greece	4.6
Iceland	3.5
Ireland	1.7
Italy	2.7
Netherlands	10.3
Norway	6.8
Portugal	3.0
Spain	7.4

Sweden	16.8
Switzerland	7.9
Average	**6.7**
Eastern Europe	
Albania	5.5
Armenia	1.4
Belarus	5.1
Bulgaria	5.3
Croatia	3.1
Czech Republic	8.3
Estonia	7.4
Georgia	0.3
Hungary	5.5
Latvia	2.8
Lithuania	1.5
Moldova	1.0
Poland	4.7
Romania	1.1
Russia	7.0
Serbia	4.0
Slovenia	13.4
Ukraine	4.8
Average	**4.6**
Islamic Nations*	** Nations in which the population is more than 50 percent Muslim*
Algeria	0.7
Azerbaijan	0.1
Bangladesh	0.0
Burkina Faso	1.6
Egypt	0.0
Indonesia	0.3
Iran	1.5

Iraq	0.3
Jordan	0.1
Kazakhstan	6.7
Kuwait	4.9
Kyrgyzstan	2.0
Lebanon	3.3
Libya	0.6
Malaysia	0.8
Mali	0.4
Morocco	0.0
Pakistan	0.0
Palestinian Terr.	1.2
Qatar	1.0
Saudi Arabia	0.0
Tunisia	0.7
Turkey	0.8
Uzbekistan	0.3
Yemen	0.0
Average	**1.1**
Sub-Saharan Africa	
Ethiopia	0.4
Ghana	0.3
Nigeria	0.2
Rwanda	0.7
South Africa	1.2
Zambia	0.5
Zimbabwe	1.3
Average	**0.7**
Asia	
China	27.0
Hong Kong	5.4[8]

India	2.5
Japan	11.3
Nepal	7.7
Philippines	0.0
Singapore	0.0
South Korea	29.5
Taiwan	17.2
Thailand	0.2
Vietnam	23.6
Average	**11.3**
Other	
Australia	16.3
Canada	6.6
Iceland	3.5
New Zealand	7.0
Average	**8.4**

A GREAT AWAKENING

Too bad that the World Polls and the World Values Surveys were not conducted in 1950. What they would show is that the world today is far more religious than it was back then. In 1950 there were about five million Christians in China. Today there are about 100 million, and millions more are converted every year. In 1950 mass attendance in Latin America was low, probably not higher than 20 percent a week anywhere. Today it is more than 50 percent in many Latin nations. Even in Islam, mosque attendance was far lower in the 1950s, and many Muslim laws were far less carefully observed.

In short, a great religious awakening has taken place around the world. Why and how this has occurred is the fascinating story to be told in the next nine chapters.

2

EUROPE:
THE GRAND ILLUSIONS

In the same interview during which he recanted his support for the secularization theory, Peter Berger noted that the world is very religious but made an additional point: "The one exception to this is Western Europe. One of the most interesting questions in the sociology of religion today is not, How do you explain fundamentalism in Iran? but, Why is Western Europe different?"[1]

This chapter answers Berger's question. In doing so, it challenges a number of the most sacred illusions of the secularization faithful.

WELCOME TO THE FUTURE?

The most frequent explanation offered for lower levels of religiousness in Europe is the so-called secularization thesis: that modernity is incompatible with religion. Therefore, because the process of modernization is further ahead in Europe than in the rest of the world, European religious institutions are fading away. As the historian of religion Jeffrey Cox has put it, "Despite the efforts of doubters, sceptics and adversaries, the most influential general account of religion in modern Europe, and in the modern world, remains the theory of secularization."[2] This theory offers a clear and parsimonious explanation of

Europe's supposed lack of religion. Moreover, it lends itself to a rather elegant statistical "proof."

The political scientists Pippa Norris and Ronald Inglehart have provided the best example of the statistical proof that modernization causes secularization.[3] In their 2004 book *Sacred and Secular: Politics and Religion Worldwide*, they assembled data on church attendance and prayer from recent World Values Surveys and correlated these measures of religiousness with standard measures of modernization, including Gross Domestic Product per capita and the Human Development Index created by the United Nations. The latter combines average life expectancy, mean years of schooling, and average income. Looking at about seventy nations, Norris and Inglehart found strong negative correlations between these measures of modernization and both average church attendance and frequency of prayer. Thus they "proved" that modernization causes secularization.

There is much less here than has been assumed, however. All that Norris and Inglehart demonstrated was what we knew all along, that Europe is the most modernized continent (aside from North America) and the least religious. But is this really a causal relationship?

The best way to find out is not to compare European nations with countries in less modernized parts of the world but to compare European nations with *one another*. European nations differ substantially in their degree of modernization as well as in their religiousness. Are the differences correlated?

I have used the same two measures of religiousness that Norris and Inglehart used; indeed, the data on prayer come from the same sources they used. The results are shown in Table 2–1.

What the data show is that *within* Europe, modernization is *not* correlated with religiousness at all. For a correlation to be statistically significant, the odds must be at least twenty to one that it is not merely a random result. In this case, all four correlations fall short—*far short*—of statistical significance. In fact, the small correlations relating to prayer go in the wrong direction: they actually suggest a *positive* (albeit statistically insignificant) correlation between frequent prayer and modernization.

Table 2–1: Correlations between Modernization and Religiousness in Europe

	Church Attendance*	Frequency of Prayer**
GDP per Capita	−0.093	0.168
Human Development Index	−0.094	0.202

* *The church-attendance correlation is based on surveys in thirty-six countries.*

** *The frequency-of-prayer correlation is based on surveys in twenty-two countries.*

There are many things about Europe that may cause its relatively low levels of religiousness, but modernization is *not* one of them. We must look elsewhere for an explanation. In fact, we must ask whether religiousness in Europe really is as low as is commonly understood.

HISTORY RECONSIDERED

For several generations, most historians embraced the secularization thesis, and by now there is a long shelf of books demonstrating (and often celebrating) the decline of religion in Christian Europe. Recently, however, a consensus has developed among historians that the secularization thesis is untenable.[4] Oxford's David Nash subtitled a 2004 article "Secularization's Failure as a Master Narrative."

Why has it failed? First, because many statistical studies showing a decline in religious practice beginning in the nineteenth century were incorrect; no significant decline set in until the 1960s, long after modernization was well established.[5] Second, because the definition of religion used to support the secularization thesis was too narrowly "churchly" and failed to consider popular and unchurched forms of religious expression, counting them instead as irreligion.[6] Margaret Loane made this point forcefully more than a century ago in her brilliant observations of working-class families:

To count up the churchgoers and chapel-goers, compare the resulting number with the population, and then, if there should be a
great disparity, argue that the neighborhood is without religion; or
to estimate the proportion of children and young persons in places
of worship and then say, "religion has no hold on them..." is a
most serious error. It is a confusion of formal outward signs and
inward spiritual graces. Many of the poor rarely attend church,
not because they are irreligious, but because they have long since
received and absorbed the truths by which they live.[7]

As Loane noted, even in the nineteenth century English churchmen and scholars were explaining a lack of church attendance as a
result of a general decline in religiousness—soon to be identified as
the secularization thesis. This explanation appealed especially to the
churchmen because it got them off the hook—if modernization was
the cause, then they were not at fault. Thus, for nearly all of the twentieth century the thesis prevailed that a decline in church attendance
proved that secularization was occurring—even if nonchurchly forms
of spirituality saw no decline or even increased. As the British scholar
Sarah Williams noted:

The simplistic identification of religion with institutional church
practice [continued]...in much of the work done in the 1960s and
1970s.... Today few historians would commit the "serious error" of
confusing "inward spiritual graces" with "formal outward signs" in
an unqualified manner. Most would nod in assent at Loane's emphasis and agree that the sum total of church- and chapel-goers is an
inadequate gauge of religious fervour and even point to the importance of popular religion in the daily lives of working-class people.[8]

Thus far, this remarkable dismissal of the secularization thesis has
been limited mainly to British historians who specialize in religion over
the past several centuries. But the points they raise are equally valid
when applied to medieval European religious history. For it is the presumed universal piety of this era, when the grand cathedrals were built
and all the great masters pursued religious subjects and themes, that

serves as the benchmark against which the European "decline" into secularism is calculated. This is another grand illusion.

THE MYTH OF MEDIEVAL PIETY

It has long been assumed that during the "Dark Ages" everyone flocked to church.[9] But, of course, there were no Dark Ages—that was actually an era of remarkable progress and innovation—and informed historians now know that few attended church during medieval times.[10] Consider this fact alone: through most of this era, when more than 90 percent of Europe's population lived in rural areas, churches were to be found only in towns and cities; therefore hardly anyone *could* have attended church. Moreover, even after most Europeans had access to a church, whether Catholic or Protestant, most people still didn't attend, and when forced to do so, they often misbehaved.

There are few statistics on medieval religious life but a surprising number of trustworthy reports from many times and places. These reports are in amazing agreement that the great majority of ordinary people seldom if ever went to church. As the political philosopher Michael Walzer put it, "Medieval society was largely composed of non-participants [in the churches]."[11]

The historian Alexander Murray's assessment of medieval Italian religious life is confirmed again and again: "Substantial sections of thirteenth-century society hardly attended church at all."[12] The Dominican prior Humbert of Romans (1200–1277) admitted that people in Italy "rarely go to church."[13] When the Blessed Giordano of Rivalto (1260–1311) arrived in Florence to preach, he suggested to a local woman that she take her daughter to church at least on feast days, only to be informed: "It is not the custom."[14] In about 1430 Saint Antonio noted that Tuscan peasants seldom attended Mass and that "very many of them do not confess once a year, and far fewer are those who take communion."[15] Saint Bernardino of Siena (1380–1444) reported that the few parishioners who came to Mass usually were late and hastened out at the elevation of the Host, "as though they had seen not Christ, but the Devil."[16]

Meanwhile, in England the anonymous authors of *Dives and Pauper* (ca. 1410) complained that "the people these days...are loath to hear God's Service. [And when they are forced to attend] they come late and leave early."[17] The English cleric Edward Topsell (1572–1625) reported that "not one young person in a thousand enjoyed prayer or preaching."[18] According to the Cambridge historian G. G. Coulton, medieval church attendance was "still more irregular in Wales, Scotland, and Ireland than in England."[19]

Extraordinary reports on the lack of popular religious participation are available for Lutheran Germany because higher church officials regularly visited local communities beginning in 1525. The distinguished American historian Gerald Strauss extracted these reports, noting, "I have selected only such instances as could be multiplied a hundredfold."[20]

In Saxony (1574): "You'll find more of them out fishing than at service.... Those who do come walk out as soon as the pastor begins his sermon."[21] In Seegrehna (1577): "A pastor testified that he often quits his church without preaching...because not a soul has turned up to hear him."[22] In Barum (1572): "It is the greatest and most widespread complaint of all pastors hereabouts that people do not go to church on Sundays.... Nothing helps; they will not come...so that pastors face near-empty churches."[23] In Braunschweig-Grubenhagen (1580s): "Many churches are empty on Sundays."[24] In Weilburg (1604): "Absenteeism from church on Sundays was so widespread that the synod debated whether the city gates should be barred on Sunday mornings to lock everyone inside. Evidence from elsewhere suggests that this expedient would not have helped."[25]

Nevertheless, it is not clear that having a large turnout at Sunday services would have been desirable. That's because when people did come to church, so many of them misbehaved. The eminent historian Keith Thomas combed the reports of English church courts and clerical diaries, finding constant complaints not only that so few came to church but also that "the conduct of many church-goers left so much to be desired as to turn the service into a travesty of what was intended.... Members of the congregation jostled for pews, nudged their neighbors, hawked and spat, knitted, made coarse remarks, told jokes, fell asleep, and even let off guns.... A Cambridgeshire man was charged with indecent behaviour in church in 1598 after his 'most loathsome farting, striking, and scoffing speeches' had occasioned 'the great offence of the good and the great rejoicing of the bad.' "[26]

Visitation reports from Lutheran Germany abound in accounts of misbehavior. In Nassau (1594): "Those who come to service are usually drunk...and sleep through the whole sermon, except sometimes they fall off the benches, making a great clatter, or women drop their babies on the floor."[27] In Wiesbaden (1619): "[During church] there is such snoring that I could not believe my ears when I heard it. The moment these people sit down, they put their heads on their arms and straight away they go to sleep."[28] In addition, dogs accompanied many parishioners inside the church, "barking and snarling so loudly that no one can hear the preacher."[29] In Hamburg (1581): "[People make] indecent gestures at members of the congregation who wish to join in singing the hymns, even bringing dogs to church so that due to the loud barking the service is disturbed."[30] In Leipzig (1579–1580): "They play cards while the pastor preaches, and often mock or mimic him cruelly to his face;...cursing and blaspheming, hooliganism, and fighting are common.... They enter church when the service is half over, go at once to sleep, and run out again before the blessing is given.... Nobody joins in singing the hymn; it made my heart ache to hear the pastor and the sexton singing all by themselves."[31]

In addition, the locals often misused the church. In 1367 John Thoresby, Archbishop of York, fulminated against holding markets in churches, especially on Sunday. According to G.G. Coulton, between "1229 and 1367 there are eleven such episcopal injunctions recorded.... Bishop after bishop thundered in vain...against those who 'turned the house of prayer into a den of thieves.' "[32] The same thing occurred again and again across the continent, as higher Church officials complained against using churches, even cathedrals, for storing crops, sheltering livestock, and indoor market days.[33]

Given their attitudes and their lack of church attendance, it is hardly surprising that most medieval Europeans were completely ignorant of the most basic Christian teachings.[34] One English bishop lamented that not only did the people know nothing from the Scriptures but also "they know not that there *are* any Scriptures."[35]

Clearly, then, it is impossible to claim that there has been a sharp decline into secularization from these "pious" bygone days. Nevertheless, these low levels of attendance and knowledge did not reflect irreligion. Nearly everyone was religious! But theirs was an *unchurched religion*— one lacking a congregational base and existing as a relatively free-floating body of supernatural culture.[36] As the influential historian Gerald Strauss put it, they "practiced their own brand of religion, which was a rich compound of ancient rituals, time-bound customs, a sort of unreconstructable folk Catholicism, and a large portion of magic to help them in their daily struggle for survival."[37] Although the people's religion did often call on God, Jesus, Mary, and various saints, as well as some pagan gods and goddesses and minor spirits such as fairies, elves, and demons, it did so only to invoke their aid. This religion concerned itself little with matters such as the meaning of life or the basis for salvation. Instead, the emphasis was on pressing, mundane matters such as health, fertility, weather, sex, and good crops.

Many Europeans today adopt an unchurched faith as well. Because so many more Europeans embrace Christian doctrines than attend church, the distinguished British sociologist Grace Davie refers to them as "believing non-belongers."[38] Moreover, unchurched and unconventional supernaturalisms and groups are widely accepted in Europe.

UNCHURCHED AND UNCONVENTIONAL RELIGIOUS AND MYSTICAL ALTERNATIVES

In 2008 the International Social Survey Project asked people in a number of European nations whether they agreed with these three statements:

- Some fortune tellers really can foresee the future. *(Fortune tellers)*
- A person's star sign at birth can affect the course of his or her future. *(Astrology)*
- Good luck charms do bring good luck. *(Lucky charms)*

The responses for each nation are shown in Table 2–2.

Table 2–2: Unconventional Supernatural Beliefs

Percentage Who Agree

Western Europe	Fortune Tellers	Astrology	Lucky Charms
Austria	28	32	33
France	37	38	23
Germany	25	32	37
Ireland	31	17	24
Netherlands	26	21	19
Portugal	27	29	45
Switzerland	35	42	36

Eastern Europe	Fortune Tellers	Astrology	Lucky Charms
Bulgaria	59	53	64
Czech Republic	68	48	45
Hungary	42	37	31
Latvia	73	58	-
Russia	57	42	44
Slovakia	65	43	49

Source: International Social Survey Project, 2008

Church attendance may be low in Europe, but unconventional supernaturalism is thriving. This is especially true in eastern Europe, but fortune tellers, astrologers and those selling lucky charms can earn a good living in western Europe as well.

In previous work, I often argued that in those places where conventional religious organizations are weak, they provide an attractive opportunity for new or unconventional religious movements to thrive,[39] as well as for unchurched religions and mysticisms to fill the void, just as they did in medieval times. This argument was in opposition to the conventional view that when people drop out of church, they are immune to all forms of supernaturalism, and that therefore unconventional religions and mysticisms can thrive only where people still believe—in places where conventional religions also remain strong.

Initial quantitative studies supported the proposition that unconventional and unchurched religions thrive where the conventional, churched religions are weakest. These studies were based on data for the fifty states and larger American cities in various eras,[40] as well as on Canadian data.[41] For example, during the 1920s, theosophy, Christian Science, and Baha'i flourished in those American states and cities with the lowest rates of membership in conventional religious bodies. Christian Science was founded in Massachusetts and maintained its headquarters in Boston, but it was far more successful along the West Coast, where conventional church membership was lowest. In Canada, too, unconventional religions did best in provinces with the lowest levels of conventional church membership.

Of course, the secularization faithful immediately challenged these findings and cited Europe as the devastating exception—that although unconventional religious movements ("cults") may flourish in America and Canada, they are so rare in Europe as to be irrelevant. These objections proved to be short-lived. A wealth of data showed that Europe had many more such groups per million population than did the United States.[42] Moreover, these statistics were based on what was known to be an *extreme undercount* of unconventional religious groups in Europe, compared with an accurate count of these groups in the United States. For example, the data showed fifty-two such movements in France; more extensive research done later found well over *seven hundred*.[43] Many of these groups in both America and Europe are tiny, as such groups typically are. But some are quite large: at present there are about 125,000 French members of Jehovah's Witnesses, 84,000 Freemasons, and about 37,000 Mormons. The number of French Mormons and of Jehovah's Witnesses has doubled in the past twenty-five years.

In addition, unchurched religion and mysticisms thrive in Europe, as Table 2–2 demonstrated. In fact, in each nation shown in Table 2–2, those who attended church weekly were significantly less likely to hold unconventional supernatural beliefs than were those who seldom or never attended. In France, for example, only 22 percent of weekly attenders believed in fortune tellers, compared with 39 percent of those who seldom or never attended.

With additional data trickling in, it now seems increasingly likely that far more Europeans actively embrace supernaturalism than it appears even from their responses to survey questions. This is so because, with the rare exception of the statements shown in Table 2–2, the survey questions are phrased in conventional "churchly" language and are focused on participation in conventional religious organizations and on belief in conventional creeds. That this scope is too narrow is illustrated by the contrasts between rates of attendance at "a place of worship or religious service" and the rates of those who said religion was "an important part of their daily life." As shown in Table 1–6 (see page 21), on average 31 percent of western Europeans report attending a religious service in the past week, but 45 percent say religion plays an important role in their daily lives. Moreover, the remarkable prevalence of religious shrines and the huge numbers of pilgrims that visit them annually is not mentioned in most discussions of European religion. The definitive study, by Mary Lee Nolan and Sidney Nolan, showed that the 6,130 active religious shrines in western Europe draw more than sixty-six million visitors a year. The Nolans' study demonstrated that some of those visitors are, of course, tourists but that most come for authentic religious reasons.[44]

In the future I anticipate asking questions designed to measure unconventional, unchurched, popular religiousness and mysticism around the world. But for now we must make do with suggestive case studies of spirituality and unchurched religions in two supposedly secularized western European nations, Sweden and the Netherlands, as well as in Russia.

SWEDEN

Sweden is almost always presented as exhibit A in the case for the triumph of secularization.[45] Church attendance is very low there, and few Swedes have much respect for the Lutheran Church, which only in 2006 was cut loose from its privileged position as the state church, funded entirely by the government. But the majority of Swedes agree with the statement "I am a Christian in my own personal way," and 70 percent say they are concerned about the "meaning and purpose of life."[46] The Swedes also think it is important to have a religious service at death (78 percent) and upon marriage (62 percent). Furthermore, large numbers of Swedes have embraced various forms of unchurched religion—a whole range of New Age and Eastern beliefs and even superstitions that the Swedish researchers Pehr Granqvist and Berit Hagekull describe as a "smorgasbord" of spirituality.[47] For example, more than 20 percent of Swedes say they believe in reincarnation; half believe in mental telepathy; and nearly one in five believes in the power of lucky charms.[48] A third believe in New Age medicine such as "healing Crystals"; 20 percent would consider purchasing their personal horoscope; 10 percent would consult a medium; and nearly two out of five believe in ghosts.[49]

Belief in unchurched spirituality is especially prevalent among the young, who are given to belief in paranormal phenomena such as premonitions and UFOs. (A similar tendency to embrace esoteric and magical beliefs has been reported for students in Germany and Austria,[50] as well as in the Netherlands.[51]) Using supernatural beliefs as the criterion, the researcher Ulf Sjödin concluded that 78 percent of "young Swedes are religious" and only 13 percent are not.[52] Sjödin concluded that to focus on the Swedish churches is to miss the reality of Swedish faith in "a kind of private or invisible religion."[53] Surely this is not a description of a secularized nation.

NETHERLANDS

Many observers regard the Netherlands as perhaps more secularized than Sweden. For one thing, it has the lowest rate of church membership of any western European nation. Only 49 percent of the Dutch acknowledge membership in an organized religion, slightly lower than the rate for France (51 percent) and much lower than that for Sweden (74 percent) or Russia (65 percent).[54] Moreover, membership is highly age related, with the Dutch under thirty being far less apt to be members. According to the Dutch scholar Jacques Janssen, "a large proportion of the Dutch population, regardless of educational level, does not know what Easter is about, let alone Pentecost or Ascension Day."[55]

But here again, moving beyond conventional religious categories reveals a more complicated picture. For example, 21 percent of the Dutch believe in astrology and 26 percent in fortune tellers. Janssen concludes: "There is much more to say on religion [in the Netherlands] than simply regarding it as a fading phenomenon. Generally, only a very few young people reject religion explicitly or prefer atheism. They still possess religious identity, but this has become a private affair."[56]

A survey of Dutch youth in their early twenties supports that statement.[57] Eighty-three percent of them say they pray, at least occasionally. Although the young people tend to shy away from the word *God* and refer instead to a "higher being" or a "higher power," fewer than one in five respondents is an atheist. New Age beliefs and activities are quite popular, and 16 percent are classified as "New Age–minded." Similar findings have been revealed by surveys of young people in England, Germany, France, and Belgium.[58]

It has been suggested that "youth is in open conflict with the established society and the authority of the past. They experiment with eastern religions and the techniques of meditation." The fact that this was written about two thousand years ago by the Roman historian Tacitus does not make it any less pertinent.[59]

Several sophisticated observers suggest that the current state of unchurched religion among young people in the Netherlands and other European nations may be a transitional stage that will serve as "a good breeding ground for a fresh form of mysticism,"[60] and "may be the basis for the refounding of religion."[61] In addition to New Age organizations, some unconventional religious groups have been gaining ground: in 2013 the Netherlands had more than nine thousand Mormons and thirty thousand Jehovah's Witnesses.

RUSSIA

As noted in the introduction, more than sixty years of intensive formal education on behalf of atheism in the Soviet Union proved to be a resounding failure: only 6.6 percent of Russians claimed to be atheists in the 1990 World Values survey. That same long era of repression had a serious impact on the Russian Orthodox Church, however. Religious attendance was impeded and sometimes punished, and the church hierarchy was somewhat discredited for collaborating with the antireligious government. The Orthodox Church has long been without significant competition in Russia. Today church attendance is lower there than in most other nations of the former Soviet Union.

On the other hand, according to the 2006 World Values survey, 65 percent of Russians think of themselves as "a religious person," up from 56 percent in 1990. In addition, two-thirds of Russians believe in "supernatural forces."[62] So did many of those employed in the Soviet regime as instructors in atheism or in the Communist Party's inner circle. It was common for Soviet leaders to consult psychics and fortune tellers, and most of them visited occult healers. Leonid Brezhnev, who ruled the USSR from 1964 to 1982, had a personal healer. A 2006 report from the Russian Academy of Sciences acknowledged that there were more occult healers than conventional medical doctors practicing in Russia, and according to one news account, "Russian newspapers are full of ads for all manner of urban witches and wizards."[63] The scholar Holly DeNio Stephens reports, "Healers and psychics frequently appear on morning and evening talk shows and recount their visions and paranormal experiences."[64] In 2008 a national survey of Russia found that 52 percent believed in faith healers and another 20 percent weren't sure.[65]

What is to be made of all this? With the scholars Mikhail Epstein and Birgit Menzel,[66] I suggest that "atheism" often constitutes a sort of vacuum in which all sorts of unchurched faiths and supernaturalisms flourish. As the aphorism often attributed to G. K. Chesterton puts it: "When people stop believing in God, they don't believe in nothing—they believe in anything." Recall that Europeans who seldom or never attended church were significantly more likely than weekly attenders to hold the unconventional supernatural beliefs shown in Table 2–2. Similarly, studies find that in the United States the irreligious are far more likely than the religious to believe in a whole array of occult beliefs such as Atlantis, Bigfoot, the Loch Ness Monster, astrology, UFOs, haunted houses, and ghosts.[67] All these beliefs are very popular in Russia. In fact, according to Birgit Menzel, during the 1990s "no less than 39 percent of all non-fiction publications in the humanities dealt with occult-esoteric topics."[68] These ideas have also deeply penetrated the sciences in Russia. The flood of conferences, classes, and textbooks filled with occult theories, from bioenergy "to UFOs and cosmic consciousness, produced by scientists at the highest academic ranks," prompted the Russian Academy of Sciences to warn against "obscure pseudoscience," but to little effect.[69] A third of Russians believe in reincarnation[70]; 42 percent believe in astrology; 57 percent believe in fortune tellers; and nearly half think that lucky charms work.

All this suggests that the low level of church attendance in Russia may represent an institutional opportunity waiting to be filled. Jehovah's Witness missionaries were allowed to enter Russia only in 1989, in the last days of the Soviet Union. By 1996 there already were 61,843 Jehovah's Witnesses in Russia; by 2013 the total had grown to 168,123. The Mormons did not begin to send missionaries to Russia until September 1990. Ten years later there were 11,092 Russian Mormons; by 2013 that number had grown to 21,709.

But the real test of the potential for church growth in Russia no doubt awaits the appearance of some vigorous and enthusiastic homegrown churches, whether offshoots of orthodoxy or Protestant denominations. Indeed, the rise of homegrown faiths may be what lies in store for the rest of Europe.

LAZY, OBSTRUCTIONIST STATE CHURCHES

Most European nations have nothing resembling a religious free market. Many still have established state churches supported by taxes. In most of the rest, a particular religion is the object of considerable government favoritism. And in nearly all European nations, the government bureaucracy engages in overt and covert interference with "outsiders" that challenge the established religious order.

There are Lutheran state churches in Denmark, Finland, Iceland, and Norway. Although the Church of Sweden (Lutheran) lost its established position in 2006, the government continues to collect a religious tax on its behalf. Germany has two state churches, the Evangelical

Church (Protestant) and the Roman Catholic Church; both are supported by taxes, and their clergy are classified as civil servants. Some cantons in Switzerland recognize Roman Catholicism as the state church; other cantons support an Evangelical Reformed state church. The Roman Catholic Church receives tax support in Austria and payments of more than six billion Euros a year in Spain. In Italy people choose the group to receive their church tax from a short list of Christian denominations. In Belgium there is no church tax, but the government provides substantial financing to Catholicism, Protestantism, Anglicanism, Judaism, Islam, and a category called "nondenominational." There is no church tax in the Netherlands, but the two major Protestant churches and the Roman Catholic Church receive large subsidies. No religious group receives direct government support in France, but the Catholic schools receive huge subsidies, and the bureaucracy shows immense favoritism to the Roman Catholic Church by repressing Protestant groups. Finally, the Church of England remains the established faith, but it is not supported by taxes or government funds, being able to sustain itself from huge endowments built up during prior centuries of mandatory tithing.

These close links between church and state have many consequences. First of all, they create lazy churches. The money continues to come whether or not people attend, so there is no need for clergy to exert themselves. Second, these links encourage people to view religion "as a type of public utility."[71] Individuals need do nothing to preserve the church; the government will see to it. This attitude makes it difficult for nonsubsidized faiths to compete. When some German evangelists attempted television ministries, they drew viewers but not contributions.[72] Religion is supposed to come free.

The existence of favored churches also encourages the government to hinder and harass other churches. The French government has officially designated 173 religious groups (most of them evangelical Protestants, including Baptists) as dangerous cults, imposing heavy tax burdens on them and subjecting their members to official discrimination in such things as government employment. Belgium has outdone France, identifying 189 dangerous cults, including the Quakers, the YWCA (but not the YMCA), Hasidic Jews, Assemblies of God, the Amish, Buddhists, and Seventh-Day Adventists.

Even groups not condemned by parliamentary action are targets of government interference. As the distinguished British sociologist James Beckford noted, all across Europe government bureaucrats impose "administrative sanctions...behind a curtain of official detachment."[73] Many Protestant groups report waiting for years to obtain a building permit for a church, or even a permit to allow an existing building to be used as a church. This is especially common in Scandinavian nations, which often rule that there is "no need" for an additional church in some area.[74] In Germany, many Pentecostal groups have been denied tax-free status unless they register with the government as secular groups such as sports clubs rather than as churches. Subsequently, the government sometimes revokes their tax-exempt status and imposes unpayable fines and back-tax demands on congregations.[75]

Nevertheless, many European scholars are adamant that their nations enjoy full religious liberty. To challenge that claim, it no longer is necessary to recite examples of state intrusions, because Brian Grim and Roger Finke have created quantitative measures of government interference in religious life.[76] They based their coding on the highly respected annual *International Religious Freedom Report* produced by the U.S. Department of State. One of Grim and Finke's measures is the Government Regulation Index, which reflects "the restrictions placed on the practice, profession, or selection of religion by the official laws, policies, or administrative actions of the state," scored from 0.0 (no restrictions) to 10.0 (only one religion allowed). On this measure, most European nations appear to offer a fair amount of religious freedom, with France having the highest level of restrictions (3.9). But Grim and Finke's second measure, the Government Favoritism Index, tells a very different story.

The favoritism index is based on "subsidies, privileges, support, or favorable sanctions provided by the state to a select religion or a small group of religions." This index also varies from 0.0 (no favoritism) to 10.0 (extreme favoritism). Taiwan scores 0.0 and Saudi Arabia and Iran each score 9.3. Afghanistan and the United Arab Emirates score 7.8, but so do Iceland, Spain, and Greece. Belgium scores 7.5, slightly higher than Bangladesh's 7.3 and India's 7.0. Morocco scores 6.3, while Denmark scores 6.7; Finland, 6.5; Austria, 6.2; Switzerland, 5.8; France, 5.5; Italy, 5.3; and Norway, 5.2. Europe has a religious "market" highly distorted by government policies of favoritism.

"ENLIGHTENED" CLERGY

In Europe, church attendance is substantially higher in Roman Catholic nations than in Protestant ones. The primary reason for the difference is that most Roman Catholic clergy still accept and preach the basic Christian message, whereas large numbers of Protestant clergy regard themselves as far too "enlightened" to do so. As will be demonstrated in the chapter on the United States, condoning an "enlightened" clergy is a sure recipe for the decline of churches. People attend church in order to worship God; if that doesn't happen, they don't go—or, in nations where there are options, they go elsewhere.

In 1963 the English Anglican bishop John A. T. Robinson published *Honest to God*. In it he dismissed the traditional image of God as a conscious being as an unbelievable "caricature," an outdated image of "an old man in the sky." He explained that "God" was nothing more than a vague aspect of human psychology. The book was an instant best-seller, strongly praised by many of Robinson's fellow English bishops. Subsequently, many other English churchmen, Don Cupitt being the most celebrated of them, have published books ridiculing the central tenets of Christianity. As noted, English historians now date the marked decline in church attendance as beginning at about this time.

It turns out that England is not unusual in the prominence of unbelieving clergy. Clerical "enlightenment" is widespread in Europe, especially in Scandinavia.

In this regard, the recent case of a parish priest in the Church of Denmark is instructive. Thorkild Grosbøll served for many years as the priest of the Danish church in Tarbaek, a town about ten miles north of Copenhagen. In 2003 he published a book in which he explained that he did not believe in God. This attracted some attention and led to an interview with a national newspaper in which Grosbøll said: "God belongs in the past. He actually is so old fashioned that I am baffled by modern people believing in his existence. I am thoroughly fed up with empty words about miracles and eternal life."[77] Subsequently, he told the *New York Times*: "I do not believe in a physical God, in the afterlife, in the resurrection, in the Virgin Mary.... And I believe Jesus was [only] a nice guy."[78] Nevertheless, Grosbøll planned to continue as a priest, obviously assuming that his beliefs were within the acceptable limits of the Danish Church. And that appears to be the case. After a hearing before an ecclesiastical court, Grosbøll resumed serving as a parish priest after reconfirming his priestly vows; he did not recant any of his views, though he was instructed not to talk to the press.

This was not a freak event. The Scandinavian state churches have been flirting with irreligion for at least a century. Consider that in Sweden the church has been largely controlled by local elected boards, the candidates being nominated by the national political parties. For several generations, then, the favored candidates were socialists, which often resulted in placing avowed atheists in charge of the church. Writing in the *Wall Street Journal*, the Swedish commentator Sven Rydenfelt reported: "Members of parish boards and the church council are elected more for their political positions and conviction than for their religious faith. No religious qualifications are required of the candidates—indeed, they need not even be baptized or confirmed. The state church is governed by a majority of nonbelievers—citizens who seldom or never attend church services."[79] For many years Sweden's minister of ecclesiastical affairs, who controlled the Church of Sweden until disestablishment was adopted in 2006, was Alva Myrdal, a well-known leftist economist and nonbeliever. She appointed a commission to compose a new Swedish translation of the New Testament, on grounds that "the timeworn Holy Bible [is] becoming increasingly marginalized in the modern, rational world view."[80] Even its ardent supporters acknowledged that this translation, published in 1981, contains "sweeping transformation[s] of accepted interpretations.... In important ways, it must of necessity run against the grain of Bible traditions."[81] This demystified translation remains the official Church of Sweden version. Is it really any wonder that by far the majority of Swedes who are in church on a Sunday attend small Protestant denominations that oppose the state church? And that brings us to the secret to strong churches: competition.

PLURALISM AND STRONG CHURCHES

A remarkable example of social scientists getting things backward is that they long have taught that competition weakens religious institutions. They argue that disagreements over doctrines erode religious certainty and thereby destroy the credibility of each religion's teachings. This thesis was first proposed by the seventeenth-century atheist Jean Bodin, who hailed the Reformation on grounds that because there now were competing faiths in Europe, each claiming to possess the truth, "all are refuted by all."[82] It seems worth noting that although Bodin ridiculed belief in God (in an anonymous publication), he was a firm believer in the Devil and in demons and even served as a judge in several witchcraft trials.

Peter Berger offered the most lucid statement of the conventional sociological version of Bodin's view that pluralism destroys the plausibility of all religions. "The classical task of religion," Berger explained, is to construct "a common world within which all of social life receives ultimate meaning binding on everyone."[83] Only where a single faith prevails can there exist a "sacred canopy" that provides that common outlook. Pluralism destroys the sacred canopy, causing confusion and doubt.

These views revealed Berger's European background; eventually his immersion in American religious life led him to accept my view that competition among religious organizations strengthens faith by weeding out the lax and unappealing denominations and energizing the others to maximize their outreach.[84] Put more formally: *the more religious competition there is within a society, the higher the overall level of individual religious participation.* Moreover, *religious groups sustaining an image of an active God who makes moral demands will enjoy substantial competitive advantages over groups that present God as a psychological construct or an impersonal "higher power."*[85]

In subsequent chapters we will see vivid examples of the importance of competition to sustaining religious participation, including in the newfound religious vigor of the Catholic Church in Latin America and in the collapse of American mainline denominations. But even in Europe, modest variations in the extent of pluralism result in substantial differences in religiousness.

The scholar of religion Laurence R. Iannaccone first applied the pluralism thesis to explain the low levels of religiousness in Europe.[86] Iannaccone initially studied fourteen major European nations—Austria, Belgium, Denmark, Finland, France, Great Britain, Germany (West), Ireland, Italy, Netherlands, Norway, Spain, Sweden, and Switzerland—plus Australia, New Zealand, Canada, and the United States. A study I published later dealt with those European nations that were more than 80 percent Catholic.[87] Both studies measured pluralism by the Herfindahl Index, a standard measure of market concentration, and gauged religiousness by weekly church attendance. The studies showed that pluralism has a remarkably strong influence on religiousness: it accounts for more than 90 percent of the total variation in church attendance across these nations. Moreover, Iannaccone's research showed that the unusually high level of church attendance in the United States is entirely consistent with America's high level of pluralism. As for the Catholic nations, several studies have found that Catholic commitment is higher to the extent that Catholics are a minority of the population—that is, where they face greater competition.[88]

Then came three subtle and persuasive studies based on Swedish data by Eva M. Hamberg and Thorleif Pettersson.[89] Pluralism is limited in Sweden, often consisting of nothing more than variations in the number and times of state church religious services. But Hamberg and Pettersson found that attendance rates increased significantly in response even to such minimal pluralism.

These studies establish that a major reason for Europe's low rates of church attendance is the stultifying effect of subsidized, monopoly churches lacking competitive challengers.

LEFTIST POLITICS

During the French Revolution, the French Encyclopedist Denis Diderot (1713–1784) proposed that freedom required that "the last king be strangled with the guts of the last priest." What this reflected, in addition to Diderot's taste for excessive rhetoric, is that in Europe the link between church and state tended to result in church support for the aristocracy in opposition to rebels and revolutionaries. As a result, in 1911 the British Socialist Party officially declared, "It is a profound truth that Socialism is the natural enemy of religion." The entire European left took this position, often expressing angry and strident atheism. Thus, in data collected in 1957 by the British Gallup Organization, supporters of the Conservative Party were almost twice as likely to attend church at least "now and again" (62 percent) than were supporters of the Labour Party (36 percent).[90] Leftism had an even stronger effect on church attendance in France at this time: 7 percent of Communist voters and 16 percent of Socialists said they were practicing their faith (Catholicism), compared with 67 percent of the Gaulists and 68 percent of the Peasant and Independent Party voters. In the Netherlands, based on data from 1956, 79 percent of voters supporting the Anti-Revolutionary Party had attended church in the past seven days, compared with 10 percent of the Labor Party.[91]

Consequently, it is the received wisdom that the popularity of leftist parties in Europe prompted substantial defections from religion, or at least from church participation. But given that participation has always been low, the success of the left in Europe probably was facilitated by the fact that churches were weak in the first place. An exception may be France, where the legacy of the revolution's militant anticlericalism lived on in the post–World War II popularity of the French Communist Party, and where the percentage of atheists is unusually high (17.1 percent). Another exception may be Spain, where bitterness going back to the Franco era still animates leftist antagonisms toward the Catholic Church.

But while support for the extreme left has greatly declined in Europe, the dominant churches—especially the state churches—have become progressively leftist. This has not brought them any resurgence in attendance.

ISLAM IN EUROPE

Recent decades have seen substantial Muslim immigration into Europe. This immigration has not had significant cultural and political impact in eastern European nations, most of which have always had Muslim minorities. But western European nations have experienced increasing difficulties involving Muslim immigrants; for example, scenes of riots by Muslim youths, during which shop windows are smashed and cars set on fire, have become all too common in cities stretching from Sweden through France. One official response has been to make it illegal to discuss these matters; the governments of most Western European nations have passed harsh laws against "hate speech" and "Islamophobia." On these grounds, a well-known Danish journalist was convicted of hate speech for criticizing the practice of "honor killing," by which Muslim families execute daughters suspected even of trivial flirtations—a practice that not only is frequent but also meets widespread approval among Muslims (see chapter 4). A second response has been the rise of political parties reflecting public concern about continuing Muslim immigration, such as the National Front in France and the Swiss People's Party.

All the political activity, legislation, and media debate surrounding Islam in western Europe is rather remarkable given the relatively small numbers of Muslims there. Table 2–3 (on the next page) shows the percentage of Muslims in western European nations, based on the Gallup World Poll results.

Only in Belgium and France do Muslims make up even 5 percent of the population. But their presence may be greatly amplified by their visibility—especially that of Muslim women, with their distinctive dress—and by incidents of terrorism in Europe. Such incidents may be few in number, but they inflame public opinion because the senseless brutality and the extremist views of their perpetrators guarantee maximum media coverage. Consider these examples:

- March 12, 2012: A Muslim terrorist chases a rabbi and three children, ages three, six, and ten, into a Jewish school in Toulouse, France, and shoots all four of them to death.

Table 2–3: Percentage of Muslims in the Population

Belgium	5.3%
France	5.1%
Greece	3.9%
Switzerland	3.0%
Netherlands	2.9%
Great Britain	2.7%
Luxembourg	2.3%
Austria	2.2%
Germany	2.0%
Sweden	1.5%
Norway	1.5%
Denmark	1.4%
Italy	1.3%
Spain	0.9%
Ireland	0.4%
Finland	0.2%
Portugal	0.1%

- May 22, 2013: Two Nigerian Muslims attack a British soldier with knives and a meat cleaver and behead him on a street in London. When taken into custody, one terrorist shouts, "We swear by Almighty Allah we will never stop fighting you."
- May 26, 2014: A gunman murders two Israeli tourists and a staff worker at the Jewish Museum in Brussels. (A fourth victim dies in early June.) Six days after the incident, the French police arrest the killer, who has a lengthy criminal record and who spent time in Syria fighting for a group associated with al-Qaeda. That, and his name, makes it obvious that he is a French Muslim, but that fact goes unmentioned in the initial press coverage.
- August 19 and September 2, 2014: Two American journalists, James Foley and Steven Sotloff, are beheaded by ISIS

fanatics, and videos of each killing are shown worldwide. The executioner speaks on the videos with a distinctive British accent and has since been identified as a Muslim born and raised near London.

- January 7, 2015: Two terrorists invade the Paris office of *Charlie Hebdo*, a satirical French magazine that ran cartoons ridiculing Muhammad. The terrorists shout, "We are avenging the Prophet Muhammad" as they murder editors and cartoonists, leaving twelve dead. The next day, another Muslim gunman seizes hostages in a Jewish kosher grocery store in Paris, demanding that police withdraw from their siege of two brothers who conducted the *Charlie Hebdo* massacre. In the end, the police kill the brothers as well as the terrorist in the kosher market, but not before he kills four Jewish hostages. All these terrorists were born in France.

- February 14, 2015: A Muslim gunman, born and raised in Denmark, opens fire on a café in Copenhagen where a group is meeting to support free speech. He kills one and wounds three. The gunman then attacks a synagogue not far from the café, killing one and wounding two.

Following each such incident, politicians and media commentators express concern that the terrorist act not result in prejudice toward Muslims. A day after the massacre at *Charlie Hebdo*, the president of France said, in a statement released through the French Embassy, "Those who committed these acts have nothing to do with the Muslim religion."

But rarely is there any mention of anti-Semitism, despite the fact that Jews were victims in many of these incidents, and in scores of other incidents of nonlethal terrorism in Europe. President Barack Obama referred to the attack on the Jewish food market by a confederate of the gunmen who attacked *Charlie Hebdo* as a "random event," but it certainly was not a coincidence that the victims were Jews. And although Muslims in Europe seem to have brought with them the nearly universal anti-Semitism of their homelands (see chapter 4), they are not alone—anti-Semitism remains quite widespread among Europeans.

ANTI-SEMITISM

As these developments suggest, religious enthusiasm is not always an unalloyed blessing for a society. Religious antagonism and intolerance frequently become problems. Anti-Semitism is one such problem. And recent surveys make it very clear that anti-Semitism persists in Europe.

In 2015 the Anti-Defamation League in New York published *Global 100: An Index of Anti-Semitism*, based on surveys in one hundred nations during 2013 and 2014. The Anti-Semitism Index is based on responses to eleven items, each a negative statement about Jews:

1. "Jews don't care about what happens to anyone but their own kind."
2. "Jews have too much control over global affairs."
3. "Jews think they are better than other people."
4. "Jews are responsible for most of the world's wars."
5. "Jews have too much power in international financial markets."
6. "People hate Jews because of the way Jews behave."
7. "Jews are more loyal to Israel than to [the country in which the interview was taking place]."
8. "Jews have too much power in the business world."
9. "Jews have too much power over the United States government."
10. "Jews have too much power over the global media."
11. "Jews still talk too much about what happened to them in the Holocaust."

People who said "probably true" to at least six of these eleven items were classified as high scorers. Table 2–4 displays the percentage of high scorers in European nations.

Nine percent of Americans score high on the Anti-Semitism Index. The average for western Europe is 22 percent, ranging from 69 percent in Greece to 4 percent in Sweden. For eastern Europe, the average is 32 percent, with Poland the highest at 45 percent and the Czech Republic

Table 2–4: Percentage Who Scored High on the Anti-Semitism Index

Western Europe	
Austria	28%
Belgium	27%
Denmark	9%
Finland	15%
France	37%
Germany	27%
Great Britain	8%
Greece	69%
Iceland	16%
Ireland	20%
Italy	20%
Netherlands	5%
Norway	15%
Portugal	21%
Spain	29%
Sweden	4%
Switzerland	26%
Average	**22%**
Eastern Europe	
Belarus	38%
Bosnia and Herzegovina	32%
Bulgaria	44%
Croatia	33%
Czech Republic	13%
Estonia	22%
Hungary	41%
Latvia	28%

Lithuania	36%
Moldova	30%
Montenegro	29%
Poland	45%
Romania	35%
Russia	30%
Serbia	42%
Slovenia	27%
Ukraine	38%
Average	33%

Source: Anti-Defamation League, *Global 100* (2015)

lowest at 13 percent. Thirty-nine percent of western Europeans agree that "Jews still talk too much about what happened to them in the Holocaust," and 24 percent in eastern Europe think that the Holocaust "was a myth or an exaggeration."[92]

Little wonder that Jews have begun to flee from Europe.[93] Of European Jewish respondents to the Gallup World Poll (combined four years 2010–13), about one out of three said that he or she would, given the opportunity, "like to move permanently to another country." The respondents were split equally between wanting to go to Israel or to the United States.

FERTILITY AND FAITH

Under modern conditions, a fertility rate of 2.05 children per average female is required to keep the population from shrinking—one child to replace each parent and a tiny fraction to cover infant and childhood mortality. It is well known that European fertility rates are far below the replacement level, even in Catholic nations such as Poland (1.39) and Italy (1.41). Were these low fertility rates to continue, eventually there would be no Europeans left in Europe.

But as is always the case, we must dig deeper into the numbers to see the flaws in the conventional wisdom. One common view is that low European fertility rates could result in a Muslim Europe. The fact is, however, that in most nations—including European nations—Muslim fertility has also dropped below replacement level or is expected to do so in the next several years (contrary to the recent Pew projections).[94]

Moreover, fertility rates are not declining uniformly across all segments of the population in Europe. On the contrary, religious Christian women in Europe continue to have children well above the replacement fertility level. Tomas Frejka of the Max Planck Institute in Germany and Charles F. Westoff of Princeton University broke down European Christians by their frequency of church attendance and determined the fertility rate for each group.[95] They merged many samples to accumulate a very large number of cases, making their study definitive. Table 2–5 shows the results.

Table 2–5: Christian Church Attendance and Fertility in Europe (Women Ages 35–44)

Women's Church Attendance	Fertility Rate
More than weekly	2.74
Weekly	2.23
One to three times a month	1.93
Less than once a month	1.83
Never	1.79

Source: Frejka and Westoff, 2008

Clearly, the most religious Christians—those who attend church at least weekly—continue to have large families. Eric Kaufmann of the University of London explored the implications of these fertility differences in his fascinating book *Shall the Religious Inherit the Earth?* (2010). Kaufmann noted that because only the irreligious sector of Europe's population is declining, while the religious sector is growing, only the irreligious European population is headed toward extinction. That differential fertility may produce a huge religious revival in Europe.

My calculations show that for Europe as a whole, the religious population will outnumber the irreligious population in about four more generations. The timespan will differ from country to country depending on the current ratio of religious to irreligious, but the eventual outcome will be the same if everything else remains constant. If the fertility rate of religious Europeans is sustained at above the replacement level, and if most children of religious parents remain religious (as they usually do), the population will grow and the churches will be full. In this way, Europe, too, may join in the global religious awakening—if indeed it really lags behind.

3

THE CHURCHING OF
LATIN AMERICA

Latin America was long regarded as, aside from the Vatican, the most
Roman Catholic area on earth, fully Christianized by missionary
monks and Spanish swords by the end of the seventeenth century.[1]
Through most of the twentieth century, official church statistics reported
that well over 90 percent of Latin Americans were Roman Catholics. For
example, the *National Catholic Almanac, 1949*, reported that Catholics
accounted for 99.2 percent of Argentina's population, 98.0 percent of
Bolivia's, 97.0 percent of Brazil's, and 99.8 percent of Chile's.

But these statistics were pure fiction. And of late they have been
used to advance another fiction: that Latin America has seen a massive
defection from the Catholic Church.[2]

Let's start with the more distant past. Although for several centuries the Roman Catholic Church was the only legal religion in Latin
America, its popular support was neither wide nor deep.[3] Many huge
rural areas lacked churches and priests, a vacuum in which indigenous
faiths persisted.[4] Even in the large cities with their splendid cathedrals,
Mass attendance was very low: as recently as the 1950s, perhaps only 10
to, at most, 20 percent of Latin Americans were active participants in
the faith.[5] Reflective of the superficiality of Latin Catholicism, so few
men entered the priesthood that across Central and South America most
of the priests were imported from abroad.[6]

Why did the Catholic Church fail to mobilize widespread commitment in Latin America? This chapter will reveal the answer.

More recent developments are equally misunderstood and raise questions of their own. The eruption of Protestantism (mostly of the Pentecostal variety) all across Latin America has enrolled millions of dedicated converts.[7] This chapter presents the first reliable current statistics on the percentages of Protestants and Catholics in each Latin American nation. It also examines the two primary Catholic reactions to the Protestant challenge. Why did the first one fail? Why did the second produce a dramatic Catholic awakening so that, together, the Protestants and Catholics have made Latin America a truly Christian region?

THE CATHOLIC MONOPOLY

During the centuries of Spanish rule, the Catholic Church in Latin America was, for all practical purposes, a branch of government. Many government positions were staffed by priests and monks, and the Church was lavishly supported by mandatory tithes that the state collected on its behalf. The Church also held huge land grants that yielded large agricultural profits. Hence, the Church "had become the dominant economic force in colonial society by the end of the seventeenth century," in the words of the scholar of religion R. Andrew Chesnut.[8] In Peru by the end of the eighteenth century, "there was scarcely an estate of any size that did not belong in whole or in part to clerics," the scholar John Lloyd Mecham wrote. "In Lima, out of 2,806 houses, 1,135 belonged to religious communities, secular ecclesiastics, or pious endowments."[9] In addition to its wealth, the Church was in complete charge of the educational system throughout Latin America. There were no public schools, only those provided by the Church.

The Church did not, however, seize these opportunities to make devout Catholics of the masses. It was unwilling to expend its resources beyond educating the urban sons and daughters of privilege. As Chesnut explained, in the judgment of the bishops "it simply made no sense to expend scarce ecclesiastical resources on the masses of impoverished laity who had no capital or real estate to donate to church coffers.... [The monopoly] church could afford to leave the financially impoverished masses to their own spiritual devices...since there was no real competition."[10]

And that's pretty much how things stood until the twentieth century.

PROTESTANT MISSIONS

The first Protestants permitted to live in Latin America were small enclaves of foreign merchants, most of them British and Americans, established early in the nineteenth century, but no Protestant churches or missionaries were allowed. To guard against unorthodox religious notions, until well into the twentieth century there even were legal bans on the sale of Bibles in most nations of Latin America, which led to the widespread misperception that only Protestants believed in the Bible.[11]

The Catholic legal hegemony began to break down in the late nineteenth and early twentieth centuries as anticolonial revolutions strained the relations between the governments and the Catholic Church—the new regimes' toleration of Protestantism being a form of political payback for the Church's having supported the conservative regimes.[12] Initially, nothing much happened to break up the Catholic monopoly. Indeed, many prominent American denominations that sustained overseas mission efforts excluded Latin American ventures on grounds that these already were Christian nations.[13] But the evangelical denominations rejected this "gentlemen's agreement" on grounds that "the Catholic Church had failed to connect with the majority of the population," according to my colleague Anthony Gill.[14] The result was a permanent split in American mission efforts (although little trace of the split now exists, since the denominations that thought it improper to send missionaries to Latin America have pretty much abandoned all missionary activities).[15] So it was that Latin America was missionized intensively, but only by conservative groups—with Pentecostal bodies soon surging ahead.

In 1900, 610 American Protestant missionaries were deployed in continental Latin America; by 1923, the total had risen to 1,627; by 1996, there were nearly 12,000.[16] To put that last total in perspective, in 1996 many Latin American nations had substantially more full-time American missionaries than Roman Catholic diocesan priests. In Honduras, for example, missionaries outnumbered priests five to one, and the figure was two to one in Panama and Guatemala. And these statistics did not include thousands of American missionaries on shorter tours.

Even more important, the number of American Protestant missionaries in Latin America has *fallen* dramatically in the past two decades. In 2004 there were only 5,116.[17] Why? Because they have been replaced by Latin Americans. In many Latin American nations today, native-born evangelical Protestant clergy far outnumber both foreign missionaries and local Catholic priests.[18]

The rapid increase in native-born Protestant clergy spurred the growth of Protestant denominations in Latin America. Although this increase is well known, statistics on actual Protestant membership have been scarce, scattered, and of suspect validity. That is no longer the case. We now have data from the Gallup World Polls on the religious makeup of Latin America.

In analyzing the data, I omitted results from five tiny nations included in the Gallup World Poll because those countries are not historically part of Latin America. Four of them are former British colonies: Guyana, Belize, Jamaica, and Trinidad and Tobago. The fifth, Haiti, is French-speaking and never was part of Latin America. I also excluded Puerto Rico, because, being an American territory, it has had a very different history from the Latin nations, and Cuba, because it lacks religious freedom. That leaves eighteen nations that are culturally and historically identified with Latin America. I have combined the surveys conducted for all years from 2007[19] to maximize the accuracy of the statistics.

All respondents were asked their religious affiliation. The results are shown in Table 3–1.

Table 3–1: Percentage Protestant and Catholic

	Protestant	Roman Catholic	Other	Secular
Guatemala	41%	55%	1%	3%
Honduras	39%	56%	3%	2%
El Salvador	39%	57%	2%	2%
Nicaragua	34%	59%	4%	3%
Brazil	26%	66%	4%	4%
Dominican Republic	24%	67%	2%	7%
Costa Rica	23%	71%	4%	2%
Chile	20%	69%	4%	7%
Panama	17%	78%	5%	0%
Bolivia	16%	81%	1%	2%
Peru	16%	82%	1%	1%
Colombia	12%	85%	2%	1%
Ecuador	12%	86%	1%	1%
Argentina	11%	82%	1%	6%
Uruguay	10%	53%	8%	29%
Paraguay	9%	89%	2%	0%
Mexico	7%	91%	1%	1%
Venezuela	8%	87%	3%	2%

Source: Gallup World Poll

These statistics reveal that Protestantism has become a major religious presence in most of Latin America. Protestants make up more than a third of the population in four of these eighteen nations, and a fifth or more in eight of them. The "Other" category includes indigenous Indian and African faiths. The "Secular" category consists of those who said they had no religion. The high total for the "Secular" category in Uruguay (29 percent) probably reflects the fact that more than 80 percent of Uruguayans are of direct European descent.[20]

The percentages of Protestant membership also reveal that even the more optimistic of the respectable claims about Protestant success in Latin America were too low. For example, in 2008 *The Economist* estimated that Protestants made up 20 percent of the population of Guatemala and 15 percent in Brazil and Chile. The correct figures are: Guatemala, 41 percent; Brazil, 26 percent; and Chile, 20 percent.

Unfortunately, the surveys do not separate the Protestants into their constituent groups. The major American evangelical groups, such as the Assemblies of God, United Brethren, Churches of Christ, and various Baptist bodies, are well represented. There are many purely local Protestant groups as well, most of them having Pentecostal roots. For example, the Jotabeche Methodist Pentecostal Church in Chile probably has more than 100,000 members; its church in Santiago can seat 18,000.[21] In Brazil, an autonomous Pentecostal body known as *Brasil Para o Cristo* (Brazil for Christ) has attracted more than a million members.[22] In addition to large Latin-born Protestant groups such as these, there are hundreds of small independent groups. Hence, the growth of Protestantism in Latin America has been the growth of meaningful pluralism.

Even as studies undercounted the presence of Protestants in Latin America, they overestimated the future growth of Protestantism. For example, in the 1990s both the anthropologist David Stoll and the distinguished theologian Harvey Cox predicted that five or six Latin nations would have Protestant majorities by 2010 and that Protestants would be on the verge of becoming majorities in several more nations.[23] Those predictions were much too optimistic; as we have seen, only in four Latin countries do Protestants constitute even a third of the population.

What nearly every published study of Protestant growth in Latin America has missed is the Catholic response. Had Catholic bishops done nothing to compete with their Protestant challengers, Stoll and Cox's predictions may well have come to pass. But that is not what happened. It is true that some Latin Catholic hierarchies still fit Adam Smith's description of established churches—that they are "altogether incapable of making any vigorous exertion in [their] defense."[24] Most, however, responded quickly and energetically.

If observers failed initially to see that the Catholic Church would vigorously respond to the Protestant challenge, it was because the initial

tactic the bishops endorsed was primarily political rather than religious—
and was a resounding failure.

LIBERATIONISTS

During the 1950s, as energetic Protestant groups began to make inroads
in Latin America, some Catholic theologians diagnosed their success as
an appeal to the material deprivations of the masses. In response they
fashioned a counterstroke that, although long on theological language
and imagery, was essentially political. Known as liberation theology, it
was a mixture of Marxism and Catholicism that aimed at "mobilizing
the poor for their own liberation."[25] The proposed tactic to achieve this
liberation was to unite small groups of lower-class Latin Americans into
a form of utopian socialist commune, wherein they would have their
political and moral awareness raised and serve as models of progress
for people in the surrounding area. These communes were called "Base
Communities" in accord with the long-range plan to rebuild societies
from below—from a new base.

The primary theorist of liberation theology was the Peruvian
Dominican priest Gustavo Gutiérrez. He redefined salvation, discard-
ing the emphasis on the individual and arguing instead that salvation is
collective, taking the form of "saving" the masses from bondage. Gutiérrez was a committed leftist who demanded "a society in which the private ownership of the means of production is eliminated." He often
expressed his admiration for the murderous Che Guevara and explicitly
linked his theology to the work of Karl Marx; not once did he criticize
the Soviet Union. As the theologian Richard L. Rubenstein noted, "Liberation theology is thus profoundly anti-American and deeply hostile to
the bourgeois capitalist world. It manifests no comparable hostility to
the communist world."[26]

Liberation theology appealed to many American priests and nuns,
especially those associated with the Maryknoll mission society. It
appealed as well to American and European intellectuals (especially
social scientists) and to many clergy in Latin America; it was officially

endorsed at a conference of Latin American bishops at Medellín, Colombia, in 1965. Although liberation theology was supposed to be a response to the poverty of the masses, in reality Catholic officials sanctioned liberationists and their programs to the extent that Protestant groups were making headway in their nations.[27]

But to no avail. Base Communities failed to arouse the masses to attempt to establish Christian socialism. There were many reasons for this failure. For one thing, most of the Base Communities never developed beyond loosely organized, nonresidential study groups that formed in urban neighborhoods.[28] In keeping with the tepid religiousness that prevailed in liberation theological circles, these Base Communities mainly attracted not poor people but the more educated.[29] Probably no more than two million Latin Americans out of a total population of nearly six hundred million ever became involved in Base Communities.[30] It even has been suggested that liberation theology "had more influence on Catholics . . . in Europe and the United States than in Latin America."[31]

Probably the primary proponent of liberation theology today is Francis, the first Latin American pope. In April 2014, Pope Francis declared on Twitter, "Inequality is the root of social evil." In May of the following year, the Vatican's charity arm, Caritas Internationalis, made the Reverend Gutiérrez one of the featured speakers at its assembly. The founder of liberation theology also appeared at an official Vatican press conference, which helped with the rehabilitation of Gutiérrez's reputation and of liberation theology.[32]

Pope Francis seems, however, to have given up on arousing the masses and calls instead for "liberation" through government decree. Addressing the United Nations in May 2014, he called for "the legitimate redistribution of economic benefits by the state."[33] In August of that year he lifted the suspension of Maryknoll priest Miguel D'Escoto Brockmann, who had been denied the right to perform his priestly duties in 1985 for serving as foreign minister in the Communist regime of the Sandinista Liberation Front in Nicaragua. A few months later Pope Francis played a major role in convincing President Barack Obama to recognize the Communist government of Cuba.

Nevertheless, liberation theology led nowhere because it was neither a revolutionary nor a religious movement; rather, it involved a weak, self-canceling mixture of each. More important, the attempt to offer religiously tinged "solutions" to material deprivations did nothing to stem the rapidly rising tide of Pentecostalism. Contrary to the consensus among social scientists (as well as bishops), compensation for material deprivations is *not* the basis of the Protestant appeal.

MATERIALIST HUMBUG

Social scientists interested in the rapid spread of Pentecostal Protestantism in Latin America have been in remarkable agreement about who is joining: they maintain that the typical convert is a poor, uneducated, married, older woman with health concerns, who lives in a rural area.[34] These scholars—an exceedingly distinguished set, it should be added—interpret such observations to demonstrate that Protestantism, especially of the Pentecostal variety, appeals primarily to "the damned of the earth."[35]

Unfortunately, most of the support for these generalizations does not come from survey data or even from personal observation of Protestant gatherings in Latin America. Instead, these claims often seem to reflect social scientific preconceptions—what "everyone knows." After all, everyone knows that religious movements are "the religious revolts of the poor"[36] and occur as "the desires of the poor to improve the material conditions of their lives . . . become transfused with phantasies of a new paradise."[37] And everyone knows that participation in *any* social movement is prompted by material factors rather than by idealism or faith. As Karl Marx explained, to suggest that people act from religious motives is to attempt to explain a "reality" by reference to an "unreality," which is "idealistic humbug."[38]

Even when scholars do not simply assume the role of material deprivations in producing Latin American Protestants and rely instead on actual observations of persons attending services, they can be badly misled. Consider that *any* crowd of Latin Americans that is fully representative of the population will contain a substantial percentage of poor, uneducated people. Hence, observing a preponderance of such people at a Pentecostal service wouldn't necessarily indicate anything except that Pentecostalism does not appeal exclusively to the rich.

Valid generalizations about the kinds of Latin Americans who convert to Protestantism require reliable surveys. And now that these surveys finally have become available from the Gallup World Poll, they refute all the material-deprivation explanations.[39] It is not just the poor who are joining; persons of all income levels are equally likely to join. Men are almost as likely as women to become Protestants, and the unmarried are not different from the married. Young people are slightly more likely than those over fifty to convert. Those with health problems are not more apt to become Protestants, and rural and urban residents are equally likely to convert. So much, then, for deprivation theory.

And so much, too, for liberation theology, since the growth of Protestantism in Latin America seems to be based on religious attractions. The best proof of this is the success of the second Catholic response to the Protestant challenge.

CATHOLIC CHARISMATICS

What has come to be known as the Catholic Charismatic Renewal movement was initiated by an outbreak of "baptisms in the Holy Spirit" that began at Duquesne University in Pittsburgh in 1967.[40] American priests took it south in the early 1970s. They "initially called themselves Pentecostal Catholics," as Andrew Chesnut observes.[41] That name was revealing: aside from some distinctive elements of Catholic culture such as an emphasis on the Virgin Mary, it is difficult to tell Protestant and Catholic charismatics apart. Both conduct vibrant, emotion-packed worship services during which clergy and members often engage in glossolalia, or speaking in tongues. Both put great stress on miraculous healing.

Having evolved into an international movement with a central headquarters in the Vatican, the Catholic Charismatic Renewal (CCR) now provides the backbone of Catholic commitment in Latin America. Although there are no reliable statistics on CCR membership broken down by nation, an estimated thirty million people in Latin America belong. In any event, their impact on the religious life of Latin America has been immense. Just as Protestant Pentecostals fill soccer stadia for massive revivals, CCR revivals fill the same stadia. In addition, the CCR has established tens of thousands of weekly prayer groups that, unlike the Base Communities, have generated intense levels of public commitment. The CRR achieved such influence not through sermons about how the Church could organize to mitigate material deprivations but by invoking the Holy Spirit. In other words, the Catholic Church activated religious motivations for religiousness.

CATHOLIC RENEWAL

Some statistics available to us suggest the energizing effect of the CCR. In 1960 only 4,093 men in the whole of Latin America were enrolled in Catholic seminaries (compared with 44,771 in the United States and Canada). By 2011 this figure had risen to 20,239.[42] Mass attendance has enjoyed a similarly huge increase, as can be seen in Table 3–2 (next page), which shows the percentage of Catholics in each Latin American nation who said yes when asked, "Have you attended a place of worship or religious service in the past seven days?"

In most of Latin America today, Catholics are attending church at a truly remarkable level. In seven of these nations the weekly attendance rate is 60 percent or higher—71 percent in Guatemala. Six more nations have Mass attendance rates above 52 percent. Compare this with Spain, where only 31 percent of Catholics say they attend Mass weekly, or Canada, where 29 percent attend Mass weekly. Argentina and Chile have attendance rates about the same as Spain's. Only in Uruguay (20 percent) is attendance at the low level thought to have been typical of Latin nations several decades ago—and Uruguay is a deviant case in many other ways as well.

Table 3–2: Current Catholic Mass Attendance in Latin America

	Attended in Past Seven Days
Guatemala	71%
Colombia	68%
El Salvador	67%
Honduras	65%
Ecuador	62%
Costa Rica	62%
Mexico	60%
Paraguay	59%
Bolivia	58%
Nicaragua	58%
Panama	57%
Dominican Republic	53%
Peru	52%
Brazil	47%
Venezuela	42%
Chile	34%
Argentina	31%
Uruguay	20%

Source: Gallup World Poll

Table 3–3 shows the percentage of the Catholics in each nation who answered yes when asked, "Is religion an important part of your daily life?" The level of subjective religiousness among Latin American Catholics is as astounding as their church attendance. Uruguay is much the lowest at only 53 percent, but that rate is higher than Spain's (44 percent).

Of course, this is precisely the effect that pluralism should have had in Latin America: Catholic Mass attendance should be higher where Protestants have been more successful.

And the data reveal that this is exactly what has happened. Where

Table 3–3: Percentage of Latin American Catholics Who Say Religion Is an Important Part of Their Daily Lives

Paraguay	92%
Honduras	91%
Panama	90%
El Salvador	89%
Brazil	89%
Bolivia	88%
Colombia	88%
Costa Rica	88%
Dominican Republic	88%
Guatemala	88%
Nicaragua	85%
Peru	85%
Ecuador	83%
Venezuela	75%
Chile	74%
Mexico	71%
Argentina	67%
Uruguay	53%

Source: Gallup World Poll

Protestants have been more successful, the Catholic response has been more energetic. Recall that for a correlation to be statistically significant, the odds must be at least twenty to one that it is not merely a random result. When we examine the percentages of Protestants who have attended church in the past seven days along with the percentages of Catholics who do the same, we find a correlation of .451, which is significant well beyond the twenty-to-one level. (For all correlations reported here, a scatterplot was examined and statistical tests performed to guard against any outlying case or cases distorting the results.)

A second test of the claim that pluralism has empowered Catholicism involves subjective religiousness: where Protestants have been more successful, Catholic subjective religiousness ought to be higher, too. And indeed, the correlation between the percent Protestant in a nation and Catholic subjective religiousness is .487.

In addition to provoking a strong Catholic response, the Protestant growth in Latin America should result in a higher overall level of public religiousness. And, in fact, the correlation between the percentage of the population that is Protestant and the overall rate of church attendance is .480. The correlation between the percentage of the population that is Protestant and the overall rate of subjective religiousness is .430.

Contrary to the sociological orthodoxy, pluralism results in active and effective churches.

RELIGIOUS HOSTILITY

Until quite recently, Latin America was a closed society insofar as religion was concerned. As noted, not only were non-Catholic faiths prohibited by law, but even Bibles were treated as contraband. In the second half of the twentieth century, the rise of Protestant sects in Latin America led the Catholic hierarchy to bitterly denounce Protestantism in terms not heard in Europe since the days of the Reformation. Even Pope John Paul II, often a voice for religious tolerance, bitterly attacked the "evangelical sects" as "voracious wolves."[43] Presumably, these attitudes shape public opinion. And Table 3–4 shows that they do.

The most recent World Values Surveys (2010–2014) included nine Latin American nations. One of the items in the survey was: "How much do you trust people of another religion?" Mistrust is rampant. On average, 55 percent of Latin Americans don't trust someone of another religion, ranging from 80 percent in Peru down to 36 percent in Trinidad and Tobago.

And the mistrust is mutual between Protestant and Catholics, there being no significant difference in their levels of mistrust in any nation (not shown in table). One can, perhaps, explain these high levels of mistrust as the expected consequence of competition. But that explanation

**Table 3–4: Percentage Who Do Not Trust
People of a Different Religion**

Argentina	39%
Brazil	40%
Chile	45%
Colombia	69%
Ecuador	65%
Mexico	71%
Peru	80%
Costa Rica	88%
Trinidad and Tobago	36%
Uruguay	47%
Average	**55%**

Source: World Values Survey

fails when one turns to the prevalence of anti-Semitism in Latin America. There are not many Jews in this region, and they certainly do not seek to convert either Protestants or Catholics. But anti-Semitism is widespread, as can be seen in Table 3–5 (next page).

Overall, about a third of Latin Americans score high on this Index of Anti-Semitism: from a high of 52 percent in Panama down to 16 percent in Brazil. Some Latin American anti-Semitism is probably a hold-over from days when Christians did teach that the Jews were outcasts, guilty of the Crucifixion.[44] But for several generations the Catholic Church and most Protestant bodies have actively renounced this position and have vigorously opposed anti-Semitism. Unfortunately, religious sources of anti-Semitism have been replaced by political sources—especially leftists such as Hugo Chavez and his successors in Venezuela. But perhaps even more important is the prevalence of pro-Arab media such as HispanTV, a Spanish-language satellite news channel operated by Iran's state media and aimed primarily at Latin America. The content is extremely anti-Semitic and anti-Israel. One result is that the long discredited hoax book *The Protocols of the Elders of Zion*, which purports

Table 3–5: Percentage Who Score High on the Index of Anti-Semitism (2013–14)

Argentina	24%
Honduras Bolivia	30%
Brazil	16%
El Salvador Chile	37%
Colombia	41%
Costa Rica	32%
Dominican Republic	41%
Guatemala	36%
Haiti	26%
Jamaica	18%
Mexico	24%
Nicaragua	34%
Panama	52%
Paraguay	35%
Peru	38%
Trinidad and Tobago	24%
Uruguay	33%
Venezuela	30%

Source: Anti-Defamation League, *Global 100* (2015)

to be the minutes of a meeting by the international Zionist conspiracy to rule the world, is suddenly widely for sale—especially in Venezuela.

This, then, is the dark side of religious life in Latin America.

FULL CHURCHES

In any event, the Catholic Church has undergone a stunning awakening in Latin America. Where once the bishops were content with bogus claims about a Catholic land and a reality of low levels of commitment, the Catholic churches in Latin America are now filled on Sundays with devoted members, many of them also active in charismatic groups that meet during the week. And the source of this remarkable change has been the rapid growth of intense Protestant faiths, which created a highly competitive pluralist environment.

Simply put, Latin America has never been so Catholic—and that's precisely because so many Protestants are there now.

This is not the first time pluralism has galvanized the Catholic Church. Toward the middle of the nineteenth century, the massive influx of Catholic immigrants to America brought with them the low levels of participation and concern that prevailed in their European nations of origin. Initially, many of these Catholic immigrants defected to Protestant groups that aggressively missionized among them. But the American Catholic clergy quickly adjusted by adopting Protestant techniques (including revival meetings), and soon the American Catholic Church was far stronger and more effective than any in Europe.[45]

In Latin America, the Catholic Church has reached new heights of member commitment by adopting major elements of their Protestant Pentecostal competitors. The Catholic Latin America of myth is truly becoming a land of Charismatic Christians.

The experience of Latin America over the past century underscores a simple truth that scholars so often fail to see: churches thrive by offering an appealing faith, not by trying to buy people off with political promises.

4

ISLAM INTENSIFIED

Muslims may never before have been as religious as they are today, and certainly not for many centuries. This new piety thrives not just among the masses making up the so-called Arab Street but even more so among the most educated and affluent.

Nor have Muslims ever been more militant and sectarian. Every day brings violent incidents somewhere in the Muslim world—Shiʻa set off bombs in a Sunni neighborhood; Sunnis machine-gun Shiʻah who are on their way home from a mosque; both groups attack those engaged in "immoral" behavior, such as girls who dare to attend school, or those who belong to another of Islam's many sects. More than 70 percent of all Muslim terrorist victims are other Muslims.[1]

Despite this bitter sectarianism, Muslims today are united in their desire for governments influenced by Shariʻa (Muslim law), and many support imposing capital punishment on blasphemers or on any Muslim who converts to another religion. Large majorities of Muslims also are united in their hostility toward Jews, and only somewhat less so toward anyone of another faith.

Islam is a faith militant.

THE GREAT MUSLIM "REVIVAL"

During much of the twentieth century, all the Western "experts"—including those employed by the CIA—assumed that Muslims were rapidly becoming secularized, in part because so many Islamic nations were ruled by what claimed to be Marxist regimes. The experts also believed that, since secularization was the wave of the future and the inevitable result of modernization, the clock could not be turned back. Thus, as the remarkable Mary Douglas gleefully pointed out,[2] no Western experts anticipated the most significant development in Muslim culture since the days of the Prophet: in the 1960s there suddenly erupted a massive revival of intense and strict forms of Islam.

This revival was reflected in a huge increase in the number making a pilgimage (Hajj) to Mecca. In the 1940s and 1950s, pilgrims numbered only about 100,000 a year. By the mid-1970s, pilgrims had risen to more than a million a year; by 2000, the total had doubled to about two million; in 2012, the total topped three million for the first time. Many more pilgrims would have come had the Saudi government not limited the available visas because of the great difficulty involved in providing food, water, and shelter for so many in the midst of the desert.

Even better data for tracking the Muslim revival are available for Turkey, still regarded as the most secularized Muslim nation. Modern Turkey emerged from a revolution that overthrew the Ottoman Empire in the aftermath of World War I. Under the leadership of Mustafa Kemal Atatürk, the Republic of Turkey was founded in 1923 as a secular state—to such an extent that in 1925 it became illegal for men to wear a fez (a round, brimless, flat-topped hat with an attached tassel) in public or for women to wear a hijab (a long headscarf) in schools or government buildings. Both items were regarded as too openly religious. Finally, the Atatürk regime prohibited the use of Arabic to give the call to prayer, requiring that it be done in Turkish instead.

The Muslim revival probably hit with less impact in Turkey than in many other Muslim nations, such as Egypt or Kuwait. Even so, it has made impressive progress there. For starters, the revival has succeeded in rolling back Atatürk-era secular measures. In 2011 Turkey lifted the ban against the hijab for universities, and in 2013 it did the same for government buildings. The Muslim faithful today regard the hijab as essential to female modesty, short of wearing a veil. Moreover, the call to prayer is once again done always in Arabic, not Turkish.

Survey data help complete the picture. In 1978 fewer than a third of the students at the elite University of Ankara held orthodox Islamic beliefs; in 1991 the overwhelming majority held these beliefs. These students have, of course, gone on to be the political and intellectual leaders of the nation.[3] The Muslim revival among the students simply reflected what was happening in the general Turkish population, as shown in Table 4–1.

Table 4–1: Increases in Religiousness in Turkey

	Percentage Who Say "Yes"		
	1990	2011	Change
"Would you say religion is very important in your life?"	83%	93%	+10%
"Would you say you are a religious person?"	73%	84%	+11%
Believe in Hell	84%	97%	+13%

Sources: World Values Surveys, 1990 and 2011

No data are available for a Muslim society prior to 1990, by which point the Muslim revival was already far along. Nevertheless, even in this rather short period that began well into the Muslim revival, we see a substantial increase in the percentage of Turks who say that religion is very important in their lives, that they are "a religious person," and that they believe in Hell—the last being something almost everyone in Turkey believed in by 2011.

Of course, it would be nice to have data on the Muslim religious revival in other nations, but the World Values Surveys did not include other Muslim nations until the year 2000, and the Gallup World Poll began only in 2005. Still, studies show dramatic shifts toward strict Islamic beliefs and practices among Muslim university students in Egypt,[4] Pakistan, Afghanistan,[5] Nigeria, Senegal, and France.[6]

More important, solid data exist demonstrating the remarkable current levels of religiousness in Muslim nations. Recall from chapter 1 that for the Muslim nations overall, 90 percent said that religion played an important part in their daily lives. As for belief, Table 4–2 is based on the Muslim nations available in recent World Values Surveys. It could not be more convincing.

It is very unlikely that belief in Hell was nearly this universal in these Islamic nations thirty years ago. We know that the belief in Hell was less widespread in Turkey, as Table 4–1 demonstrates.

Finally, the most recent World Values Surveys asked respondents to agree or disagree with the statement "Whenever religion and science conflict, religion is always right." Table 4–3 (next page) shows the results.

Table 4–2: Percentage Who Believe in Hell

Algeria	100%
Egypt	100%
Jordan	99%
Pakistan	99%
Iraq	98%
Saudi Arabia	98%
Turkey	97%
Iran	94%
Bangladesh	94%
Lebanon	92%
Libya	91%

Sources: World Values Surveys, most recent year question was asked

Table 4–3: "Whenever science and religion conflict, religion is always right"[7]

Percentage Who Agree

Qatar	98%
Jordan	97%
Pakistan	96%
Yemen	96%
Egypt	95%
Tunisia	94%
Palestinian Territories	93%
Algeria	92%
Libya	92%
Iraq	88%
Kuwait	84%
Lebanon*	75%
Turkey	70%

Muslims only

Sources: World Values Surveys, 2010–14

What an overwhelming consensus! The Muslim revival is real.

This revival is often described as a return to medieval ideals and practices, as represented by bearded mullahs in ancient attire who officially condone "honor killings" of female family members suspected of immorality, and by terrorists who detonate their explosive vests among the "godless." Western observers committed to the secularization doctrine cannot grasp how these religious developments could be anything but a regression to backward times.

But there is nothing medieval about any of this. Although a central aspect of the Muslim revival involves a call for a return to imaginary "good old days," that revival is occurring among people who are essentially modern and urban. As the historian of Islam Ira Lapidus put it, "This is a return to the Qur'an in the way that the Protestant Reformation was a return to the Bible—a turn to the past to look for inspiration for adaptation to current and future conditions."[8] Those who embrace the strict forms of Islam that flourish today are not "traditionalists"; as the French scholar Olivier Roy points out, these Muslims "live the values of the modern city—consumerism and upward social mobility; they left behind the old forms of conviviality, respect for elders and for consensus, when they left their villages."[9]

Anti-Westernism is another important aspect of the Muslim revival. Anti-Western sentiment grew out of anticolonialism, but it has been inflamed by the immorality of popular Western culture—which even offends millions of religious Westerners. When asked if exposure to Western culture was a serious problem, 92 percent of Jordanians and 83 percent of Egyptians said it was.[10] This, too, is an urban, modern reaction in that all forms of Western culture are nearly invisible in the villages. Consequently, it is the most educated and modern Muslims who are most offended.

Survey data give the lie to the claim that the Muslim revival is occurring overwhelmingly among the poor and uneducated. As Table 4–4 shows, weekly mosque attendance is not unique to the lower class. In fact, in eleven of the fourteen Muslim nations surveyed, the most educated have the *highest* percentage of people who attend mosque weekly.

RULE BY SHARI'A

As the centerpiece of its political demands, the Muslim revival aims to establish Shari'a as the basis of the legal system. Shari'a is the moral code and religious law of Islam. Strictly speaking it is divine law, derived from the Qur'an and from the examples set by Muhammad. Shari'a is extremely comprehensive, extending to politics and economics as well as to crime and personal matters such as sex, hygiene, diet, prayer, and fasting. Moreover, it is considered to be infallible, to be laws directly given by Allah.

The main motive of Muslim terrorists is to enforce Shari'a in circumstances where the government does not sustain it. To produce,

Table 4–4: Education and Weekly Mosque Attendance

	Percentage Who Attended in Past Week		
Education	Elementary	Secondary	Higher Ed.
Afghanistan	65	81	77
Algeria	53	50	52
Bangladesh	79	85	90
Egypt	52	66	70
Iran	50	44	41
Iraq	52	50	53
Kuwait	90	90	92
Libya	66	69	72
Morocco	65	62	74
Pakistan	52	66	69
Palestinian Terr.	51	50	58
Saudi Arabia	69	64	74
Turkey	52	58	46
Yemen	44	64	72

Source: Gallup World Poll

serve, or consume alcohol is a sin—hence the bombing of bars. Sex, except within marriage, is a sin—hence honor killings. To abandon the True Faith is an abomination—hence beheading neighbors suspected of reading the Bible. All other religions are false—hence attempts to blow up huge statues of Buddha and the burning of churches. Of course, as with all law, Shari'a must be interpreted and applied to particular cases, and that places immense authority in the hands of *imams* and *ulama*, the elite clerics.

It is the primary goal of militant Muslim groups to establish Shari'a everywhere. What do most Muslims think about that?

Table 4–5 (next page) tells the story.

Table 4–5: Percentage of Muslims Who Endorse Shari'a

	Believe Shari'a must be the only source of legislation	Believe Shari'a must be a source of legislation	Combined
Saudi Arabia	72%	27%	99%
Qatar	70%	29%	99%
Yemen	67%	31%	98%
Egypt	67%	31%	98%
Afghanistan	67%	28%	95%
Pakistan	65%	28%	93%
Jordan	64%	35%	99%
Bangladesh	61%	33%	94%
United Arab Em.	57%	40%	97%
Palestinian Terr.	52%	44%	96%
Iraq	49%	45%	94%
Libya	49%	44%	93%
Kuwait	46%	52%	98%
Morocco	41%	55%	96%
Algeria	37%	52%	89%
Syria	29%	57%	86%
Tunisia	24%	67%	91%
Iran	14%	70%	84%

Source: Gallup World Poll

As can be seen from this table, nearly everyone in these Muslim nations wants Shari'a to play a substantial role in their governance. There are, however, marked national differences in the degree to which they want to be governed by Shari'a. Thus, while 72 percent of Saudis want to be governed *only* by Shari'a, a mere 14 percent of Iranians agree with them—evidence that the mullahs in Iran rule a more "secular" people than is allowed to express itself in public. Many will be surprised where Egypt stands on this issue, being far more similar to Saudi Arabia, Yemen, and Afghanistan than to its neighbors Libya, Algeria, and Morocco. But this is consistent with how high Egypt stands on other extremist issues, as will be seen. Despite these variations, nearly every Muslim in each of these nations wants Shariʻa to play a significant role in governance—Iranians are lowest at 84 percent.

EXCLUDING UNBELIEVERS

Diversity is not regarded as a virtue in Muslim nations, at least not when it comes to religion. The Muslim revival has resulted in near unanimity that "the only acceptable religion is my religion," as recent World Values Surveys show.[11] It has also led to an exodus of Christians and Jews from many Muslim nations. Table 4–6 (next page) examines Christian flight since 1975.

Over the past four decades the percentage of Christians has declined in fifteen of the seventeen Muslim nations surveyed. In one, Pakistan, the percentage remained the same. Only in Syria did Christians increase their portion of the population. The growth of the Christian community in Syria reflects the fact that, for all its flaws, the Syrian regime has been tolerant, and even protective, of its Christian minority, which is made up primarily of Greek and Eastern Orthodox Christians. Some Christians who fled other Middle Eastern nations have settled in Syria.

But the recent bloody civil war has fallen especially hard on Syria's Christians; many of the rebel groups have committed atrocities against Christian communities. By 2013 jihadist forces were overrunning Christian enclaves in Syria. When rebels took control of Maaloula, one of Syria's oldest Christian communities, they burned down the town's churches and drove out Christian residents.[12] As the BBC News reported, in areas the jihadist group ISIS has seized, "Christians have been ordered to convert to Islam, pay jizya (a religious levy), or face death." ISIS forces abducted more than two hundred Syrian Christians in February 2015. The Islamist threat has forced thousands of Christians from their homes. Jihadist rebels have kidnapped senior Christian clerics as well.[13]

Table 4–6: Changes in the Percentage
of the Christian Population

	1975	2014	Change
Algeria	0.8%	0.2%	–0.6%
Bahrain	3.7%	1.1%	–2.6%
Bangladesh	0.5%	0.4%	–0.1%
Egypt	18.2%	5.1%	–13.1%
Iran	0.9%	0.1%	–0.8%
Iraq	3.8%	1.4%	–2.4%
Jordan	5.1%	1.7%	–3.4%
Kuwait	4.5%	1.5%	–3.0%
Lebanon	61.1%	37.8	–23.3%
Libya	2.3%	0.1%	–2.2%
Morocco	0.7%	0.0%	–0.7%
Pakistan	1.8%	1.8%	—
Palestinian Territories	4.7%	1.1%	–3.6%
Saudi Arabia	0.5%	0.2%	–0.3%
Syria	9.4%	11.0%	+1.6%
Turkey	0.6%	0.2%	–0.4%
Yemen	0.1%	0.0%	–0.1%

Sources: 1975: Barrett (1982); 2014: Gallup World Poll

As those examples suggest, intolerance of other religions in Muslim nations can manifest itself in the most violent forms. Consider the two nations where by far the most dramatic decline in the percentage of Christians has taken place: Egypt and Lebanon. Attacks on Christians are endemic in Egypt. Upon taking office in 2014, Egyptian president Abdel Fattah el-Sisi called for unity and tried to protect Coptic Christians. But the persecution escalated once again in 2015. In one incident, a Muslim mob descended on the homes of Coptic Christians, throwing rocks. After ISIS forces captured twenty-one Egyptian Christians in Libya and beheaded them on video, a mob attacked Christians in the Egyptian village that had been home to thirteen of the twenty-one murdered.[14] Little wonder, then, that the Christian percentage of Egypt's population has declined so precipitously over the past four decades. Sources typically indicate that Christians account for about 10 percent of the Egyptian population, but the Gallup World Poll data (based on 13,816 interviews) place the Christian community at only half that size. These new data suggest that Christian flight has been even more considerable than most people have realized.

As for Lebanon, in 1975 Christians made up nearly two-thirds of its citizens. Today they make up little more than a third. This exodus resulted from a civil war that began in 1975 and continued until 1990. During that time Muslim militias murdered thousands of Christians and razed their villages. Nor did Christians stop fleeing when the war ended. In 2007 the *Telegraph* of London reported that sixty thousand Christians had left Lebanon in less than a year, and a poll showed that nearly half of the country's Maronite Christian population was considering emigrating. The rise of radical Islam and increasing tension between Sunni and Shi'a Muslim factions were driving Christians away.[15]

As for the decline in Jews living in Muslim nations, the Gallup World Polls can offer no useful data because Jews have become too few to be estimated reliably by survey samples. The Gallup samples for the seventeen nations shown in Table 4–6 total 124,171 respondents. Of these respondents, only 5 were Jews—and in fifteen of the seventeen nations, not a single Jewish person responded.

But we can gauge the flight of Jews from Muslim nations by looking at census data. Table 4–7 (next page) is based on census data published in 2015 by the *Wall Street Journal*.[16]

As the data show, the exodus has produced remarkable changes: in 1948 nearly 850,000 Jews lived in the nine Muslim nations studied; today there are fewer than 5,000.

Table 4–7: The Flight of Jews from Muslim Nations

| | Total Number of Resident Jews | | |
	1948	2015	Percentage Decline
Algeria	140,000	0	–100%
Egypt	75,000	50	–99.93%
Iraq	135,000	10	–99.99%
Lebanon	5,000	100	–98%
Libya	38,000	0	–100%
Morocco	265,000	2,500	–99%
Syria	30,000	50	–99.83%
Tunisia	105,000	1,500	–98.57%
Yemen	55,000	100	–99.82%
Total	**848,000**	**4,310**	**–99.49%**

Source: Lagnado, 2015

RELIGIOUS HOSTILITY

Quite simply, anti-Semitism is rampant in Muslim nations. This is hardly surprising given the constant expressions of hatred toward Jews by the Muslim media and in Muslim schools. For example, a TV program aimed at young children sponsored by the Palestinian Authority has a giant cuddly bee character that encourages young viewers to attack Jews; in one episode a young girl says she wants to grow up just like her uncle and be a policeman who "shoots Jews."[17] Should Saudi Arabian parents ask their children in the eighth grade, "What did you learn in school today?" the kids might quote the following from one of their required textbooks: "They are the people of the Sabbath, whose young people God turned into apes, and whose old people God turned into swine to punish them. As cited in Ibn Abbas: The apes are Jews, the keepers of the Sabbath; while the swine are the Christian infidels of the communion of Jesus."[18] Saudi students in the ninth grade will read this in their textbook: "The annihilation of the Jewish people is imperative."[19] Given all this, Table 4–8 should come as no surprise.

Table 4–8: Percentage Who Score High on the Index of Anti-Semitism (2013–14)

Algeria	87%
Bahrain	81%
Egypt	75%
Iran	56%
Iraq	92%
Jordan	81%
Kuwait	82%
Lebanon	78%
Libya	87%
Morocco	81%
Oman	76%
Palestinian Territories	93%
Qatar	80%
Saudi Arabia	74%
Tunisia	86%
Turkey	69%
United Arab Emirates	80%
Yemen	88%
Average	**80%**

Source: Anti-Defamation League, *Global 100* (2015)

Overall, eight out of ten people in these eighteen Muslim nations score high on the Index of Anti-Semitism. In the Palestinian Territories, where children's TV approves of shooting the Jews, 93 percent score high. Iran, at 56 percent, has the fewest high scorers. Significantly, 65 percent of the respondents in these eighteen nations blame Jews "for most of the world's wars," and 63 percent say the Holocaust "was a myth or an exaggeration."

Another common method of measuring religious hostility is to ask whether someone would object to having people of a different religion as neighbors. Table 4–9 shows responses to that question in Muslim nations.

Table 4–9: Percentage Who Would Not Want People of a Different Religion as Neighbors

Bangladesh	66
Libya	54
Yemen	53
Palestinian Territories	50
Jordan	50
Algeria	43
Saudi Arabia	40
Iran	38
Morocco	36
Iraq	35
Turkey	35
Lebanon	34

Sources: World Values Surveys, most recent survey in each nation

Unfortunate as these numbers are, be aware that many respondents who were willing to have members of another religion next door had in mind Muslims of a different sect, not Christians, Jews, Buddhists, or Hindus.

Indeed, when asked specifically whether they would want to have any Jews living nearby, 83 percent of people in Iraq and 62 percent of those in Egypt volunteered that they would not.[20]

DEADLY CONVERSION

On May 15, 2014, the government of Sudan sentenced twenty-seven-year-old Meriam Yehya Ibrahim to death for having become a Christian. In addition, she was sentenced to one hundred lashes for adultery because her marriage to a Christian was considered invalid. She was to be flogged before being hanged.

Under intense pressure from Western diplomats, the Sudanese government finally permitted this young woman to leave for the United States. But her conviction and death sentence were not peculiar to this African nation. Apostasy is outlawed by Shari'a, and anyone who defects from Islam can be sentenced to death in many Islamic nations, including Egypt. In fact, in some nations, including Afghanistan and Saudi Arabia, death is the *mandatory* sentence for quitting Islam.

The Pew Forum on Religion and Public Life has published surveys in which Muslims were asked whether they favor or oppose the death penalty for people who leave the Muslim religion. As Table 4–10 demonstrates, support for killing defectors from the faith is depressingly high in most Muslim nations. In Egypt, *88 percent* approve. Jordanians (83 percent) are nearly as favorable. Only in Tunisia (18 percent), Lebanon (17 percent), and Turkey (8 percent) is there little support, and these are three of the most "secular" Muslim nations. Remarkably, 31 percent of Muslims living in Great Britain approve.[21]

Table 4–10: Percentage of Muslims Who Favor the Death Penalty for Anyone Who Leaves the Muslim Religion

Egypt	88%
Jordan	83%
Afghanistan	79%
Pakistan	75%
Palestinian Territories	62%
Djibouti	62%
Malaysia	58%
Bangladesh	43%
Iraq	41%
Tunisia	18%
Lebanon	17%
Turkey	8%

Source: Pew Forum, *The World's Muslims* (2013)

GENDER INEQUALITIES

The situation of women in Islamic nations is much in the news. It certainly is true that Muslim women do not enjoy the freedom that prevails in the West and that many aspects of their situation greatly offends Western sensibilities. It also is true that the primary basis for their situation is religion. But Western critics almost completely ignore how Muslim women feel about many of these arrangements. Consider Table 4–11.

Table 4–11: "How Important Is It for Women to Wear a Veil in Public Places?"

	Percentage Who Say It Is "Important"	
	Men	Women
Egypt	95%	95%
Saudi Arabia	92%	91%
Iraq	89%	92%
Iran	88%	85%
Jordan	83%	83%
Bangladesh	76%	75%
Algeria	75%	74%
Indonesia	70%	71%
Turkey	14%	9%

Sources: World Values Surveys, 2000–2014

Only in Turkey are women even slightly less likely than men to favor veils; in every other nation, veils are favored overwhelmingly and equally by both men and women. This should come as no surprise. In all societies men and women tend to have similar ideas about proper sex roles because they were socialized into a common culture. That is, both boys and girls are taught similar lessons about how boys and girls, and then men and women, are supposed to behave. Therefore most

Muslims, male and female, embrace the sex role differences sustained by Islam.

HONOR KILLINGS

Too often, families kill wives or daughters (and rarely a son) because they believe they have dishonored the family, usually by being suspected of sexual misdeeds. Many of the cases are truly bizarre: A young girl strangled by her family for having been raped by her cousins. A girl killed by her brother when he discovered she owned a cell phone—he assumed she must be using it for immoral purposes. A young woman beaten to death by her brothers for wearing slacks. A couple hanged from a tree—while the neighbors laughed—because the young man and young woman had eloped without the permission of the girl's family. Each of these incidents was reported by the press in 2012.

In 2013 the Pew Forum's global survey of Muslims asked respondents to what extent it is justified for family members, to protect the family's honor, to kill a woman who engages in premarital sex or adultery. Table 4–12 (next page) shows the percentage of Muslims in each country who responded that such killings were sometimes justified or often justified.

Only in Afghanistan (60 percent) and Iraq (60 percent) do the majority endorse honor killings. But in most nations a substantial minority of Muslims support honor killings, which helps explain why authorities in most of these nations have proved unwilling to prosecute those who commit such murders. For example, honor killings occur regularly in Pakistan, where 41 percent of Muslims approve of the practice. According to a report by the Human Rights Commission of Pakistan, 913 girls and women were known to have been "honor-killed" in Pakistan during 2012.[22] The report said that 604 were killed after being accused of having illicit relations with men. Another 191 were killed for marrying without the approval of their family. Often the killings were approved by local tribal courts.

**Table 4–12: Is It Justified for Family Members, to
Protect the Family's Honor, to End the Life of a Woman
Who Engages in Premarital Sex or Adultery?**

	Percentage of Muslims Who Responded Sometimes/Often Justified
Afghanistan*	60%
Iraq*	60%
Jordan	41%
Lebanon	41%
Pakistan	41%
Egypt	38%
Palestinian Territories	37%
Bangladesh	36%
Tunisia	28%
Turkey	18%
Morocco	11%

*In these countries, the question was modified to: "Some people think that
if a woman brings dishonor to her family it is justified for family members
to end her life in order to protect the family's honor. Do you personally
feel that this practice is often justified, sometimes justified, rarely
justified, or never justified?"*

A significant number of honor killings have occurred even in
Europe, the United States, and Canada.[23] Moreover, the incidence
of honor killings appears to be rising—although this may partly be
the result of greater willingness of authorities to prosecute. Unfortunately, public discussion of honor killings often arouses angry attacks
from Muslim organizations and from well-meaning advocates of inter-
religious harmony.

ISLAMOPHOBIA?

Efforts to deny any significant link between violent acts of terrorism and Islam are widespread, especially in the news media and government circles. Thus, although Major Nidal Malik Hasan shouted "Allahu Akbar" while he gunned down his victims in a murderous outburst at Fort Hood in 2009, the U.S. government denies that this was an act of terrorism, insisting it was only an incident of "workplace violence." The words *Muslim* and *jihad* never appear in the official Department of Defense report on this incident (*Protecting the Force*: *Lessons from Fort Hood*), and the word *Islam* appears only once, in a footnote. In similar fashion, a study of terrorism issued by the Department of Homeland Security (*Evolution of the Terrorist Threat to the United States*) mentions Islam only once. Former attorney general Eric Holder, when testifying before Congress, refused to admit that the actions of various Muslim terrorists could be linked to religious motives. The underlying issue here has nothing much to do with who did what or why but everything to do with the highly charged concept of Islamophobia—of which no one wants to be guilty.

The standard definition of Islamophobia is "prejudice against, hatred towards, or irrational fear of Muslims."[24] Leading proponents of this definition, most of whom apply it whenever any links are drawn between terrorism and Islamic radicalism, are primarily western European intellectuals who participate in international commissions and forums, and leading Muslim spokespersons living in the West. And, of course, Islamophobia is enshrined in the many "hate speech" statutes that abound in Europe. Undoubtedly, some people are Islamophobic, just as some are anti-Semitic and others hate evangelical Christians. Trouble arises when the charge of Islamophobia is used to silence all comments on the obvious religious motivation of so many terrorists. Thus, in the immediate aftermath of the murderous attack on the staff of the French satirical magazine *Charlie Hebdo* that left twelve dead, the prominent former Democratic Party chairman Howard Dean appeared on MSNBC to condemn all references to "Muslim" terrorists, saying, "They're about as Muslim as I am," since their actions were contrary to "what the Koran says." *New York Times* columnist Nicholas Kristof quickly agreed: "Let's avoid religious profiling." And President Barack Obama, Secretary of State John Kerry, and various White House spokespeople avoided any mention of the fact that these terrorists were Muslims.

What, then, are we to make of claims by prominent Muslims in the Middle East who praise terrorists for doing their duty for Allah? Omar Bakri, a Muslim cleric living in Lebanon, said that the two who beheaded a British soldier on a London street were "courageous and brave.... I don't see it as a crime as far as Islam is concerned."[25]

I am fully aware that millions of Muslims are not motivated by their faith to hate, let alone to kill those who do not fully share their religious outlook, and that many Muslim clerics teach that Islam is a religion of peace. But it is absurd to ignore the fact that most current religious terrorists are Muslims who justify their actions on religious grounds.

Responses to Muslim terrorism have long generated confessions that terrorism exists because Americans, and Westerners in general, have offended Muslims in so many ways, including by supporting Israel, that they really have only themselves to blame. In the immediate wake of the 9/11 attack, former president Bill Clinton cited the Crusades as one of "our" crimes against Islam. More recently, while speaking at the National Prayer Breakfast in Washington, and in the aftermath of televised beheadings by ISIS terrorists, President Obama also stressed Christian guilt for the Crusades. This is twisted history,[26] but rather than dispute that claim here, it seems sufficient to point out that most Muslim terrorism is against *other Muslims*. It seems unlikely that even the most ardent apologists for Islam would suppose that either Western or American misdeeds are the reason why Sunni Muslims kill and are killed by Shi'a.

MODERN MUSLIMS

Contrary to what the secularization faithful would have predicted, the rise of a far more intense and militant Islam seems primarily to have been a response to modernization. The traditional Islam sustained in the isolated village cultures of most Muslim nations at the end of the nineteenth century was relatively lax and accommodated to worldliness. Then, as modernity broke down the isolation within and across Muslim nations, the result was not the proliferation of "enlightened" irreligiousness but rather the rise of national and international Islamic leaders and movements. Partly in response to Muslim economic and industrial "backwardness," and partly in reaction against the forces of secularization, these emerging leaders and movements generated widespread, militant commitment to a variety of strict forms of Islam. This intensification of Islam is not a regression into a pious past. Whatever else it may be, this is "modern" Islam.

It was not only among Muslims that modernity resulted in a great increase in religiousness. That happened in Sub-Saharan Africa, too. Only here, modernity provoked not an intensification of prevailing faiths but a massive conversion to Christianity.

5

SUB-SAHARAN AFRICAN PIETY

When people refer to "Africa," they seldom mean to include the Arab nations lining the Mediterranean Sea, an area identified as North Africa. What they usually mean by Africa is the area south of the Sahara Desert.

And even when they specify Sub-Saharan Africa, people typically exclude the northern countries—such as Sudan and Chad—that are contiguous with the Arab states and that have long been Islamic societies. What usually is meant by Sub-Saharan Africa is the huge southern region where as recently as 1900 nearly everyone still pursued a tribal religion. This region proved to be an incredibly fertile field for Christian missionaries.

Today nearly everyone in the region has become a Christian. But some might wonder what's really new here. Are the people of southern Africa really any more religious, or did they simply trade their tribal religions for Christianity?

The religious shift in southern Africa has been massive. In fact, nowhere has the global religious awakening been more dramatic than in southern Sub-Saharan Africa. Consider that among active Christian churchgoers, more live in this region than anywhere else on earth. As noted in chapter 1, an average of *71 percent* of people in Sub-Saharan Africa report attending religious services within the past seven days.

This rate of church attendance is astonishingly high—much greater than can be found anywhere else.

The conversion of Sub-Saharan Africa has brought important changes—for example, it has significantly improved the situation of women, as will be seen. Unfortunately, religion has not mitigated the frequency or severity of civil wars or made Sub-Saharan nations less subject to brutal, tyrannical rule.

Still, how southern Africa's religious transformation came about is a remarkable story, one that involves a wide variety of actors. It is a story that illustrates the dynamics of religious awakening, especially the importance of competition and pluralism.

INTO AFRICA

For centuries Sub-Saharan Africa was defended against Western intruders by a microorganism to which native-born Africans were somewhat immune. Beginning with a Portuguese expedition to explore the Congo in 1485, Westerners had to abandon one venture into Africa after another because of appalling death rates from malaria. For example, in 1832 the British merchant-adventurer Macgregor Laird sailed a steamboat up the Niger River. Of the forty-eight Europeans aboard, only nine returned—the rest having died of disease, mainly of malaria.[1] Of eighty-nine English missionaries who went to West Africa between 1804 and 1825, fifty-four died and fourteen went home in ill health.[2] The historian Philip Curtain reported staggering death rates of 48 percent of British military personnel stationed in Sierra Leone between 1817 and 1836, and of 67 percent for troops assigned to the British installation on the Gold Coast.[3]

Then came quinine. During the seventeenth century Jesuits in Peru had discovered the effectiveness of the bark of the cinchona tree for treating malaria (the bark is a natural source of quinine). But few European physicians accepted claims made for the ground bark, and for many years an amazing array of quack treatments were preferred. Only in the 1830s did clinical tests by French army doctors demonstrate that quinine worked. Soon cinchona bark became a major export from Latin America, rising from two million pounds in 1860 to twenty million in 1881.[4] With the widespread use of quinine, Sub-Saharan Africa was no longer the "white man's grave," and the rush of Europeans began—explorers, treasure hunters, settlers, colonizers, and missionaries.

In 1870 about 10 percent of Africa, including the Arab North, was under European control. By 1914 this had risen to 90 percent; only Ethiopia and Liberia remained independent. Even though ruled by Europeans, the Muslim nations were both dangerous and unrewarding areas for Christian missionaries. In contrast, the southern region of Sub-Saharan Africa was both relatively safe and a fertile mission field, as shown in Table 5–1 (next page).

In 1900, South Africa (42 percent), Madagascar (39 percent), and Ethiopia (37 percent) already had large Christian populations, and Ethiopia (26 percent) and Nigeria (26 percent) had substantial numbers of Muslims. But elsewhere nearly everyone pursued one of the traditional tribal religions. These traditional faiths offered little resistance to the spread of Christianity.

ROMAN CATHOLIC MISSIONS

The first Catholic missionaries went to Sub-Saharan Africa as part of the explorations dispatched by Prince Henry the Navigator of Portugal (1394–1460). But these expeditions were unable to penetrate inland because of the malaria barrier. Serious Catholic missionizing efforts did not begin until the availability of quinine led to the European rush to colonize the whole subcontinent. Thus, Catholic missionaries had no significant head start over Protestant missionaries. The religious preference of various European colonial nations shaped missions. For example, Catholic missionaries were welcomed in French colonies and Protestants were given preference in British colonies. Both French and British colonial authorities were, however, often in conflict with the missionaries, who tended to side with the local population in disputes.

In any event, Roman Catholic missionaries poured into Africa from about 1870 on. By 1910, there were 1,843 European Catholic priests and 41 local priests serving in Africa. They were assisted by 1,389 brothers

Table 5–1: Religious Composition of
Southern Sub-Saharan Africa, 1900

	% Muslim	% Christian	% Tribal Faiths
Angola	1	0	99
Benin	1	7	92
Botswana	14	0	86
Burundi	0	0	100
Cameroon	0	5	95
Central African Republic	0	1	99
Belgian Congo	3	0	97
Ethiopia	26	37	37
Gabon	0	7	93
Ghana	5	5	90
Ivory Coast	5	0	95
Kenya	3	1	96
Lesotho	0	11	89
Liberia	2	11	87
Madagascar	1	39	60
Malawi	3	2	95
Mozambique	3	1	96
Namibia	0	9	91
Nigeria	26	1	73
Rwanda	0	0	100
South Africa	1	42	57
Swaziland	0	1	99
Tanzania	7	2	91
Togo	4	1	95
Uganda	2	7	91
Zambia	0	0	100
Zimbabwe	0	4	96

Source: Barrett, 1982

and 3,718 sisters, many of them Africans. Together they staffed 3,383 churches and chapels, 3,673 mission stations and outstations, and 3,377 schools. And in 1910 the Vatican claimed 952,520 African members,[5] a total that continued to grow rapidly.

PROTESTANT MISSIONS

Given that Britain had colonized by far the largest portion of Sub-Saharan Africa, Protestant missionaries (most of them British and American) had a far larger mission field than did the Catholics, and they marshaled even greater resources. By 1910 there were 4,091 foreign Protestant missionaries stationed in Sub-Saharan Africa, assisted by 1,496 ordained Africans. These missionaries maintained 12,136 elementary schools, 60 hospitals, and 10 medical schools. This impressive and extremely expensive infrastructure achieved results. The missionaries claimed that in 1910 there were 12.3 million Protestant Christians in the region.[6]

Although the vast majority of Protestant missionaries initially came from Britain, by the end of World War I (in 1918) most were coming from America. At the time, the majority of Protestant missionaries came from what are now identified as liberal denominations. British missionaries were dominated by Anglicans, and 90 percent of all American missionaries were sponsored by the Congregationalists (today known as the United Church of Christ), the Presbyterians, the Methodists, and the Episcopalians. But by 1935 these denominations were sending only half of the American missionaries, and their proportion had declined to 25 percent by 1948. Today these denominations are sending fewer than 4 percent.

Why the decline? The liberal denominations stopped sending missionaries because they lost their faith in the validity of Christianity.

LIBERAL MISSIONS ABANDONED

By the start of the twentieth century, some Protestant denominations had begun to lose faith—not merely in missions but even in Christianity. Increasingly, their elite seminaries were dominated by theologians who doubted the existence of a conscious, active God and who rejected most traditional Christian doctrines as outmoded from the standpoint of modern science and knowledge.[7] Soon these views prompted grumbling about the propriety of sending out missionaries. Led by Daniel Johnson Fleming of New York's Union Theological Seminary and the Harvard Divinity School's William Ernest Hocking, the liberal theologians charged that Christianity had no greater claim to religious truth than did other religions. In January 1930 a blue-ribbon commission (funded by John D. Rockefeller Jr.) was convened to "re-think" Christian missions. When the final report appeared in 1932, it attracted national attention and was widely read. Composed by Hocking and signed by all thirteen other commission members, *Re-Thinking Missions* charged that "it is a humiliating mistake" for Christians to think their faith is superior, for there is nothing unique in Christianity, and anything in its teachings that "is true belongs, in its nature, to the human mind everywhere."[8] The report argued that if "the Orient is anywhere unresponsive," the fault lies with missionaries who attempt to teach complex doctrines that "are too little Christian, too much artifacts of our Western brains."[9] The commission warned against missionizing to the slogan "Our message is Jesus Christ," lest natives fail to realize that this is merely symbolic language "marking loyalty to a tradition."[10] The report then denounced all teachings that credit "intrusions from the supernatural" into "realms of natural law"[11]—that is, miracles.

As can easily be inferred from the report, the basis for Hocking's objection to missions, widely shared by his fellow liberal theologians,[12] was that he could no longer acknowledge God as an aware, conscious, concerned, active being. Rather, in his book *The Meaning of God in Human Experience: A Philosophic Study of Religion*, Hocking devoted nearly six hundred pages to debunking traditional conceptions of God, leaving a God with only vague, symbolic properties. He concluded that all religions are reflections of the same God, albeit in somewhat idiosyncratic ways.

Despite this conclusion, and perhaps because of the huge missionary apparatus in place, Hocking and his commission felt that missions were valuable and should continue. But to do what? Perform social services!

The Hocking commission's recommendation reflected what many missionaries already believed by this time. Missionaries traditionally came from the ranks of East Coast college students, and many of these young idealists had embraced the Social Gospel. Indeed, to the young people who signed up as missionaries now, "phrases like 'evangelization of the world'...had become downright embarrassing," in the words of the historian William R. Hutchison.[13] They instead believed that missionaries should witness on behalf of worldly good deeds—bringing sanitation rather than salvation.

Whatever the theological virtues of these views, they are sociologically naive. It soon became obvious that people will seldom face the hardships of missionary service merely to do good deeds. Without the conviction that they were bringing priceless truths to those in need, the mission spirit quickly dissipated in liberal Protestant circles. Missionary recruitment flagged on college campuses; Hutchison writes that the "Student Volunteer Movement attracted declining numbers to its conventions, to the signing of pledge cards, and to actual missionary service."[14]

As the liberals deserted the mission fields, missionary work became the domain of conservative denominations. The result is that Protestantism in Africa is overwhelmingly conservative. This is true even of African Anglicans whose bishops barely speak to their counterparts in Britain.

Today Africa still receives various missionizing foreign faiths, such as the Mormons, Seventh-day Adventists, and Jehovah's Witnesses. The Mormon missions began only recently, but they already have attracted 420,000 converts. The Adventists have been active for nearly a century and have enrolled about 3 million members. The rapidly growing Jehovah's Witnesses have 1.2 million followers in Sub-Saharan Africa, including more than 350,000 in Nigeria and 189,000 in the Democratic Republic of the Congo (Kinshasa).

But on the whole, missionaries no longer play a significant role in African Christianity. The extraordinary Christianization of Sub-Saharan Africa was accomplished mainly by Africans and sustained by new denominations they originated.

INDIGENOUS DENOMINATIONS

Europeans are amazed by the extent of American denominationalism, but it is rather modest by comparison with that of southern Sub-Saharan Africa. In 1968, David B. Barrett, the distinguished expert on African religion, counted 5,031 distinct African Initiated Churches (AIC)—that is, Protestant denominations of African origins.[15] By 1995, Barrett estimated that the number of AICs had reached more than 11,500.[16] The emergence of these groups raises two questions. First, what advantage did such churches have over those represented by the missionaries? Second, why have they continued to proliferate?

As Barrett pointed out, Africans who responded enthusiastically to the Christian missions were bound to experience some disappointment. Their conversion did not convey to them what Barrett called the "mysterious power of the whites"—financial and cultural power.[17] Instead, the African converts found their material situations mostly unchanged, and even the missionaries excluded them from authority and treated them as inferior. As one South African theologian noted, "Many African Christians felt that the church was not interested in their daily misfortunes and concrete problems."[18] Meanwhile, both white missionaries and colonial administrations were challenging traditional aspects of African culture, including polygamy, indigenous slavery, worship of spirit ancestors, body and facial scarring, witch doctors, and female circumcision.

But a key turning point in African Christian history occurred early in the twentieth century, when the Bible was translated into the major African languages. Today at least portions of the Bible have been translated into more than 650 African languages. And as my colleague Philip Jenkins noted so insightfully: "Once the Bible is in a vernacular, it becomes the property of that people. It becomes a Yoruba Bible, a Chinese Bible, a Zulu Bible."[19] When Bibles translated into their tribal languages became available, Africans began to study scripture and often to conclude that various aspects of their traditional ways were legitimate—for example, that the Bible approved of polygamy, slavery, and belief in the existence of witches—and that the missionaries had misrepresented scripture, imposing their own cultural biases on it. Thus, there arose a multitude of African Christian innovators, who formulated and preached an Africanized gospel message and founded organizations with no ties to missionaries. Many new denominations have retained aspects of African culture such as polygamy and belief in witches. The distinguished historian of Christianity Mark Noll refers to these new Christian groups as "indigenized."[20]

From the start, such groups proliferated. Consider some famous African Christian innovators and the remarkable movements they initiated.

ISAIAH SHEMBE (CA.1870–1935)

In 1870, Isaiah Nloyiswa Mdliwamafa Shembe's father took his family from the Zulu kingdom and resettled in the Afrikaner Orange Free State.[21] In his youth, Shembe was employed by a Boer farmer near Harrismith. The outbreak of the first Boer War (1880–1881) disrupted his circumstances and prompted young Shembe to migrate to the Rand, where he began to attend the African Native Baptist Church. Returning to Harrismith in 1906, Shembe took up a career as an itinerant evangelist, receiving a preacher's certificate in 1908. In 1910 he became a follower of the influential white Pentecostal evangelist John G. Lake. Shembe led Lake on two evangelizing tours of the area and carefully observed Lake's preaching techniques and his faith healing. When Lake left Africa to continue his evangelism in the United States, Shembe struck out on his own, beginning with a mission to the Zulus. He sent messengers ahead of him to proclaim that a "man of heaven" had been sent to the Zulus; a day or two later Shembe would arrive in that community to preach and perform faith healings.

Shembe became an extremely effective evangelist and soon organized the Nazareth Baptist Church, which attracted tens of thousands of followers. After Shembe's death in 1935, his son Johannes Galilee Shembe took over the church. When he died in 1976, the church split into two groups, each led by one of Shembe's grandsons. In 2009 the two groups broke into four. Altogether, these factions of the Nazareth Baptist Church have about four million members today.

From the start, Shembe's church was distinctively African. He composed many hymns in Zulu, adapted traditional sacred dances, and designed sacred costumes. Shembe imposed new dietary laws (prohibiting chicken as well as pork) and initiated observance of the Sabbath on Saturday rather than Sunday. He also greatly deemphasized Jesus (Christmas is not celebrated) in favor of the exclusive worship of the Jehovah of the Old Testament. The church now reveres Shembe as an African Messiah—"the Christ of the Zulus," whom many believe to have risen from the dead.[22]

WILLIAM WADÉ HARRIS (CA.1860–1929)

William Harris may have been the most effective evangelist of his day.[23] He did not found a new denomination, directing his huge number of converts to the established mission churches, including the Roman Catholic. But Harris practiced and preached so many African aspects that after his death his followers had little choice but to create new churches.

Harris was raised in Liberia by his Methodist mother and then spent his teenage years in the home of his maternal uncle, a Methodist pastor and schoolmaster. At this time a bitter conflict developed between the native Liberians and the immigrant, Americanized blacks whose corrupt administration ruled the nation. Harris believed that Liberia would be far better off ruled as a British crown colony; the British were admired for their honest and relatively enlightened administrations and for their expensive investments in educational and medical institutions in their colonies. To this end, Harris participated in a failed coup d'état and ended up serving a brief term in prison. It was there that he received a vision that he was called to be a prophet and first spoke in tongues.

Upon his release in 1913, the new prophet went forth. He wore a white robe and a turban, and carried a Bible, a bamboo cross, and an African gourd rattle. Harris identified himself with the prophet Elijah. In addition to preaching a traditional Christian message, he focused on destroying the traditional African fetishes; he often burned them on a large brass tray when people brought them to him. Harris approved of polygamy and was always accompanied by two female assistants (who may or may not have been his wives) and who also wore white robes and carried gourd rattles. Within a year Harris baptized an estimated

120,000 Africans in the Ivory Coast and Ghana. That these "converts" received no prior instruction in Christianity worried many missionaries, but subsequent to their baptism they seem to have been eager to accept instruction.

All this activity upset local French colonial administrators as well as missionaries. Toward the end of 1914, Harris and his female assistants were arrested, beaten, and deported from the Ivory Coast. Returning to Liberia, Harris lived in relative obscurity until his death in 1929. Shortly before his death Harris authorized three young men to start a new church. Thousands of those Harris had baptized flocked to the church because it incorporated a great deal of African culture—hymn singing in African languages and style, dancing, and approval of polygamy. French authorities, egged on by both Catholic and Protestant missionaries, quickly drove the new movement underground. But the church survived, and today it has about 200,000 members.

GARRICK SOKARI BRAIDE (1882–1918)

As a young man, Garrick Braide worked as a fisherman.[24] Despite his lack of education, he became a missionary for the Anglican Church. He soon gained a reputation among his fellow Nigerians as a prophet and healer, and from 1912 to 1916 he drew huge numbers of converts into the Anglican faith. Many locals called him the Prophet Elijah II, and he even was thought to have the power of rainmaking. Eventually this aroused the opposition of the Nigerian Anglican bishop and the colonial authorities. Braide's frequent remarks that Africans needed to take responsibility for themselves was falsely interpreted as inciting anti-colonial feelings. So the bishop denounced him as a heretic and encouraged the colonial administrators to arrest him—which they did. Braide spent the next two years in jail and died in 1918 during the great influenza epidemic that swept the world. While he was in prison, nearly fifty thousand of his followers founded the Christ Army Church.

JOSEPH AYODELE BABALOLA (1904–1959)

Joseph Babalola was a heavy-equipment driver employed to build roads when, at age twenty-four, he came to believe that God had called him to preach the faith. As he gathered a following he was dismissed from the Anglican Church, in part because he persisted in speaking in tongues. He then affiliated with the Faith Tabernacle of Nigeria and began holding revivals. His Great Revival of 1930 attracted some two million people in a matter of just weeks. This outpouring prompted an American missionary to say, "Joseph Babalola has been able to accomplish more in six weeks than the Anglican Church has been able to do in sixty years."[25] Babalola eventually founded the Christ Apostolic Church, which now has branches even in many Western nations.

SIMON KIMBANGU (1887–1951)

Simon Kimbangu was born in the western Congo and in his youth was baptized into the Baptist Mission Society.[26] In 1918 he believed he had been called during a dream to be an evangelist, but the Baptist missionaries would not accept him into service on grounds that he could not read well enough. But in 1921 Kimbangu began an unsanctioned evangelical crusade and achieved instant fame for performing miracles. During his first service he was credited with healing a paralyzed woman, a blind man, a deaf man, and a crippled girl. Soon thereafter he was believed to have raised a young girl who had been dead for three days. Thousands flocked to hear him and to become his followers.

This alarmed the Belgian authorities, who soon acted to suppress the movement as having a tendency toward "pan-Africanism" and thus being anticolonial. The army was directed to suppress the movement. Kimbangu proved difficult to arrest—stories of his narrow escapes abounded. Eventually he surrendered voluntarily. What followed was all too typical of Belgian colonial practices. Kimbangu was tried by a military tribunal, with no opportunity to defend himself, and was found guilty of sedition. His sentence was 120 lashes and then death. The Baptists pleaded to the Belgian king for mercy, and the death sentence was commuted to life in prison. So after receiving 120 lashes, Kimbangu was clapped into solitary confinement, never allowed any visitors, and died in prison after thirty years.

But not even military force was sufficient to suppress the Kimbanguist movement. Now known as the Church of Jesus Christ on

Earth by the Prophet Simon Kimbangu, it has more than seven million members.

These are but a few of the most significant early founders of Africanized Christian groups. Like these founders, most of the thousands who followed them have been uneducated and initially associated with a mission organization before they experienced a "call." Most have spoken in tongues, and nearly all have devoted much time and attention to healing. Moreover, miracles, such as those attributed to Joseph Babalola and to Simon Kimbangu, are typically believed about most founders. African founders also have been responsive to the widespread fear of witchcraft and have offered rituals and ceremonies designed to reveal and overcome witchcraft spells.

WITCHCRAFT

Despite having embraced Christianity, Sub-Saharan Africans still believe in witchcraft, although most oppose it. This is confirmed by two questions the Gallup World Poll asks (only in this region):

- Do you personally believe in witchcraft?
- Do witch doctors do good things or bad things to people?

Table 5–2 (next page) show the results.

In most Sub-Saharan nations the overwhelming majority believe in witchcraft. Only in Burundi, Rwanda, and Uganda do most people not believe. Interestingly, in many nations more people believe witch doctors do bad things than believe in witchcraft. I take this to mean that they believe that witch doctors don't have supernatural powers but that they often attempt to do harmful things. Not surprisingly, the higher the percentage of Christians in a nation, the less likely people are to believe in witchcraft.

Table 5–2: Witchcraft

	% Believe	% Do Good	%Do Bad
Angola	70	13	67
Benin	86	30	32
Botswana	48	20	43
Burundi	31	6	84
Cameroon	77	4	67
Central African Republic	71	23	50
Congo (Kinshasa)	73	10	72
Congo (Brazzaville)	76	15	55
Ghana	76	11	60
Ivory Coast	95	1	89
Kenya	31	5	74
Liberia	72	16	37
Madagascar	92	15	58
Malawi	69	16	60
Mozambique	61	9	37
Nigeria	59	4	68
Rwanda	16	4	89
South Africa	53	13	37
Swaziland	54	10	68
Tanzania	60	16	67
Togo	77	37	35
Uganda	16	6	72
Zambia	52	15	55
Zimbabwe	59	7	63

Sources: Gallup World Polls

WOMEN'S RIGHTS

Many of the early founders of AICs advocated an improved status for women. For example, William Harris featured two women as his coevangelists and urged discontinuation of such practices as isolating women in special huts during their menstrual periods. In addition, women founded some successful AICs, and women have always made up "the great majority of their members," notes Allan Anderson.[27]

Consequently, the Christianization of Sub-Saharan Africa seems to have resulted in remarkable levels of gender equality in many nations. The Global Gender Gap Index, prepared by the United Nations and the World Health Organization, uses various economic, political, educational, and health criteria to assess gender equality. The highest possible score a country can achieve is 1 (equality); the lowest possible score is 0 (inequality). In the most recent index, published in 2014, Rwanda (ranked seventh in the world, with a score of .7854), South Africa (.7527), and Burundi (.7565) all finished ahead of the United States (.7463) and Canada (.7464). Mozambique (.7370), Malawi (.7281), and Kenya (.7258) were not far behind.

The Gallup World Poll allows another view of women's rights in Sub-Saharan Africa. Gallup asked more than 85,000 respondents, "Do you agree or disagree with the following statements?"

- Women should be allowed to hold any job for which they are qualified outside the home.
  Agree: 92%
- Women and men should have equal legal rights.
  Agree: 83%
- Women should have the right to initiate divorce.
  Agree: 67%

Agreement with the first two items is as high as it is in most Western nations. The lower agreement for the third item mostly reflects the fact that many Africans don't think either men or women should be able to file for divorce.

The data demonstrate a simple fact about Sub-Saharan Africa: the higher the percentage of Christians in a country, the more people there favor women's rights. We know this because we can look at how many respondents from dozens of nations agree that women should be able to hold any job, have equal rights, or initiate divorce. Whether people agree with these statements is strongly correlated with the percentage of a nation's population that is Christian: for all three questions, the correlation is at least .5 and is statistically significant. And on a fourth statement, about whether female circumcision is normal for all women, there is a strong negative correlation (–.51) between the percentage of a nation's population that is Christian and whether people agree with the statement.

Unfortunately, Christianity has not had similarly positive effects on politics.

WAR AND TYRANNY

War and terrorism are chronic throughout the Sub-Saharan region. Of the thirty-seven nations listed in Table 5–3, only six did not have a major war or armed conflict between 1990 and 2010. Many have had such conflicts almost annually.[28] In fact, the thirty-seven nations have on average been at war or engaged in serious armed conflict for 8.2 years, or nearly half of that twenty-year interval.

Although sometimes conflicts erupt between Muslims and Christians, for the most part religion is not involved. When a million people were slaughtered in three months during the Rwandan genocide, both the Tutsi victims and their Hutu killers were Christians. The far bloodier Congo civil wars, which have killed more than five million people, also pitted Christians against Christians. Muslim and Christian nations are equally likely to suffer from war and conflict.

Wars and armed conflicts probably have much to do with the lack of democracy in Sub-Saharan Africa. Not a single one of these thirty-seven nations is rated as democratic by *The Economist*'s Intelligence Unit; nineteen are ranked as total autocracies. Although we cannot trace a direct connection to religion in these matters, democracy is positively correlated with the Human Development Index, and development, in turn, is strongly correlated with religion—positively with Christianity and negatively with Islam. A major factor in Sub-Saharan politics is the lack of education and the persistence of tribalism, both of which may be reduced by religious organizations eventually. But the fact remains that democracy is a fragile institution.

WHAT THE CHANGES MEAN FOR AFRICA

What does all this mean for Africa? We know, first, that although northern Sub-Saharan Africa remains overwhelmingly Muslim, southern Sub-Saharan Africa was almost completely Christianized during the twentieth century. Considering that (as Table 5–1 showed) tribal faiths dominated Africa in 1900, it is remarkable to see the huge percentages of Christians in southern Sub-Saharan Africa today.

Table 5–3 (next page) tells the story. This table demonstrates the immense power of pluralism. The Christianization of southern Africa was speeded by the proliferation of African Initiated Churches and by the complete Africanization of the Roman Catholic mission effort. Consider that in 1960, only 2,087 African seminarians were preparing for the Roman Catholic priesthood. By 2011, that number had surged to 27,483.[29] This remarkable achievement is reflected in the fact that the College of Cardinals now includes sixteen Africans.

But there is also a profound mystery concerning African Catholicism. The official Catholic statistics claim far fewer members in many African nations than are revealed by the Gallup surveys. For example, the 2014 *Catholic Almanac* claims that 27 percent of the population of Cameroon are Roman Catholics, but the Gallup findings, based on self-reports, show that 41 percent are Catholics. The official figure for Ghana is 12 percent Catholic, whereas the Gallup figure is 22 percent. In Botswana the Church claims 5 percent and Gallup finds 28 percent. Similar contrasts exist for most nations in the region. Moreover, most of these nations have seen no increase in the official Catholic membership statistics for at least five years. These are hardly trivial differences.

Table 5–3: Muslims and Christians in Sub-Saharan Africa, 2014

	% Muslim	% Christian	(% Catholic)
Northern Region			
Burkina Faso	58	34	(27)
Chad	62	36	(18)
Djibouti	99	0.2	(0.1)
Guinea	88	11	(7)
Mali	94	3	(2)
Niger	99	1	(0.2)
Senegal	96	4	(3)
Sierra Leone	70	29	(11)
Sudan	96	3	(1)
Southern Region			
Angola	1	95	(48)
Benin	33	51	(29)
Botswana	1	89	(28)
Burundi	3	97	(71)
Cameroon	21	76	(41)
Central African Republic	10	89	(39)
Congo (Brazzaville)	2	94	(48)
Congo (Kinshasa)	4	94	(37)
Ethiopia	28	72	(1)
Gabon	6	91	(53)
Ghana	19	78	(22)
Ivory Coast	38	49	(26)
Kenya	9	90	(30)
Lesotho	0.1	99	(57)
Liberia	14	84	(14)

Madagascar	1	92	(39)
Malawi	14	85	(23)
Mozambique	5	88	(47)
Namibia	0.1	99	(25)
Nigeria	37	61	(19)
Rwanda	3	96	(59)
South Africa	2	88	(27)
Swaziland	1	96	(27)
Tanzania	41	58	(30)
Togo	18	60	(39)
Uganda	16	83	(38)
Zambia	1	98	(36)
Zimbabwe	1	90	(25)

Sources: Gallup World Polls

Drawing on various contacts, I tried to learn whether Vatican officials had an explanation for these discrepancies. They did not. The best anyone could come up with is that growth has so overwhelmed the capacity of the local priests to keep up with such vital matters as baptisms, confirmations, and confessions that they have neglected their record keeping.

Even after looking at the changes occurring in Sub-Saharan Africa, some might argue that the tens of millions of new Christians aren't really more religious than they were a century ago, that all they have done is abandoned their tribal religions for Christianity. But the fact is that the Christians of southern Africa pursue their new faith with far greater intensity than they did their tribal religions. For one thing, all across the region church attendance rates are significantly higher than anywhere else. At the high end, *90 percent* of Nigerians report attending religious services within the past seven days; even the lowest rate in the region, Botswana's 49 percent, exceeds that of the United States, which is often seen as very religious. And for most congregations in southern Africa, the sedate Sunday service familiar to Westerners is almost unknown. Instead, the typical service resembles what most Westerners would call a revival meeting. The whole congregation participates. They sing, dance, testify, shout, break into tongues and otherwise fully express their deep religious feelings.

In short, southern Africa has undergone a seismic religious shift.

6

THE "UNCHURCHED" JAPANESE

Some observers have identified Japan as an unusually religious society because the nation's religious statistics add up to far more than 100 percent. They do so because nearly everyone adheres to Shinto and most people also pursue Buddhism. But few Japanese regard either Shinto or Buddhism as their religion, since neither of these faiths requires any formal membership. Hence, although as many as 90 percent of the Japanese visit Shinto shrines and nearly as many have a Buddhist altar in their homes,[1] only 4 percent of Japanese say they are active in a church or religion, and only about 20 percent consider themselves to be "religious."[2] This has led many of the secularization faithful to the erroneous conclusion that Japan is a "postreligious society."[3]

Nonsense. Only 11 percent claim to be atheists, and as will be seen, most Japanese are deeply involved in unchurched religions. Consequently, Japan provides an opportunity to compare the moral effects of churched and unchurched religions.

SHINTO

Shinto is the traditional Japanese religion—there are references to it from as early as the sixth century. The word itself means the "way of the gods" and involves the study of *kami*, which are not only gods but also spirits resident in rocks, trees, animals, and places. Shinto is so quintessentially Japanese that one of its central teachings concerns the creation of the islands of Japan and entails the creation of a pantheon of gods and goddesses.

This creation story begins with a god (Izanagi-no-Mikoto) and a goddess (Izanami-no-Mikoto). Together they stirred the ocean with a spear, and when it was withdrawn, water dripped from the spear point, creating an island from nothingness. The god and goddess then lived in a huge palace on the island and gave birth to two additional islands, but they found them imperfect and destroyed them. Then, having done the ritual correctly, they gave birth to the eight perfect islands of Japan. Hence, unlike other nations, Japan was created by the gods. In addition to these two progenitor divinities, the Shinto pantheon is a typical array of nature gods, including a Sun Goddess, Storm God, Wind God, Sea God, and the like.

The Shinto conception of the afterlife is an unattractive house of the dead like the Greek notion of Hades. But Shinto also includes the belief that after death a person becomes a family spirit, and these are venerated, often by daily rituals.

There is no single Shinto faith; it is divided into a multitude of factions and worship groups. According to Nobutaka Inoue,[4] Shinto can be distinguished into:

Shrine Shinto, the main tradition, which embraces both public shrines and those within the home.

Imperial Household Shinto, in which religious rites are performed only by members of the imperial household at the three shrines on the palace grounds.

Folk Shinto, which consists of a variety of practices, including divination and shamanic healing.

Sect Shinto, which, as the name suggests, involves recent offshoots often led by a founder offering innovative (heretical) teachings.

Following the Meiji Restoration in 1868, which overthrew the shogun and restored the emperor to full power, Shinto and Japanese imperialism became inseparable—so much so that the phrase *State Shinto* came into common usage. State Shinto taught that the emperor was a divine ruler who had taken on human form. The emperor's portraits served as shrines, which were ubiquitous not only in government buildings but also on all military posts and every ship in the Imperial Navy. The most important duty of the captain of a sinking ship was to ensure that the emperor's portrait was removed to safety.

Worship of the emperor reached its peak during World War II, when it inspired countless suicide attacks. But when the Japanese were defeated in 1945, a major clause in the surrender document required Emperor Hirohito (1901–1989) to go on the radio and tell the nation that he was not divine and that the people would no longer be allowed to worship him.

Today Shinto has about 100,000 shrines in Japan, and these are served by about 20,000 priests.[5] But only about 1 percent of Japanese report to survey interviewers that Shinto is their religion. That is because, like the Chinese, they limit the word *religion* to churched religions, to organized groups to which people *belong*. The Japanese do not belong to Shinto; they merely *use it*.

JAPANESE BUDDHISM

Buddhism came to Japan from China in about the sixth century, but for centuries it attracted few followers. Then, when the shoguns came to power in the twelfth century, Buddhism became popular. It remained the "official" religion under the shogun until the Meiji Restoration returned full power to the emperor, whereupon the government became hostile to all forms of Buddhism and fully committed to Shinto. Buddhism survived, as the Japanese people merely adopted both faiths.

Whereas Shinto abounds in gods, originally Buddhism was a nontheistic, or godless, religion. But it turned out that a godless faith could be sustained only by a small intellectual elite, and popular Buddhism now abounds in gods and spirits and is "an extremely theistic religion," as the *Oxford Dictionary of World Religions* notes.[6] Indeed, Buddha himself is worshipped in his many temples.[7]

The Buddhism that arrived in Japan by way of China was (and is) much different from the original, or Theravāda, Buddhism. Buddha regarded the world as evil and placed all hope in an escape from the illusion of existence—to Nirvana, a state of nonexistence. In China this was changed to conceive of Nirvana as a heavenly *place*, a literal, physical paradise known as the Pure Land where the virtuous go after death. As this form of Mahāyāna Buddhism became popular among ordinary people, intellectuals turned away and returned to the original notion of Nirvana and to meditation as the essential religious activity. This became known as Zen Buddhism. Both forms flourished in Japan. So, too, did a form of Buddhism that was originated in Japan by a Buddhist monk named Nichiren (1222–1282). His was a much more radical school of Buddhism, dedicated to the Lotus Sutra and implacably opposed to all other forms of Buddhism.

RUSH HOUR OF THE GODS?

Immediately after World War II, with an official end to State Shinto, there was an explosion of religious movements in Japan; so many new groups appeared that observers spoke of "the rush hour of the gods."[8] It has generally been assumed that this religious fervor resulted from the devastation and suffering caused by the war. But no similar religious activity took place in postwar Germany or in the Soviet Union, where devastation and suffering surely equaled that of Japan's. There also was a religious "rush hour" in South Korea, which was hardly touched by the war. At the end of the war, South Korea was liberated from Japanese rule—but so was Taiwan, which did not experience any outburst of new faiths.

The common element was newly granted religious freedom in postwar Japan and Korea and the lack thereof in Germany, the Soviet Union, and Taiwan. State churches suppress religious competition and dampen religious enthusiasm. The German state church apparatus remained intact in the Western Zone of Germany. In the Eastern Zone, the Soviets repressed all religion, as they did in the USSR as well. Thus, new groups could not prosper in either Germany or the Soviet Union. In Japan, though, the "MacArthur" constitution inaugurated complete religious freedom in a nation where the government had strictly repressed all but a few traditional religions, primarily State Shinto and Buddhism. In South Korea, too, a policy of religious freedom replaced the prior Japanese religious repression. In both nations the emergence of new religious movements took place almost at once. The end of Japanese rule brought no similar eruption of new religions in Taiwan because its new Nationalist Chinese rulers did not condone religious freedom.

The notion that the war caused Japan's "rush hour" is further refuted by the fact that nearly all of what became the leading new religious movements in the postwar period originated *prior* to the war—sometimes long before. Konkō-kyō was founded in 1885 and Reiyukai Kyōdan in 1925; the immensely successful Sōka Gakkai movement was organized in 1930, as were PL Kyōdan and Seichō no Ie; and Risshō Kōsei-kai began in 1938.[9] Back in those days, however, government repression was sufficient to limit them all to small groups of followers, often in a single village or neighborhood. Thus, Neill McFarland described these groups as "innumerable captive and incipient religious movements" and noted that the new constitution allowed "their voices to be heard."[10] As Aiko Moroto put it, what was new after the war was that "these groups came out into the open."[11] But, as will be seen, to the extent that these were "churched" religions, their success was limited.

CHURCHED RELIGIONS

The Japanese restrict the word *religion* to churched religions. Consequently, 67 percent deny that they have a religion—as is shown in Table 6–1. Nearly a third claim to be Buddhists (far fewer than actually engage in Buddhist worship). Meanwhile, 2 percent report that they are Christians; 1 percent give their religious preference as Shinto (although nearly all Japanese have a Shinto shrine in their home); and 1 percent mention other faiths, most of them being groups involved in the "rush hour."

Table 6–1: Japanese Religious Affiliation, 2014

None	67%	85.3 million
Buddhist	29%	36.9 million
Christian	2%	2.5 million
Shinto	1%	1.3 million
Other	1%	1.3 million
Total	**100%**	**127.3 million**

Sources: Gallup World Polls

SŌKA GAKKAI

By far the largest and most aggressive of the "new" religions that erupted in Japan with the advent of postwar religious freedom is Sōka Gakkai, founded in 1930 and based on the writings of the Nichiren Buddhist sect. In its early days, Sōka Gakkai was careful to acknowledge the emperor: "We must make our children thoroughly understand that loyal service to their sovereign is synonymous with love of country," as an official publication put it in 1933.[12] But the group denied the emperor's divinity, for which its leaders were arrested and imprisoned during World War II.

After the war, Sōka Gakkai launched an aggressive membership drive—so aggressive that it aroused a great deal of opposition for "forced" conversions. For example, sometimes members of Sōka Gakkai surrounded the home of intended converts and made loud noises for a day or two until the people inside agreed to sign a membership pledge. Sōka Gakkai members often resorted to threats of divine retribution or even physical violence in their proselytizing efforts.[13] In 1952, Sōka Gakkai was required to agree to a government demand that it would no longer employ such aggressive methods.

However it sought members, Sōka Gakkai was quite successful and by the 1960s had attracted perhaps as many as a million converts. At that time the group also launched a political party (the Clean Government Party) and managed to elect some members of parliament. Subsequently, Sōka Gakkai initiated an international membership drive and established congregations in many Western nations, including the United States.

In recent times, the movement has attracted far less attention and fewer members. Sōka Gakkai leaders claim to have five million members in Japan (equal to 4 percent of the population), but survey findings suggest their followers cannot number more than a tiny fraction of that total. As for other Japanese-originated churched religions, they are far too small to be of any social significance.

CHRISTIANITY

Japan nearly became the first Christian nation in Asia. The remarkable early spread of the faith began in 1549 with the arrival of Francis Xavier, cofounder of the Jesuits, at the port of Nagasaki. Xavier was well received by the local lords, and soon there were many Catholic missionaries in Japan. But, following the pattern that had been used in the conversion of northern Europe, the missionaries focused on converting the nobility with the expectation that the people would follow. Consequently, when the Tokugawa clan seized power in 1603 and installed rule by the shogun, Japanese Christianity lacked the mass following needed to resist the anti-Western policies that ensued. The shogun outlawed Christianity and by killing or cowing the Christian nobility effectively destroyed the church.

With the overthrow of the shogun in 1868, Christian missionaries were allowed to return to Japan. By 1910 there were 1,029 Protestant missionaries in Japan, nearly all of them from Great Britain and the United States. All together, Protestant missions reported having 82,000 Japanese members. The Protestants were joined by 1,917 Catholic missionaries—66 of them ordained Japanese priests. Catholic missions claimed 125,000 Japanese converts, for a total of 207,000 Christians.[14] The rise of Japanese imperialism, and Japan's invasion of China in 1931, caused growing tensions with Western powers, which resulted in government suppression of missionary efforts and made life unpleasant for Japanese Christians. How many remained Christians during World War II is unknown, but even after vigorous mission efforts resumed, by 1950 there were only about 120,000 Catholics and 200,000 Protestants in Japan, or about 0.4 percent of the population.[15] More than sixty years later, about 2 percent of the Japanese are Christians.

The primary barrier to Christian growth has been intense Japanese nationalism. Christianity is viewed as a foreign faith that devalues Japanese culture, and by claiming to be the one true faith, it denigrates traditional Japanese religions as false. In addition, by stressing individual responsibility, Christianity conflicts with the Japanese emphasis on the group. Oddly, though, the Christian emphasis on participation in an organized group—the congregation—is seen as alien by people who have always regarded religion as an unchurched, informal activity. Of course, the Japanese face social pressure to observe the outward forms of these unchurched faiths, which conflict with Christian practice.

Following World War II, the Jehovah's Witnesses initiated an energetic missionary campaign in Japan. Today they have 3,056 congregations and 216,472 members, an increase of nearly 400 percent since 1980.[16] The first Mormon missionaries arrived in Japan in August 1901, but results were few until after World War II. The Book of Mormon was translated into Japanese in 1957, and today Japan has two Mormon temples and 279 congregations, with a total of 126,981 members.[17]

UNCHURCHED RELIGIONS

Although 67 percent of the people in Japan give their religious affiliation as "none" and 89 percent say they are not active "in a church," this is not a secularized nation.[18]

Consider that 88 percent of households maintain Buddhist altars, which are believed to shelter the spirits of their deceased ancestors.[19] Most Japanese frequently perform rites before these altars and offer gifts (including food) to the spirits. In addition to a Buddhist altar, nearly all Japanese homes contain a *kami-dana*, or Shinto home shrine, before which they perform rituals each morning and evening.

Japanese life is drenched in religious assumptions and practices. When one buys a new car, it is customary to drive to the nearest Shinto temple to have the vehicle blessed by a priest (a similar practice of getting cars blessed by Catholic priests has sprung up in Belgium).[20] Everyone in Japan who seeks a loan to build a house will be sent a form by the government listing normal closing expenses. These include a substantial payment of several thousand dollars for a Shinto ceremony to "purify" the land spiritually. It might be possible to persuade a lender to forgo such a ceremony, but no responsible Japanese would consider doing so because few Japanese would be willing to buy or occupy a home built without it. Should it be necessary to remove a tree, no action will be taken without a religious service to appease the spirit of that tree. This, too, requires the service of a Shinto priest and does not come cheap.

These are not the beliefs and actions of an irreligious nation.

Table 6–2 demonstrates the overwhelming extent to which the individual Japanese express their commitment to unchurched religion.

Table 6–2: Unchurched Religiousness in Japan

"Do you regularly visit a family grave at least several times a year?"			
	Yes: 75%	No: 25%	
"After death a person's spirit remains with the family."			
	Agree: 58%	Unsure: 16%	Disagree: 26%
"Do you pray on certain occasions when you need assistance?"			
	Yes: 64%	No: 36%	
"Have you visited a temple recently to pray for a positive outcome in your life?"			
	Yes: 54%	No: 46%	
"Do you keep a good luck charm or amulet around?"			
	Yes: 63%	No: 37%	
"Do you feel that rivers and mountains have spirits?"			
	Yes: 59%	No: 41%	
"Do you think palm reading is a reliable way to tell the future?"			
	Yes: 53%	No: 47%	
"When a person is born and when a person dies are predetermined."			
	Agree: 73%	Unsure: 8%	Disagree: 19%
"Without reference to any established religion, do you believe it is important to have spiritual beliefs?"			
	Yes: 72%	Unsure: 14%	No: 14%

Source: Tenth Annual Japanese Character Study, Institute
of Statistical Mathematics (Sakamoto, 2000)

This is hardly a portrait of a secularized society. It is, rather, evidence of the extent of unchurched religion in Japan. Three out of four make regular visits to family graves. Most believe that after death a person's spirit remains with the family. About two-thirds pray for benefits and more than half have recently done so in a temple. Nearly two-thirds possess good luck charms. Fifty-nine percent believe that mountains and rivers have spirits—a standard Shinto belief. More than half accept the reliability of palm reading. About three-fourths believe that life and death are predetermined, and all but a very few think it is important to have spiritual beliefs.

Although it cannot be argued that the Japanese have become more religious than they were, say, fifty years ago, clearly theirs is a religious nation. Equally clearly, unlike the nations of Latin America, Islam, and Sub-Saharan Africa, the Japanese mainly pursue unchurched religions. Does that matter?

This is a question that social scientists have long ignored, probably because they have seldom bothered to distinguish types of religion. But, as we shall see, there are excellent reasons to doubt that churched and unchurched religions have similar social consequences.

UNCHURCHED RELIGION AND MORALITY

Religion functions to sustain the moral order.[21] This classic proposition is regarded by many as the closest thing to a law that the social scientific study of religion possesses.

This proposition comes from the founders in the field. In his famous book *The Religion of the Semites*, W. Robertson Smith (1846–1894) explained that "even in its rudest form Religion was a moral force, the powers that men revered were on the side of social order and moral law; and the fear of the Gods was a motive to enforce the laws of society, which were also the laws of morality."[22] The revered French sociologist Emile Durkheim (1858–1917) argued that religion exists *because* it unites humans into moral communities and that, although law and custom also regulate conduct, religion alone "asserts itself not only over conduct but over the *conscience*. It not only dictates actions but ideas and sentiments."[23] And the equally famous Bronislaw Malinowski (1884–1942) held that "every religion implies some reward of virtue and punishment of sin."[24]

In one form or another, this proposition appears in practically every social scientific textbook discussion of religion. But it's wrong—and these three famous founders should have known better. Since all three had a classical education and were well versed in Greek and Roman mythology, how could they ignore the blatant fact that the Greco-Roman gods were quite morally deficient? These gods and goddesses were said to do terrible things to one another and to humans as well—sometimes merely for amusement. And although they were quite likely to do wicked things to humans if the humans failed to propitiate them, the Greco-Roman divinities had no interest in anything (wicked or otherwise) that humans might do to one another. Indeed, since the famous classical philosophers, including Aristotle, taught that the gods were incapable of caring about mere humans, they would have ridiculed the claim that religion reinforces the moral order.

All along, some famous social scientists have acknowledged that many religions say nothing about morality. Edward Tylor (1832–1917), the founder of British anthropology, noted that the claimed linkage between religion and morality "simply falls to the ground" because most religions of "primitive" peoples are "devoid of that ethical element." Such religion, Tylor said, "is not immoral, it is unmoral."[25] Herbert Spencer (1820–1903), founder of British sociology, likewise noted that many religions ignore moral issues. Many anthropologists have echoed this view. For example, the celebrated Ruth Benedict (1887–1948) argued that to generalize a link between religion and morality "is to misconceive" the "history of religions." She suggested that such a linkage probably is typical only of what she called "the higher ethical religions."[26] And the remarkable Mary Douglas (1921–2007) flatly asserted that there is no "inherent relation between religion and morality: there are primitives who can be religious without being moral and moral without being religious."[27]

Unfortunately, these challenges to the claim that religion sustains morality were dismissed, probably because most social scientists had little interest in "primitive" societies and it seemed obvious that the proposition held in more advanced societies. That Judaism, Hinduism, Christianity, and Islam all sustain conceptions of the supernatural as conscious, concerned, and dedicated to codes of morality is obvious. Moreover, empirical research has frequently confirmed a strong correlation between commitment to one of these faiths and morality.[28]

But social scientists failed to realize that the exception applied not only to "primitive" societies but also to unchurched religions, including Buddhism, Shinto, and Taoism, and therefore to some large modern societies, including Japan.

The Tao does not advise humans to love one another, and the spirits resident in mountains and rivers do not issue commandments. Like the Greco-Roman pantheon, the *kami* of Shinto are many, of small scope, and lacking in concern for humans. They might be persuaded to grant favors, but issues of morality are not germane to pleasing them.

In all its forms, Buddhism lacks a conception of a God as conscious and concerned—in fact, as one scholar puts it, "Buddhists have even gone so far as to say that belief in such a God often leads to ethical degradation."[29] Of course, Buddhism soon abounded in gods, but they also are like the Greco-Roman divinities, being of small scope and displaying no concern for human behavior. Therefore, whatever its ethical positions, Buddhism lacks a spiritual mechanism for sustaining moral conformity. Although belief in God and devotion to religion are highly correlated with morality in most of the world—including even Europe—there is no reason to suppose that such correlations will hold in Japan.

The data support this hypothesis. Table 6–3 is based on five measures of morality. Each respondent in the World Values Survey conducted in Japan in 2010 was asked:

> Please tell me for each of the following actions whether you think it can always be justified, never be justified, or something in between:
> - Stealing property.
> - Cheating on taxes if you have a chance.
> - Someone accepting a bribe in the course of their duties.
> - Avoiding a fare on public transport.
> - Claiming government benefits to which you are not entitled.

As the table shows, Japanese who say they believe in God are not even slightly more likely to say these actions are never justified than are Japanese who say they do not believe in God. The lower half of the table shows the same lack of effect for a different measure of religiousness: whether a respondent would identify herself or himself as a "religious person," as "not a religious person," or as an "atheist."

There is simply no relationship between religion and morality in Japan. Which is not to say that the Japanese are not moral, but only that their morality seems not to be influenced by religion. Hence, at least these unchurched religions seem unable to sustain the moral order. Nor, perhaps, can they sustain a modern culture.

Table 6–3: Religion and Morality, Japan

Believes in God:	Yes	No
Percentage Who Say Never Justified		
Stealing property	94%	94%
Cheating on taxes	88%	87%
Taking a bribe	83%	84%
Avoiding fare	84%	83%
Cheating on gov't benefits	63%	66%

	Religious Person	Not Religious	Atheist
Percentage Who Say Never Justified			
Stealing property	94%	93%	93%
Cheating on taxes	87%	87%	86%
Taking a bribe	81%	83%	81%
Avoiding fare	84%	83%	81%
Cheating on gov't benefits	65%	63%	67%

Source: World Values Survey, 2010

CULTURAL MALAISE

In recent years, many observers have become concerned that something seems to have gone wrong with the Japanese culture. A general feeling of malaise is evident; a large proportion of Japanese seem to have lost their sense of purpose. Consider these symptoms:

Suicide. Japanese have always regarded suicide as the honorable way to atone for various shortcomings and failures, or as the way to achieve a glorious death. The ritual suicides (*seppuku*) of the samurai became famous, and the tradition culminated in the suicidal attacks by kamikaze pilots toward the end of World War II. Today Japan's suicide rate is high—according to the World Health Organization, 18.5 suicides occur in Japan for every 100,000 people (compared with a rate of 12.1 per 100,000 for the United States).[30] But very few of these suicides are "honorable" deaths. Rather, nearly all of them are rejections of life as not worth living. Whole groups and families now commit suicide together. Many suicide groups are recruited on the Internet.[31]

Family. Japan's fertility rate is far below replacement level and falling rapidly. There were 2.2 births per average woman in 1965, but only 1.4 in 2014. The marriage rate continues to plummet—from 12 per 1,000 population in 1972 down to fewer than 6 in 2014.[32]

Sex. According to a national survey conducted in 2011 by the Japanese Family Planning Association, an astonishing 36 percent of males aged sixteen to nineteen, and 59 percent of females that age, say they are uninterested in or even averse to sex.[33] A survey conducted in 2001 by a condom manufacturer found that Japan ranked far last among twenty-eight advanced nations in the average frequency of marital sex—about three times a month.[34]

It seems plausible that the widespread cultural malaise that these many symptoms reflect is at least partly related to a disjuncture between Japan's traditional unchurched religions and its advanced modernity. Both Buddhism and Shinto are oriented to the past, rather than the future, and consequently they are somewhat incompatible with the immense progress that has taken place in Japan. And since both are lacking in congregational life, they offer no network of social support against loneliness and despondency. This is a cultural problem in many other Asian societies, too, as will be pursued at length in chapters 7 and 8. But nowhere else has it resulted in the cultural crisis that seems to have arisen in Japan.

7

CONVERTING CHINA

By the end of the nineteenth century, many "sophisticated" Americans held Christian missionaries in contempt, as naive fanatics who imposed misguided morality on natives by convincing women to cover their breasts, urging couples to limit their sex lives to the "missionary position," and thereby despoiling more innocent cultures.[1] As Mark Twain put it in 1872, Hawaiians enjoyed an idyllic life "before the missionaries braved a thousand privations to come and make them permanently miserable by telling them how beautiful and blissful a place heaven is, and how nearly impossible it is to get there."[2] It also soon became de rigueur to dismiss the missionary converts as opportunists; the several million who attended church in China were said to be merely "rice Christians," cynical souls who frequented the missions only for the benefits they provided.[3]

Attacks on missionaries intensified in the twentieth century. Even Pearl Buck, daughter of missionaries and winner of the Nobel Prize for Literature (in 1938) for her novels about China, joined the chorus, expressing her agreement with the authors of *Re-Thinking Missions* that the Christian doctrines that motivated missionaries were outdated superstitions. Any college student who enrolled in Introductory Anthropology was (and unfortunately still is) almost certain to be told in detail how the intrusive missionaries had destroyed more authentic "native cultures."

In 1949 the Chinese Communist Party came to power and soon expelled all Western missionaries. With the launch of the Cultural Revolution in 1966, the Chinese Communists outlawed religion entirely. All temples, pagodas, shrines, mosques, and churches were destroyed or converted to secular uses. Anyone detected in religious activity was subject to persecution and even death.

Meanwhile, Western scholars came to dismiss the work missionaries had done as ineffective. Writing in 1974, Harvard's John K. Fairbank claimed that by the time Chinese Communists came to power it had "become evident that few Chinese people were likely to become Christians and that the missionaries' long-continued effort, if measured in numbers of converts, had failed."[4] Moreover, at that time it was widely agreed among the Western secularization faithful that China soon would be a model of the postreligious society.

But it wasn't to be. In the past thirty years, after several decades of severe repression, religion has been springing up everywhere in China. Tens of thousands of temples have been reopened or rebuilt. Millions have returned to Buddhism, and once again huge numbers of Chinese are pursuing their traditional folk religions and worshipping at their ancestral shrines. As the University of Chicago's Daniel Overmyer described it, "wherever local conditions permit, religious activities come bubbling to the surface, festivals to the gods are held, traditional funerals and burial rituals are restored, destroyed images and shrines are replaced, priests appear to perform rituals, and congregations meet to worship."[5]

Meanwhile, with no Western missionaries involved, tens of millions of Chinese have embraced Christianity; thousands more convert every day and scores of new churches open every week (not counting new underground congregations).[6]

Some of this Chinese religious activity could be called a revival— the return of participation in the folk religion, for example. But the rapid expansion of Christianity is something new in Chinese history. It may be more appropriate to call what is going on in China today a religious awakening.

Unfortunately, most discussions of the religious developments in China have not been based on reliable statistics, properly interpreted.

This has encouraged a good deal of nonsense. Some experts say there are 16 million Chinese Christians; others put their number at 200 million. Moreover, all the textbooks on comparative religion, and most discussions of religion in China, include Taoism as a major faith. That is because many scholars regard a religion as a set of writings rather than as an activity engaged in by people; the best data available suggest that there are virtually no Taoists in China.

Two surveys provide the statistical heart of this chapter. The first was conducted in 2001 by the Research Center for Contemporary China at Peking University and was released as part of the World Values Surveys. It is based on one thousand face-to-face interviews. The sample was selected from a large "master sample" created for another survey in 1998. Persons under age eighteen and older than sixty-five were excluded. The data are freely available to anyone.

The second survey was conducted in 2007 by Horizon Ltd., China's largest and most respected polling firm. It consists of a national multistage probability sample of mainland China. Respondents were sixteen or older and had lived at their current residence for at least three months prior to the survey. The data were collected by face-to-face interviews with 7,021 Chinese conducted by Horizon's regular staff of interviewers. The data were made available to the Institute for Studies of Religion at Baylor University by a generous grant from the John Templeton Foundation.

These groundbreaking surveys allow a more accurate view of China's religious landscape.

THE DECLINE IN "IRRELIGION"

Not so long ago people in China were well advised to claim that they had no religion, and although the government has ceased attacking all manifestations of faith, it remains an officially atheist regime that occasionally, if unpredictably, punishes religious activities. Consequently, many religious Chinese continue to conceal their faith, especially from strangers such as survey interviewers.

Of even greater importance, most Chinese who currently deny that they are religious do so because, like the Japanese, they limit the definition of religion to churched religions. Consequently, the overwhelming majority of Chinese honestly tell survey interviewers that they are not religious, even though they also acknowledge that they engage in a whole host of activities and hold beliefs that Western observers would tend to define as religious.

For example, the 2007 Horizon Survey found that 72 percent of those who said they had no religion had, during the past year, "venerated ancestral spirits by their graves." Ten percent of these same respondents who claimed they had no religion said they believed in the God in Heaven (the Jade Emperor), and 2 percent even said they believed in Jesus. Similarly, 22 percent of Chinese who say they believe in Buddhism also say they do not have any religious beliefs. Consider, too, that the folk religion blends elements of Buddhism, Taoism, and Confucianism with ancestor worship, belief in the Jade Emperor and many other traditional gods, and in ghosts and demons. It is housed in a huge number of temples, most of them having been recently rebuilt or restored, where crowds gather to pray and to place offerings of food and incense before images of various gods. Most Chinese patronize the folk temples, but most also seem to believe that this is not a religion! Only 4 out of the 7,021 Chinese respondents gave the folk religion as their religion; most of the others involved in folk religion said they had no religion.

Or consider Confucianism. Many Chinese officials and academics are adamant that Confucianism is merely a philosophy and not a religion—a claim that has been ratified by many Western scholars.[7] But when Anna Xiao Dong Sun visited a number of temples in China, she observed many visitors earnestly praying to statues of Confucius for a variety of blessings and benefits.[8] Even so, most of these "worshipers" probably would have said they had no religion, as seems to be reflected in the fact that only 12 of 7,021 Chinese in the 2007 survey identified Confucianism as their religion.

All this stems from the fact that most Chinese define religion as belonging to an *organized religious group* such as Islam or Christianity, rather than consisting of practices such as praying in temples or of belief in the supernatural.

Given this very narrow definition of religion, it is not surprising that a huge majority of Chinese call themselves irreligious. But a shift is occurring. China experienced an immense decline in irreligiousness between the 2001 and the 2007 surveys. In the first survey, 93 percent gave their religion as "none"; six years later that number fell to 77 percent. It seems implausible that a change of such great magnitude in such a short time reflects conversions. Rather, it seems that more Chinese are willing to admit to having a religion, being less fearful of government repression.

PRACTICING FOLK RELIGION

The most basic form of Chinese folk religion involves ancestral spirits. Traditionally, Chinese venerate the spirits of their ancestors each year on grave-sweeping day, or the Qingming Festival, held on the 104th day after the winter solstice—usually around April 5. On that day, observant Chinese gather at the graves of their ancestors; sweep and clean the tombs; make offerings of flowers, food, and drink; and pray to the spirits of the departed. For many, the holiday takes the form of a family celebration, and there often is dancing, kite flying, and fireworks.

The Qingming Festival was discouraged and sometimes punished at the height of Chinese religious persecution, during Mao Tse-tung's rule, but it was reinstated as a national holiday in 2008. In the 2007 survey, 72 percent of the respondents said they had "venerated ancestral spirits by their graves" during the past year. Of these, three-fourths had done so only during the Qingming Festival; the rest had done so more often (1 percent did it weekly). Keep in mind that although most Westerners would define this as a religious event, most Chinese do not. In fact, 36 percent of Chinese Christians venerated their ancestors' graves. It should be acknowledged that Matteo Ricci (1552–1610), the extraordinary Jesuit scholar who missionized in China, decided that veneration of ancestors was not inconsistent with Catholic faith and permitted his converts to continue doing so. The Vatican later denounced this view, but reversed itself in 1939. In any event, ancestor worship involves supernaturalism, which is why it was defined as religious—hence wicked—during the Cultural Revolution.

Besides venerating ancestors at their graves, 12 percent of the Chinese keep ancestral tablets in their homes, slightly more than the 11 percent who display a portrait or statue of Chairman Mao. In addition, 18 percent of the Chinese surveyed in 2007 reported that they had a portrait or statue of various gods in their home, such as the God of Wealth, God of the Kitchen, or the Earth God.

The McGill University scholar Kenneth Dean put it well when he said that the traditional Chinese folk religion "has revived with great force...[and] is practiced by hundreds of millions of people."[9] Still, hardly anyone in China admits to membership in what all the comparative religion textbooks present as major Chinese faiths: the 2007 survey found 0.6 percent were Taoists, 0.2 percent were Confucianists, and the same tiny percentage were classified as Others. Then there is Buddhism.

THE BUDDHIST REVIVAL

Buddhism came to China from India in about the first century AD, and changed dramatically. As described by Buddha, based on his "discovery" that the world is mere appearance, lacking all point or purpose, Nirvana is a state of nonbeing that releases an individual from the cycle of rebirths. In contrast, as noted in chapter 6, the Buddhism that succeeded in China conceived of Nirvana as a heavenly place, a physical Paradise known as the Pure Land where the virtuous go after death. Moreover, to attain Nirvana it is not necessary to lead a life of ascetic meditation; the Pure Land can be reached by ordinary people through faith and devotion alone. Hence, the popular Chinese Buddhism came to be known as Pure Land Buddhism.

But after having achieved great success in attracting the Chinese masses, Buddhism was all but destroyed in 845 when the government seized all Buddhist land, emptied the temple treasuries, razed more than

40,000 temples, and forced 265,000 monks and nuns back to lay life.[10] It was a blow from which Chinese Buddhism never recovered. Buddhism lived on primarily within the expansive embrace of the folk religion, whose temples include statues of Buddha and Confucius along with hundreds of traditional gods. Then, in 1966, the Chinese Communist government prohibited Buddhism along with all other religions.

Not surprisingly, then, only 2 percent of Chinese said they were Buddhists in the 2001 survey. But rather remarkably, *18 percent* did so only six years later, and 12 percent said they had recently worshipped in a Buddhist temple. Here, too, the explanation cannot be a huge wave of conversions. Instead the change must reflect the increased willingness of Buddhists to come into the open, greatly encouraged no doubt by the government's legitimation of Buddhism, as reflected in its sponsorship of a World Buddhist Forum in 2006. Since then it has been far safer and less socially stigmatized to admit being a Buddhist, as this is not regarded as a "foreign" faith in the same way that Islam and Christianity are. In any event, Buddhism very likely is the largest of the faiths most Chinese regard as religions.

ISLAM

Both the 2001 and the 2007 surveys report that Muslims make up fewer than 0.5 percent of the Chinese, which seems accurate despite the fact that official figures from the 2000 census reported that Muslims make up about 2 percent of Chinese.[11] The discrepancy is due to the fact that most Chinese Muslims live in border areas, including Inner Mongolia and Tibet, counted by the census but not included in the surveys. Geographical concentration remote from central China enabled the Islamic communities to sustain themselves during the most intense periods of government persecution of religions.

But conflict with the government persists. Muslims are often seen as foreigners, a judgment that is reinforced by marked ethnic contrasts— many Muslim communities do not speak Chinese. In response, Muslim communities frequently protest against their conditions. In March 2014

a group of knife-wielding Muslim terrorists attacked commuters await-
ing their train in a station in Yunnan Province. According to worldwide
press accounts, at least 34 people were murdered and nearly 150 were
wounded. Chinese press accounts revealed that there had been several
hundred Muslim attacks on Chinese residents in Xinjiang Province in
the past year. Worse yet, according to official Chinese press reports,
terrorist attacks by Muslim nationalists seem to be accelerating and
becoming more lethal.

THE RISE OF CHRISTIANITY

It turns out that the Chinese Christians of 1949—those ridiculed in the
West as rice Christians—were so "insincere" that they endured decades
of bloody repression during which their numbers grew substantially.
And, as official repression has slacked off, Christianity has been growing
at an astonishing rate in China. Unfortunately, there is a great deal of
disagreement over just how astonishing the growth has been: are there
now 16 million or 200 million Christians in China? Both numbers have
been asserted with great confidence, but neither is credible.

The 2007 survey found that 2.5 percent of Chinese said they were
Protestants and 0.2 percent reported that they were Roman Catholics;
that would suggest about 30 million Chinese Christians (about 2 million of them Catholics). But all surveys are subject to random error—the
results may vary from the true value by a certain amount known as
the confidence interval. The size of the confidence interval depends on
the size of the sample. In this instance, being based on seven thousand
cases, the confidence interval is plus or minus 0.55 percent. Thus, the
true percentage of Christians in China might be as low as 2.15 percent
or as high as 3.25, purely as a function of random variation.

Of course, the calculation of the confidence interval assumes that
100 percent of those selected in the sample were successfully interviewed. But surveys almost never achieve a 100 percent completion rate,
and in this instance only 62 percent of the original cases were interviewed. That means the results could be greatly biased, depending on

whether Christians were more or less willing to be interviewed than were non-Christians.

In this instance, the results significantly *underestimate* the number of Christians in China.

My suspicions that only those most openly Christian had responded were aroused by the fact that nearly all who said they were Christians also reported that they displayed a cross or a portrait of Jesus in their homes. A follow-up study by sociologists at Peking University demonstrated that Christians were far more likely than non-Christian Chinese to refuse to be interviewed and that a substantial number of Christians who were interviewed falsely denied being Christians, probably because the interviewer was a stranger whom they did not trust. Drawing on contacts with the Christian community, those conducting this study obtained random samples from the active membership rolls of Christian house churches in many of the same areas used in the original sample. Then interviewers called on each person drawn in these samples—the interviewers were unaware of the purpose of the study, so they conducted themselves in the usual way. Of the Chinese approached, all of whom were known to be Christians, 62 percent declined to be interviewed, compared with 38 percent of all respondents in the original study. Of those who agreed to be interviewed, 9 percent did not admit that they were Christians.

Adjusting for these sources of underreporting yields an estimate that 4.5 percent, or about 50 million Chinese over age sixteen, were Christians in 2007, about 3.5 million of them Catholics. But of those interviewed in 2007, 5.1 percent said they believed in Jesus Christ. If we assume that everyone who claimed to believe in Jesus Christ was a Christian, then, with the adjustment applied, 6.7 percent of Chinese, or 73 million people, were Christians in 2007. Taking all these factors into account, my best estimate is that there were slightly more than 61 million Chinese Christians in 2007. But even if the lowest of these estimates of China's Christian population is more accurate, there has been a phenomenal rate of growth.

The best available statistics place the number of Christians in China in 1950, as the new Communist regime consolidated its power, at about

4.2 million. In 1980, after several decades of repression, the number of Christians in China was probably about 10 million. If we accept that there were about 61 million Chinese Christians in 2007, then the rate of growth from 1980 through 2007 averaged about 7 percent a year. If that same rate of growth were to hold until 2030, there would be more Christians in China than in any other nation: 295 million.

Why has Christianity been growing so rapidly in China?

EDUCATION AND CHRISTIANITY

A number of observers have noticed the high rate of conversion to Christianity taking place among Chinese graduate students at American universities.[12] Many also have remarked on the very Christian climate that prevails at the leading Chinese universities, where many students as well as many faculty openly express their faith.[13] In fact, a survey conducted at elite Renmin University of China found that 62 percent said they were "interested" in Christianity.[14] This is remarkable given that the great majority of students belong to the Communist Party or to the Party's Youth League and are, thereby, officially prohibited from having any religion; the Christians among them (and there are some) would be unlikely to admit their religious beliefs except to confidants. In addition, a fine study by Purdue's Fenggang Yang reported the prevalence of well-educated Chinese among urban Christians in China.[15] Nor is this anything new. In Beijing during the 1930s, Watchman Nee's numerous Christian converts consisted almost entirely of "top honor students from Yenching, Ching Hua, Peking Union Medical College, [and] Peking University."[16]

No one has adequately explained why Christianity seems to have such great appeal to the most-educated Chinese. Indeed, if true, the special appeal of Christianity to the educated Chinese is quite inconsistent with the still-prevailing notion among sociologists that religion functions primarily to compensate the lower classes for their worldly deprivations.

And the most-educated Chinese *are* more likely than the less educated to become Christians and to reject Buddhism.

Table 7–1 shows the relationship between education and reporting oneself to be a Christian or a Buddhist. Keep in mind that the very small percentage of Christians reported in China at the time of the 2007 survey statistically squeezes the possible relationship between education and Christianity. It also is necessary to use the "uncorrected" data on Christian membership, since it is impossible to know how the correction factor might be related to education. Nevertheless, the results show that college-educated Chinese are more apt to be Christians than are the less educated, even though the least educated are second highest in their Christian membership, which probably reflects in part their greater willingness to be interviewed and to admit their Christian affiliation. Although the percentage point differences in the Christian column are not large, the results are statistically significant—they are very unlikely to be a random artifact. The relationship with Buddhism, which is far less compressed for lack of variation, is stronger and linear. The least educated are almost twice as likely to be Buddhists as are the college educated, a relationship that is highly significant statistically.

Table 7–1: Education and Religion in China
Members of Communist Party and Communist Youth League Excluded

Education	% Christian	% Buddhist
College	4.04%	11.62%
Vocational School	2.81%	15.07%
High School	2.76%	17.35%
Less Than High School	3.61%	20.31%

Source: Horizon Ltd. Survey, 2007

SPIRITUAL DEPRIVATION

Social scientists seem unable to free themselves from the iron grasp of deprivation theory as they continue to teach that the primary social function of religion is to provide people with relief from their material misery.[17] Perhaps amazingly, the data have never properly supported this view. For more than fifty years, studies in the United States and other Western nations have consistently found that the lower classes are conspicuously absent from the churches on Sunday morning.[18] Moreover, the major religious movements that have erupted throughout the centuries, in both the East and the West, were generated not by the suffering masses but by dissatisfied elites.

Buddha was a prince; fifty-five of his first sixty converts were from the nobility, and the other five may have been nobles, too—we simply don't know their backgrounds.[19] The early Taoists as well as the Confucianists were recruited from the Chinese elites.[20] Or consider two small sects that appeared in ancient Greece: the Orphics and the Pythagoreans. According to Plato, both movements were based on the upper classes: their priests "come to the doors of the rich...and offer them a bundle of books."[21] Of course, Moses was raised as a prince, and the prophets of the Old Testament all belonged "to the landowning nobility,"[22] as did most members of the Jewish sect known as the Essenes.[23] It is now widely accepted that early Christianity "spread first among the educated more rapidly than among the uneducated," as W. M. Ramsay wrote in his classic study.[24] As for the great Christian sect movements, most, if not all, were based on people with considerable wealth and power: the nobility, the clergy, and well-to-do urbanites. For example, the Cathars enrolled a high proportion of nobility,[25] as did the early Waldensians.[26] Luther's Reformation was supported not by the poor but by princes, merchants, professors, and university students—Luther despaired at ever reaching the peasants and villagers.[27] The Methodists were founded by John Wesley and his classmates at Oxford. Finally, of 428 medieval Roman Catholic ascetic saints, three-fourths were from the nobility—22 percent of them from royalty.[28]

It is difficult to explain why so many social scientists continue to ignore these well-known historical facts and to stress that religion is, as Marx famously put it, "the sigh of the oppressed creature...the opium of the people." Perhaps it is because they have never been rich or powerful that scholars fail to realize that wealth and status often do not satisfy all intense human desires. But, as the great Nobel laureate economist

Robert William Fogel pointed out, "throughout history...freed of the need to work in order to satisfy their material needs, [the rich] have sought self-realization."[29]

Deprivation theory needs to be extended. It is not merely that people will sometimes adopt religious solutions to their thwarted material desires (as probably helps explain why the least-educated Chinese become Christians) but also that people will pursue or initiate religious solutions to their thwarted spiritual desires—a situation to which the privileged are especially prone, since they are not distracted by immediate material needs. Thus, it is people of privilege who are most apt to give serious attention to the great intellectual and existential questions: Does life have meaning? What can we hope for? Does virtue exist? Is death the end? When people are dissatisfied with their society's conventional answers to these questions, or discover that there are no traditional answers to questions raised by changing conditions, they suffer from *spiritual deprivation* and often seek to alleviate it by formulating or embracing an alternative religion or philosophy.

What causes spiritual deprivation? Obviously, it can arise in many ways. But here I will focus on cultural incongruity.

MODERNIZATION AND CULTURAL INCONGRUITY

Culture consists of all the material and intellectual elements of a society (the latter consisting of the people and their interrelationships). Perhaps the most significant feature of culture is that it is created by humans. This is not to say that the members of any given society created all, or even nearly all, of that society's culture, for in most instances much of a society's culture is borrowed from other societies—a process known as diffusion. Importing culture can be risky in that important elements of the subsequent culture may not fit together, resulting in *cultural incongruity*. In recent times, the process of rapid modernization of non-Western societies is a major source of cultural incongruity.

The primary impediment to modernization in Asia was devotion to the past, as symbolized by "ancestor worship." It was believed that history traced a descent from more enlightened times. Thus, when serious efforts to modernize China began early in the twentieth century, they collided with the prevailing culture, which not only lacked a belief in progress but also was committed to the idea that modern times were inferior to the past. It was precisely this commitment to the past that had caused China, once the most advanced society on earth, to have fallen so far behind the West. Mao resorted to many of his excesses partly to rid China of these antiprogressive, traditional attitudes and customs. To the extent that Mao succeeded, he may have facilitated China's entry into its current era of rapid industrialization and modernization, but by persecuting all signs of religion, old or new, he also helped to create a moral and spiritual vacuum. Although thousands of the temples Mao closed have since reopened and many new temples have been built, this has not satisfied the spiritual needs of many Chinese, who recognize that these faiths, which celebrate the past, are rather incongruous with modernity.

But where are the Chinese to turn for spiritual enlightenment? What are the grounds for morality? What is the meaning of life? These are precisely the questions Christianity addresses directly, eloquently, and effectively.

Since modernity came to China from the West, many Chinese have looked westward seeking spiritual answers. In the words of one of China's leading economists: "In the past twenty years, we have realized that the heart of your culture is your religion: Christianity. That is why the West is so powerful. The Christian moral foundation of social and cultural life was what made possible the emergence of capitalism and then the transition to democratic politics. We don't have any doubts about this."[30] One can hear this line of thought on many Chinese campuses.[31] Hence the appeal of Christianity to the most-educated Chinese, who are most sensitive to the incongruity between traditional Chinese faiths and industrial and technical modernity. I hasten to add that people may join religious movements for a variety of reasons, and these may well differ substantially on the basis of privilege.

But if *spiritual* deprivation explains the growth of Christianity among more-educated Chinese, then we should expect to see similar trends in other Asian nations. The most obvious example to choose is Japan, where the major unchurched religions—Shinto and Buddhism—are out of kilter with the nation's advanced modernity. And even though Christianity is not growing rapidly in Japan, here too it should have its greatest appeal to the more educated.

Sure enough, as Table 7–2 reveals, in Japan the college educated are four times as likely to be Christians, and much less likely to be Buddhists, than are those with less than high school educations.

Table 7–2: Education and Religious Affiliation in Japan

Education	% Christian	% Buddhist
College	3.2%	22.9%
High School	1.9%	28.7%
Less Than High School	0.8%	38.2%

Source: Gallup World Poll

In the next chapter we will look at four other rapidly modernizing Asian societies to test the spiritual deprivation explanation.

MORALITY

What about morality? Despite the growth of Christianity, religion in China still is overwhelmingly unchurched—folk religions and Buddhism. Therefore, the arguments developed in chapter 6 ought to hold in China as well as in Japan, for these religions are based on gaining benefits from gods who do not impose moral demands—indeed, they do not offer theologies concerning matters of ultimate meaning.

And Table 7–3 (next page) shows that there is no correlation between religion and morality in China. Those who say they believe in a god are not more inclined to condemn stealing, cheating on taxes, taking bribes, avoiding fares on public transportation, or taking government benefits to which one is not entitled. The lower half of the table uses another measure of religiousness—whether the respondent identifies himself or herself as a "religious person," as "not a religious person," or as an "atheist"—and shows similar results. Unchurched religions with small gods do not support the moral order in either Japan or China.

Table 7–3: Religion and Morality, China

Believes in God:	Yes	No
Percentage Who Say Never Justified		
Stealing property	56%	58%
Cheating on taxes	45%	45%
Taking a bribe	48%	53%
Avoiding fare	36%	38%
Cheating on gov't benefits	24%	25%

	Religious Person	Not Religious	Atheist
Percentage Who Say Never Justified			
Stealing property	64%	68%	68%
Cheating on taxes	54%	50%	58%
Taking a bribe	61%	60%	65%
Avoiding fare	45%	40%	48%
Cheating on gov't benefits	28%	26%	34%

Source: World Values Survey, 2012

THE FUTURE

At the moment it appears that China is playing a significant role in the global religious awakening. In fact, if the percentage trend holds for another few years, there will be more Christians in China than in any other nation. But, of course, these trends may not hold. For one thing, the Chinese government may attempt to crack down on the Christians, if for no other reason than that the Communist regime may perceive them as a growing threat to party rule.

An unpredictable factor here is that just as Christianity has greater appeal to the more educated Chinese, it has been making serious inroads among Communist Party officials. Although party members are prohibited from having any religion, clearly many of them do. Those living in the cities are careful to appear irreligious, but out in the rural areas many party members are openly religious. In one sample, 21 percent of village party members admitted to student survey interviewers that they were Christians; some of them even displayed crosses on the walls in their homes. In this same sample, 75 percent of party members said they observed the Qingming Festival, which involves ancestor worship.[32] In addition, many student Christians at Chinese universities are the daughters and sons of party members. These factors may mitigate potential anti-Christian government actions. Or not.

What is certain is that, whether or not it becomes a Christian nation, China will remain a religious nation. It remained so even during the vicious excesses of the Cultural Revolution.

8

FAITH IN THE
"FOUR ASIAN TIGERS"

S oon after the end of World War II, four small Asian nations began
an extraordinary era of rapid industrialization, and within a few
years all four were among the world's most economically developed
nations. Based on their superb economic achievements, these nations—
Taiwan, Hong Kong, Singapore, and South Korea—became known as
the "Four Asian Tigers." Given their relatively small populations, religious activities within these countries can have little effect on the global
religious situation. But they provide an excellent opportunity to continue to examine the effects of unchurched religions on morality and to
further test the hypothesis that Christian growth in Asia is a response
to cultural incongruity between the traditional religions and modernity.

The most effective way to proceed is to treat each of the Tigers
separately.

TAIWAN

The island of Taiwan, once known as Formosa, has an area of 13,855
square miles (slightly larger than the state of Massachusetts) and lies 110
miles off the coast of mainland China. Taiwan was occupied by Japan
beginning in 1895 and then, at the end of World War II, was restored

to China. In 1949, when the Communists came to power in China, an estimated two million Chinese took refuge on Taiwan, including leaders of the deposed Nationalist government led by Chiang Kai-shek, many leading Chinese families, and nationalist troops. Industrialization soon began, and by the mid-1970s only Japan was experiencing more rapid economic growth than was Taiwan. Today, with a population of twenty-three million, Taiwan has one of the world's strongest economies, with a GDP per capita only slightly below that of Canada, Sweden, and Denmark, and above that of Japan, France, and the United Kingdom.[1]

Although Chinese nationalists and their descendants make up only a small minority of the population—about 14 percent—nearly all Taiwanese who were residents of the island before 1949 are also Chinese. Thus, it is no surprise that 35 percent of the population of Taiwan identify themselves as Buddhists (Table 8–1). What does seem surprising is that, although almost no one in China claims to be a Taoist, a third of Taiwanese do so. In addition, 8 percent report their religion as one of four sects based on Chinese folk religion: Yiguandao, Tiandism, Miledadao, and Zailiism. Christians make up only 4 percent of the Taiwanese, and 18 percent have no religious affiliation. The "Other" category includes 60,000 Muslims, 51,000 Mormons, 20,000 Scientologists, and 16,000 Bahá'is.

Table 8–1: Religious Affiliation in Taiwan

Buddhist	35%	8 million
Taoism	33%	7.6 million
Folk Religion Sects	8%	1.8 million
Christianity	4%	0.9 million
Other	2%	0.5 million
None	18%	4 million

Source: Government statistics

These official government statistics are somewhat misleading in that most Taiwanese actually are religiously unaffiliated in any exclusive sense. That is, most actually have some involvement in both Buddhism and Taoism, and they also observe some aspects of one or another form of Chinese folk religion. The *CIA World Factbook* assigns 93 percent of Taiwanese to this "mixture."[2] Moreover, as is typical in China, many Taiwanese who are assigned one of these religious preferences in the government data tell survey interviewers that they have no religion—the Gallup World Poll classified 27 percent of Taiwanese as "Secular." Thus, only a small proportion of Taiwanese belong to a churched religion—mainly the few Christians.

Given the advanced level of modernity of their society, the most-educated Taiwanese ought to be experiencing some degree of cultural incongruity, and some of them should have responded by becoming Christians, others by rejecting the traditional faiths of Buddhism and Taoism. Table 8–2 shows that to be the case. College-educated Taiwanese are significantly more likely to be Christians than are the less educated, and they are markedly less likely to be Buddhists or Taoists. Thus, the hypothesis is supported in a third Asian society.

Table 8–2: Education and Religious Affiliation in Taiwan

Education	% Christian	% Buddhist	%Taoist
College	8.3%	27.1%	21.2%
High School	6.9%	35.9%	25.7%
Less Than High School	5.2%	47.8%	29.2%

Source: Gallup World Poll

As in Japan and China, religion in Taiwan, being unchurched, ought not to support the moral order. And Table 8–3 (next page) shows that it does not.

Table 8–3: Religion and Morality, Taiwan

Believes in God:	Yes	No
Percentage Who Say Never Justified		
Stealing property	79%	81%
Cheating on taxes	64%	57%
Taking a bribe	72%	67%
Avoiding fare	47%	43%
Cheating on gov't benefits	30%	29%

	Religious Person	Not Religious	Atheist
Percentage Who Say Never Justified			
Stealing property	77%	80%	76%
Cheating on taxes	64%	65%	59%
Taking a bribe	74%	73%	66%
Avoiding fare	47%	51%	42%
Cheating on gov't benefits	30%	31%	30%

Source: World Values Survey, 2010

HONG KONG

Although Hong Kong has officially been a part of China since 1997, for some time it was allowed to retain considerable independence. More recently, however, Chinese authorities have interfered in Hong Kong life, building up local resentments. In late 2014 a series of massive student demonstrations challenged Chinese authority, demanding greater local political freedom and democracy. Eventually, the students were put down with force, and as of this writing it is unclear just how the Chinese authorities will proceed. So far, however, the government has not significantly interfered with religious practice.

This former colony of Great Britain is tiny, having an area of little more than four hundred square miles or about six times the size of Washington, D.C. Hong Kong was invaded by the Japanese during World War II, and its population plummeted from about 1.6 million in 1941 to 600,000 in 1945. With British rule reestablished, during the 1950s Hong Kong began to industrialize, initially by the manufacture of textiles, and it soon became one of the most industrialized and modern nations in the world, and a leading center of international finance. Between 1961 and 1997, Hong Kong's GDP increased by eighty-seven times, and the population grew to 7.1 million by 2011.

It is difficult to establish a reliable religious profile of Hong Kong. The profile published by the government is clearly incorrect. It places Christian membership at 12 percent, but the Gallup World Poll (based on 4,296 cases) shows that 20 percent are Christians and the 2013 World Values Survey (based on 1,000 cases) puts Christian membership at 19 percent. And whereas the government statistics claim that 21 percent of people in Hong Kong are Buddhists, the Gallup data show that only 13 percent are Buddhists and the World Values Survey puts the figure even lower, at 11 percent. Unfortunately, we can't simply substitute the Gallup or the World Values data for the official statistics, because both have shortcomings. For example, both Gallup and the World Values Survey fail to identify some important categories, such as Chinese folk religion, dumping them into the "Other" category, which the government places at 49 percent. Moreover, both greatly overstate the "None" category, since so many clearly religious Asians deny that they are religious. Table 8–4 (next page) presents my estimates of the current religious profile of Hong Kong, based on both surveys and on the official statistics.

As is true in both China and Japan, unchurched folk religions, which involve local gods and ancestor worship, represent the largest religious affiliation in Hong Kong (37 percent). Christianity (20 percent) is the second-largest religious affiliation. Unlike China, but like Taiwan, Hong Kong has many residents (14 percent) who profess to Taoism. And 13 percent claim to be Buddhists. Even so, the huge majority of Hong Kong's citizens are unchurched.

Table 8–4: Religious Affiliation in Hong Kong

Chinese folk religions	37%	2.6 million
Christianity	20%	1.4 million
None	15%	1.1 million
Taoism	14%	1.0 million
Buddhism	13%	0.9 million
Other	1%	0.07 million

Sources: Government statistics; Gallup World Poll; World Values Survey, 2013

The thesis that cultural incongruity is a major factor in Christian conversion predicts that in Hong Kong, the more educated will be more likely to be Christians and least likely to still be Buddhists. Sure enough, that is the case, as Table 8–5 demonstrates.

Table 8–5: Education and Religious Affiliation in Hong Kong

Education	% Christian	% Buddhist
College	30.8%	4.1%
High School	21.3%	9.8%
Less Than High School	12.3%	27.1%

Source: Gallup World Poll

In Hong Kong, the college educated are more than twice as likely to be Christians as are those with less than a high school education. Conversely, the least educated are almost seven times as likely to remain Buddhists as are those who went to college.

What about morality? Does Hong Kong's experience support the hypothesis that unchurched religion does not sustain it? The data on Hong Kong are limited, making it more difficult to test the hypothesis there. The 2013 World Values Survey of Hong Kong was obviously in error about atheism and probably on other religious variables as well. The survey done in 2013 reported an absurd claim that 55 percent of people in Hong Kong were atheists, a rate about twice as high as that of the second-highest nation and ten times higher than the number reported for Hong Kong in 2005. Changes of that magnitude in so few years on significant characteristics simply do not occur. Consequently, the data in Table 8–6 are from 2005. Unfortunately, in that wave of the World Values Surveys, neither the question on belief in God nor the one on stealing was asked. But even within those limitations, the data show no consistent religious effect.

Table 8–6: Religion and Morality, Hong Kong

	Religious Person	Not Religious	Atheist
Percentage Who Say Never Justified			
Cheating on taxes	67%	59%	54%
Taking a bribe	71%	66%	63%
Avoiding fare	62%	61%	60%
Cheating on gov't benefits	49%	48%	57%

Source: World Values Survey, 2005

SINGAPORE

Like Hong Kong, Singapore was founded as a British colony; Sir Stamford Ruffles set it up in 1819 as a trading post of the East India Company. Today this tiny nation consists of a main island and sixty-two small islets, making up 277 square miles. Singapore fell to the Japanese during World War II. After being liberated, it was once again a British colony, but it became an independent nation in 1963. Singapore soon began to industrialize; today it is ranked as the world's fourth-leading financial center, and its port is one of the five busiest in the world—all this with a population of only about 5.5 million.

Table 8–7 (next page) presents a profile of religious affiliations in Singapore, based on official statistics, which are fully in accord with Gallup World Poll findings but which offer some additional categories.

Singapore's religious composition is rather different from that of the preceding Asia nations. It has much higher proportions of Christians (18 percent), Muslims (15 percent), and Hindus (5 percent). Buddhists are the largest group (33 percent), and a substantial number (17 percent) claim to have no religion.

Table 8–7: Religious Affiliation in Singapore

Buddhism	33%	1.8 million
Christianity	18%	1 million
No Religion	17%	0.9 million
Muslim	15%	0.8 million
Taoism	11%	0.6 million
Hinduism	5%	0.3 million
Other	1%	0.05 million

Source: Government statistics

Table 8–8 demonstrates more support for the hypothesis concerning cultural incongruity. The college educated are more than five times as likely to be Christians as are those with less than a high school education; the less educated are far more likely to be Buddhists or Taoists.

Table 8–8: Education and Religious Affiliation in Singapore

Education	% Christian	% Buddhist	% Taoist
College	32.7	25.2	0.8
High School	17.2	39.1	1.7
Less Than High School	6.3	51.9	3.7

Source: Gallup World Poll

Religion in Singapore differs from that in Japan, China, Taiwan, and Hong Kong in that a substantial number (38 percent) belong to churched religions: Christianity, Islam, and Hinduism. When only those Singaporeans who say they are religious are considered, 45 percent belong to one of these three churched religions. Consequently, it seems reasonable to expect that in Singapore, religion will influence morality. And that is the case, as can be seen in Table 8–9. All ten of the relationships are linear and positive. Taken together, these findings are overwhelmingly statistically significant.

Table 8–9: Belief in God and Morality, Singapore

Believes in God:	Yes	No
Percentage Who Say Never Justified		
Stealing property	56%	47%
Cheating on taxes	53%	43%
Taking a bribe	53%	47%
Avoiding fare	41%	34%
Cheating on gov't benefits	36%	32%

	Religious Person	Not Religious	Atheist
Percentage Who Say Never Justified			
Stealing property	58%	54%	47%
Cheating on taxes	57%	48%	42%
Taking a bribe	54%	52%	47%
Avoiding fare	42%	38%	34%
Cheating on gov't benefits	37%	36%	28%

Source: World Values Survey, 2010

SOUTH KOREA

Korea was a Japanese colony from 1905 until 1945, when the Japanese were driven out, whereupon it was divided into two nations, an

American-backed democratic south and a Soviet-backed communist north—a division that remains. Following the Korean War (1950–1953), South Korea began to industrialize. Today, with a population of about fifty million, South Korea has one of the world's strongest industrial economies, ranking sixth in the total value of its annual exports.

Although there are proportionately more Christians in South Korea than in China, Japan, or any of the other Four Tigers, the history of Christianity in Korea is bloody.[3] Roman Catholic missionaries arrived in Korea from China in the seventeenth century and slowly built a following. But in 1758 Catholicism was outlawed as an evil practice. In 1785 Catholic missionaries returned and began again. Then, in 1801, a new era of anti-Catholic persecution resulted in the martyrdom of many missionaries, and Korean Christians were subjected to abuse. Nevertheless, Catholics soon resumed their mission efforts—and in 1866 at least eight thousand Korean Catholics were killed, as were nine French missionaries. The Japanese colonization of Korea in 1905 reinforced the official hostility to Christianity.

It is estimated that when the Japanese left in 1945, only 2 percent of Koreans were Christians. Since then, Christianity has achieved remarkable growth: today about 30 percent of Koreans are Christians, as can be seen in Table 8–10. The data in this profile of religions in South Korea are based on official statistics, which were fully in accord with Gallup World Poll findings.

Table 8–10: Religious Affiliation in South Korea

No Religion	47%	22.6 million
Christianity	30%	14.7 million
Buddhism	22%	10.8 million
Other	1%	0.5 million

Source: Government statistics

The other aspects of the table are typical of Asian nations. Most people claim to have no religion, although most of these Koreans probably take part in Buddhist activities, including worship in temples, and the statistics make no mention of folk practices such as ancestor worship, although they are quite common.

Table 8–11 shows that in South Korea, too, the college educated are somewhat more likely than those without high school diplomas to be Christians, and less likely to be Buddhists. So again the cultural incongruity hypothesis is confirmed.

Table 8–11: Education and Religious Affiliation in South Korea

Education	% Christian	% Buddhist
College	39.1%	17.0%
High School	35.3%	20.1%
Less Than High School	32.5%	27.7%

Source: Gallup World Poll

What about morality?

The data in Table 8–12 (next page) show that there is no relationship between religiousness and morality in South Korea. The results are, if anything, negative—that is, the less religious are slightly more likely to condemn immoral actions, although the individual results are not statistically significant.

Hence, despite the prevalence of Christians, religion has no effect on morality in South Korea. In fact, when denominational effects were examined, Christians did not differ from the Buddhists or those with no religion. Why Christianity lacks moral implications in South Korea must, for now, remain a mystery.

EASTERN FAITH

This concludes a three-chapter tour of the Far East. In every nation traditional folk religions and Asian faiths such as Buddhism retain widespread support, and the cultural incongruity associated with rapid modernization has prompted many people, particularly the more educated,

Table 8–12: Belief in God and Morality, South Korea

Believes in God:	Yes	No
Percentage Who Say Never Justified		
Stealing property	69%	73%
Cheating on taxes	68%	73%
Taking a bribe	34%	38%
Avoiding fare	72%	76%
Cheating on gov't benefits	37%	42%

	Religious Person	Not Religious	Atheist
Percentage Who Say Never Justified			
Stealing property	75%	69%	72%
Cheating on taxes	72%	69%	72%
Taking a bribe	76%	71%	76%
Avoiding fare	42%	30%	38%
Cheating on gov't benefits	41%	36%	43%

Source: World Values Survey, 2010

to convert to Christianity. The growth of Christianity differs greatly across these nations—from very slow in Japan to very rapid in China. It is true that the East is still dominated by religions lacking in moral implications, but there is no lack of spirituality and mysticism. The secularization thesis finds no support here.

9

THE HINDU REVIVAL

When India became an independent nation in 1947, its political establishment assumed that Hinduism was in its last days. Most of India's new leaders had been educated in Great Britain, where they were exposed to true believers in secularization. Thus, Jawaharlal Nehru (1889–1964), India's first prime minister and a graduate of Trinity College, Cambridge, "believed that industrialization would erode the influence of religion."[1] But nothing of the sort happened. India began to industrialize rapidly, but this was accompanied by a massive Hindu revival. Today fully 80 percent of India's population—nearly a billion people—identify as Hindu. And 67 percent of Indians say they have attended a religious service in the past week, while 85 percent acknowledge religion as important in their daily lives. Atheists are scarce.

India is also home to many religious minorities—Muslims, Christians, Sikhs, Buddhists, and Jains. Thus, unlike most other Asian countries, India is largely a land of *churched* religions. That makes it an interesting test case for the connection between churched religions and morality.

The Hindu revival has not come without its problems, however. As we will see, it has led to growing conflicts with India's many religious minorities.

HINDUISM

It is not surprising that the origins of Hinduism are unknown, since most of the religious history of India is little remembered. Consider that it was not until some stubborn Englishmen dug into various ruins and bribed several members of the hereditary Brahman priesthood to teach them the secret, sacred language of Sanskrit that it was discovered that Buddhism had originated in India and that Buddha was an Indian prince. The Indians had forgotten a millennium of active and quite successful Buddhism so completely that the large shrine marking Buddha's birthplace was not rediscovered until 1896 by the English soldier-turned-archaeologist Alexander Cunningham and his companions.[2] In any event, Hinduism in India may date as far back as 1500 BC, although a bitter conflict continues as to whether it was then of local origins or imported from abroad. While this is fodder for scholarly disputes, it is irrelevant to the nature of the Hindu religion, its future, and its moral effects.

Before briefly sketching the elements of Hinduism, let me dismiss a charge raised by some religious studies professors, most of them in the grip of postmodernism: that "Hinduism" was "invented" by Western colonialists.[3] Their case rests on two points. First is the claim that Western colonials coined the word *Hindo*, or *Hindoo*, as it often was spelled early in the nineteenth century. Second, they condemn Hinduism as a false "construction" imposed on an "extravagant variety"[4] of Indian sects, doctrines, gods, and rituals—an array the Indians themselves are said not to have regarded as having any common core until "educated" in this view by British imperialists and missionaries.

As to the first claim, although Westerners named the oceans and the continents, that doesn't falsify geography. More to the point, *Hindu* occurred in Muslim texts before the British even knew where India was.[5] The word actually derives from *Sindu*, the local name for the Indus River, which became *Hind* or *Hindu* in Persian languages and reentered Indian languages as Hindu.[6] As to the second claim, variations within Hinduism do not exceed those within Judaism, Christianity, or Islam. Like the multitude of disputatious groups within those three faiths, the

Hindu variations are explicitly based on a common core of scripture, doctrine, and practice.[7] Hinduism embraces three sets of scriptures, the Vedas, the Upaniṣads, and the Bhagavad-gītā.

The Vedas date back to about 1500 BC. They embrace a set of gods and stress that humans must frequently perform a set of rituals in order "to ensure the orderly functioning of the world."[8] Since only the priestly upper caste of Brahmans could perform the needed rituals, it gave them immense power—the continued existence of the world depended on them. For more than three millennia, the Vedas were regarded as so secret that not a line was written down. This immense text was transmitted orally from one generation to the next, and only male Brahmans were allowed to hear it—should a lower-class person or a woman happen to hear any portion of the Vedas being recited, her or his ears were to be filled with molten lead. The written Vedas were created by the British, who bribed some Brahmans to dictate them to a stenographer.

During the Vedic era, Hindus worshipped thirty-three divinities, all of them typical nature gods. Then, in the sixth century BC, came more than two hundred new scriptures known as the Upaniṣads. These scriptures also were kept secret, but they were written. More important, they transformed Hinduism by introducing the concept of sin. Not that they depicted the gods as concerned about human morality, but they introduced the doctrine of *karma* and the transmigration of souls.

Vedic-era Hinduism had little or nothing to say about death or an afterlife. But the Upaniṣads proclaimed that upon death we are reborn and our situation in each life is determined by our behavior in our previous life. That is, immoral behavior is punished by rebirth into an unpleasant existence and good behavior is rewarded by rebirth into privilege. Thus was the caste system sanctified—the exalted status of the Brahmans is *earned* in previous lives, and those born into the lowest castes are getting what they *deserve*. But this is a hopeful doctrine for the lowest castes in that they can aspire to being privileged in their next lives. The Upaniṣads also tended to minimize the importance of the gods, stressing the idea that all the gods are within the individual.[9]

Finally, in the third century BC came the Bhagavad-gītā, a beautiful, poetic work that restored the full pantheon of gods, but with an amazing twist: that somehow they all are one, or nearly so. Modern Hinduism embraces a supreme god known as Brahmā, the creator. He is part of a Divine Trinity, also including Vishnu (the preserver) and Shiva (the destroyer), thus representing the three primary forces of the universe. But most Hindu teachers regard the Trinity not as separate gods but as three aspects of the same god, hence a sort of monotheism. Of course, modern Hindus also recognize a host of lesser gods, but it is claimed that they tend to worship only one of these gods, or at least only one at a time.

Observant Hindus engage in daily rituals at home before a family shrine, and this often includes lighting a lamp and offering food before images of a god. Hindus also worship in temples—two-thirds say they do so weekly. And they are expected not to eat beef (cows are regarded as sacred), and about a third of them are vegetarians.

REVIVAL

Contrary to predictions, industrial development did not lead to the demise of Hinduism in India. In fact, since that nation's long tryst with socialism subsided and an emerging free market spurred rapid economic growth, Hinduism has boomed. As the distinguished Meera Nanda points out in the subtitle of her fine book *The God Market*, "globalization is making India more Hindu"; Nanda writes that "secularism is retreating" and "the 'gods are back' in ever greater force in the private and the public spheres."[10]

One quantitative measure of the revival is pilgrimages. In 1986 about 1.3 million Indians visited the Vaishno Devi Shrine, high in the hills of Kashmir; by 2000 the number of pilgrims had reached about 5 million; by 2012 that number had doubled again to 10 million, some of whom booked helicopter flights to avoid the steep climb. The shrine is devoted to the Goddess Durga, and it is believed that petitioners may gain many material benefits.

There is nothing unique about the increase of pilgrims to the Vaishno Devi Shrine—it is, rather, the rule. In 1989 the Amarnath cave temple was still rather unknown, drawing only about 12,000 pilgrims that year. In 2007 it drew 400,000.[11] In 2012 a total of 622,000 pilgrims came.[12]

No doubt the world's largest pilgrimage occurs every three years during the eight-week Kumbh Mela, which involves bathing in the Ganges River at an appointed place (four places rotate over a twelve-year period). In 2001 the estimated total of bathers was 50 million. In 2013 the total was placed at 100 million. As for the Tirumala Venkateswara Temple, it has become the most visited place of worship in the world, with up to 100,000 pilgrims a day. Indian tourist agencies report that "religious trips account for more than 50 percent of all package tours."[13]

All across India there has been a huge boom in sacred building. In Delhi alone, the number of registered religious buildings increased from 560 in 1980 to 2000 in 1987. Many Hindu orders have reported doubling and redoubling their number of ashrams.

A national survey conducted in 2007 found that a third of Indians said they had become more religious in the past five years (only 5 percent said they had become less religious).[14] In India today, as Shikha Dalmia reports, "Women and men wear necklaces and bracelets adorned with Hindu religious symbols, without a trace of self consciousness. Figurines of gods adorn dashboards; posters of deities drape store walls; garlanded idols are prominently displayed in professional offices; and religious songs blare constantly into the air from places of worship and loud private ceremonies."[15]

The Hindu revival is not primarily rooted in the lower castes. To the contrary, everyone agrees that it is especially popular among the more privileged, the very persons who the secularization thesis assumes will be the first to reject religion.[16] The National Election Survey conducted in 2004 found that 60 percent of middle- and upper-class Hindus said they prayed "every day in temples or in family shrines, while only 34 percent of the very poor and 42 percent of the poor did so."[17] This is confirmed by Table 9–1 (next page). The upper-income group is significantly more likely than those with less income to say that they pray and also that religion is very important in their lives.

Table 9–1: Income and the Importance of Religion

Income:	Upper	Middle	Lower
Percentage who pray	85%	79%	71%
Percentage who say religion is "very important"	55%	48%	46%

Source: World Values Survey, 2006

INDIA'S RELIGIOUS MINORITIES

As Table 9–2 shows, India's religious minorities consist of Muslims (13 percent), Christians (3 percent), Sikhs (1 percent), Buddhists (1 percent), and Jains (0.5 percent).

Table 9–2: Religious Affiliation in India

Hindu	80%	963 million
Muslim	13%	157 million
Christian	3%	36 million
Sikh	1%	12 million
Buddhist	1%	12 million
Jain	0.5%	6 million
Other and None	1.5%	18 million

Source: Indian Census, 2001

Let's consider some of these religious groups.

CHRISTIANITY

In 1910, India was the largest Christian foreign mission field. There were more than 4,600 Protestant missionaries in India that year, the majority of them from Britain, but with Americans close behind. Although India was a British colony, the Roman Catholics also sustained a huge mission effort there, with more than 6,000 missionaries (including 1,755 native Indian priests). The Protestants operated 37 colleges and universities in India, 141 normal schools (devoted mainly to teacher training), and 11,503 elementary schools. In addition, Protestant missions served 170 hospitals and 26 medical schools. The Catholics probably matched these numbers, although no statistics are available. Finally, the Protestant mission churches claimed 1,471,727 Indian members and the Roman Catholics claimed 1,060,369[18]; together they accounted for about 1.6 percent of the population.[19]

At present, Christians make up about 3 percent of the population of India. But India's Christians tend to be privileged. As can be seen in Table 9–3, they are twice as likely as Hindus, and six times as likely as Muslims, to have entered college.

Table 9–3: Education and Religious Preference

	Percentage to Have Entered College
Christians	12%
Buddhists	8%
Hindus	6%
Other	6%
Muslims	2%

Source: Gallup World Poll

SIKHISM

Sikhism was founded in the Punjab region of India in the fifteenth century by the Guru Nanak in reaction against those aspects of Hinduism involving ritual, the worship of many gods, and support for the caste system. Its central teaching is the "oneness of God."[20] It is a warrior's faith in that all males are required to always carry a sword—although in modern times the sword may be no more than a small dagger. Sikhs are not permitted to cut any of their hair—not on their heads, nor their beards, nor anywhere on their bodies; women may not pluck their eyebrows. Male Sikhs wear their hair in a knot, covered by a turban; female Sikhs often wear head scarves, while some wear turbans.

Unlike Hindus, Sikhs oppose religious rituals, including pilgrimages and fasting. They reject animal sacrifices and *sati*—the practice of placing living widows on their husbands' blazing funeral pyres. Sikhs are discouraged from being beggars or living as celibates. They have no priests.

Through the centuries the Sikhs established a reputation as fierce warriors, and by the start of the nineteenth century they had established a large empire including what now are Afghanistan, Pakistan, and northern India. Soon came a long war with the British Raj. Faced with Western-style armed forces, the Sikhs were defeated and their empire came under British rule. The partition of India in 1947 was a catastrophe for the Sikhs: they were attacked by both Hindus and Muslims, and before order could be restored, perhaps as many as a million Sikhs were murdered. Peace has never been fully restored. Sikh nationalists continue to rebel against the governments, thus prompting repressive attacks, as we will see shortly.

JAINISM

Although its origins were entirely forgotten until modern times, Buddhism began in India. It was founded by Siddhartha Gautama, who became known as Buddha, an Indian prince who was born in the fifth century in Lumbini, a tiny village on the border of Nepal. At about the same time, in a village about a hundred miles away, Mahāvīra, the founder of Jainism, was born. There is some evidence that they knew of one another—three Buddhist scriptures mention Mahāvīra—and their biographies are quite similar. Both were of the nobility. Both married and fathered one son. At about age thirty, both abandoned their families and their privileged lives to become wandering ascetics—although Buddha eventually abandoned asceticism, while Mahāvīra became an increasingly severe ascetic. Both drew most of their followers from the nobility in the immediate area in which they were born—neither is thought to have ever traveled more than about fifty miles from his birthplace. Both were greatly influenced by early Upaniṣads, and both proclaimed that the goal of all spirituality was release from the cycle of rebirth. But whereas Buddha thought Nirvana was to be achieved through meditation, Mahāvīra favored asceticism.

Mahāvīra taught that he was but the last of twenty-four *Jinas*, or teachers, on how to achieve Nirvana. Upon his death, the Jains (followers of the *Jinas*) split into two antagonistic groups. The Digambaras practiced complete nudity (Mahāvīra had gone naked), while the Shvetambaras believed it was appropriate to wear clothing so long as it was white. The Shventambaras won out, although small groups of Digambaras still exist.

Jainism is, perhaps, the most ascetic faith to sustain millions of followers. Because of their reverence for living things, Jains not only are vegetarians but also reject fruits with seeds, avoid anything fermented (yeasts are living), strain their water so as not to swallow organisms, and wear masks so as not to breath in insects. They cannot farm because they cannot uproot weeds or kill insects that attack crops.

Jains acknowledge the existence of many Hindu divinities but dismiss them as minor spirits having no relevance for attaining Nirvana. Nevertheless, Jain temples contain large statues of the twenty-four *Jinas*, including Mahāvīra, and they conduct elaborate ceremonies in front of them that an outsider would certainly identify as "worship." Indeed, the faithful place offerings in front of these statues.

RELIGION AND MORALITY

India's religious landscape differs from that of most other Asian nations. Hinduism is a churched religion. Membership is exclusive: Hindus do not dabble in Buddhism, Shinto, folk religions, or any other faith. And Hinduism has a strong emphasis on sin. In addition, virtually all the minority faiths in India also are churched religions with explicit concerns about sin.

Consequently, we should expect religion to be linked to morality in India. And it is. The data for India must come from the 2006 World Values Survey because India was not included in the 2012–14 wave. In 2006 the question about God was not asked, nor was the question about stealing. But Table 9–4 (next page) shows a strong linear relationship between the religious-person question and the other four morality items.

Table 9–4: Religion and Morality

	Religious Person	Not Religious	Atheist
Percentage Who Say Never Justified			
Cheating on taxes	56%	50%	30%
Taking a bribe	58%	52%	30%
Avoiding fare	55%	43%	23%
Cheating on gov't benefits	54%	46%	30%

Source: World Values Survey, 2006

RELIGIOUS CONFLICT

In the days of rule by the British Raj, India was much larger than it is today, as Pakistan and what later became Bangladesh were included. What that meant was that a huge population of 359 million Hindus confronted about 80 million Muslims. The intense hatred between these two populations made it impossible for the British to abandon a united India. Fortunately, the two populations tended to be settled in different locales, so independence from the British Raj could be accomplished by partitioning India into two new nations: India and Pakistan. (Bangladesh was originally part of Pakistan, but, the two being separated by more than 1,300 miles, Bangladesh seceded in 1971.) Even after the partition, an estimated 200,000 to 500,000 people were slaughtered in widespread attacks and riots, and more than 14 million displaced refugees fled—Muslims from Hindu areas and Hindus from Muslim areas.

Although this left few Hindus in Pakistan, many are still in Bangladesh, and of course there are a huge number of Muslims still in India. A great deal of antagonism remains—and not just between Hindus and Muslims. Table 9–5 (next page) shows how prevalent are feelings that one does not want neighbors of a different religion.

With the exception of Jews (whose percentage is based on a small number of cases), about half the members of the other four religious

Table 9–5: Percentage who "would not like to have people of a different religion as neighbors"

Hindus	56%
Muslims	47%
Christians	49%
Buddhists	55%
Jews	15%

Source: World Values Survey, 2014

groups in India do not want someone of a different religion living near them. This may be a realistic judgment given the realities of the bitter religious conflicts that continue.

In June 1984 units of the Indian army launched Operation Blue, an attack on rebellious Sikh nationalists who were occupying a small group of buildings in the Punjab. As so often happens, the Indians employed forces (including tanks, heavy artillery, and chemical weapons) far out of scale to the needs of the operation. The attack spread to all Sikhs in the general area and resulted in the burning of a Sikh library and severe damage to the Golden Temple of Amritsar, the Sikhs' holiest place. During the conflict as many as five thousand Sikhs may have been killed.

Subsequently, many Sikhs resigned from government positions, and others returned honors they had received from the government. Nevertheless, Prime Minister Indira Gandhi dismissed these as the acts of a few fanatics and rejected suggestions that she replace her personal bodyguards, all of whom were Sikhs—selected because the Sikhs are famous as solders. On October 31, only about four months after the destruction of their temple, two of Gandhi's Sikh bodyguards shot her more than thirty times for her complicity in Operation Blue. In the next several days, thousands of Sikhs were killed by Hindu rioters.

This was not an isolated incident. Indeed, the destruction of the Babri Mosque in Uttar Pradesh is sadly similar. The mosque was constructed in 1527, and in modern times the claim arose that a Hindu temple on that site had been demolished so the mosque could be built there. That claim is disputed, as is a claim by Jains that the Hindu temple had itself been built over a Jain temple in the seventh century. In 1992 a riot involving about 150,000 Hindus resulted in the destruction of the mosque. This touched off riots in other Indian cities during which several thousand were killed, most of them Muslims. In Bangladesh, Muslims responded by destroying hundreds of homes and shops of Hindus, and leveling a number of Hindu temples.

Conflicts between Hindus and Muslims in India have worsened since Muslim terrorist groups have gained some support among Indian Muslims. In November 2001 three Muslim suicide bombers attacked the provincial assembly in Srinagar, Kashmir, killing thirty-eight. In December of that year a squad of five terrorists, armed with automatic weapons and wearing suicide vests, attacked the Indian Parliament and killed nine before dying. In February 2002 Muslim militants burned a train carrying Hindu pilgrims; this precipitated the Gujarat Riots, during which an estimated two thousand Muslims and several hundred Hindus were killed.

In 2007 Hindu militants objecting to Christmas celebrations burned nineteen Christian churches in Odisha. In 2010 came the Deganga Riots, during which hundreds of Hindu businesses and homes were looted and burned by angry Muslims. And thus it continues.

LOOKING HOMEWARD

By now we have examined religion around the globe—from Europe to South America to the Middle East to Africa and on to Asia. Almost without exception, religion is on the rise in these places, contrary to the claims of ardent secularists.

But what about closer to home? Is secularism really on the march in the United States, as is so often said? Let us turn to the religious landscape in America.

10

RELIGIOUS AMERICA

Depending on how you look at it, American religion is either highly diverse or quite monolithic. While the nation sustains as many as 1,500 different Protestant denominations,[1] few Americans belong to non-Christian religions—as can be seen in Table 10–1 (below).

In addition, nearly all Americans say they believe in God; 80 percent believe in heaven; half pray daily (29 percent pray more than once a day), and only 13 percent do not pray at all.[2]

Table 10–1: American Religious Affiliation

Christian	78%	247 million
Protestant	48%	152 million
Catholic	27%	86 million
Other	3%	9 million
Jewish	2%	6 million
Other	4%	13 million
Unaffiliated*	12%	38 million
None	4%	13 million

Most of them Christians without a denominational preference
Sources: Gallup World Polls, 2006–14

Nevertheless, many critics challenge the notion that America is a religious nation. For example, the Canadian philosopher Charles Taylor has received international acclaim (including the Templeton Prize and Japan's Kyoto Prize) for his thesis that secularization is far advanced not only in Europe but also in the United States and Canada, even if most people still profess their faith in God. Why? Because they do not experience the world as "enchanted"—Westerners no longer live in a "world of spirits, demons, and moral forces."[3] Hence, although they are not yet militant atheists, according to Taylor today's Europeans, Canadians, and Americans are immune to deep, mystical, religious experiences, being in tune only with "naturalistic materialism," which is the scientific understanding of reality.[4]

Taylor's views are compatible with the rather superficial character of most survey research questions devoted to religiousness, which might seem to reflect the lack of depth in the faith of those surveyed. One can be rather close to nonbelief and still answer "yes" when asked "Do you believe in God?" But that criticism cannot apply to these results from the 2007 Baylor National Survey of Religion, conducted by the Gallup Poll.

Please indicate whether or not you have had any of the following experiences:

I was protected from harm by a guardian angel. *Yes:* 55%

What an unexpected and extraordinary finding. Many will no doubt try to explain away this result by claiming that people did not mean their answers literally—that this is merely a figure of speech by which people acknowledge getting a lucky break. But it seems likely that people actually meant what their answer says, given that 61 percent of respondents to the survey believed that angels "absolutely exist" and another 21 percent think they "probably" exist. Indeed, 82 percent told Gallup that "I am sometimes very conscious of the presence of God," 44 percent said they have "felt called by God to do something," and 20 percent said, "I heard the voice of God speaking to me."

When I mentioned the finding about guardian angels in passing at a press conference, two different reporters, one from TV, the other from a major newspaper, pulled me aside and in whispers told me it had happened to them! One said that she had been very pregnant and had stepped off a curb and started to fall, "when two hands grabbed me and put me back on the curb. But there was nobody there." I am not prepared to say whether this incident really happened as she explained it. I am prepared to claim that for her and for most Americans, the world remains "enchanted"—a subject I will pursue later in this chapter.

Nor has Europe become disenchanted. Recall from chapter 2 that multitudes of Europeans believe in ghosts, lucky charms, occult healers, wizards, fortune tellers, *huldufolk*, and a huge array of other aspects of that enchanted world that Taylor believes has long since vanished. What Taylor really demonstrates is that from nowhere is one's vision of modern times so distorted as from the confines of the faculty lounge.

Taylor is hardly alone in "discovering" that, despite appearances, America really is a secularized society. One of the most faithful secularizationists, Oxford's Bryan Wilson, did so by claiming that American religiousness is an illusion because of "the lack of depth of many religious manifestations in the United States," which disguises the fact that "religion [there] is in decline."[5] The equally dogmatic Roy Wallis said that America's high levels of religious participation are not really about religion at all but about ethnic loyalty.[6] Hence, German-Americans keep on being Lutherans in order to keep on being Germans, and English-Americans keep on being Episcopalians for the same reason. What Wallis overlooked was that most German-Americans have left the Lutheran churches for others having no ethnic identity,[7] and, given the small and declining number of Episcopalians, most English-Americans have long since departed. The most rapidly growing American denominations have no ethnic ties at all.

Most other determined secularizationists have settled for claiming that America's journey into modern secularity has simply been delayed, and therefore they grasp at any hint that the decline has finally begun. What is surprising is the instant credibility that clergy and presumably religious media so frequently give to "bad news" claims about American religiousness. Let's consider some of the most alarming reports.

THE BAD NEWS BEARERS

Young people are leaving the churches in droves! This is so generally believed that nearly everything written about it in periodicals such as *Christianity Today* is to explain why the exodus is happening and what can be done to reverse the trend. In 2012 the Barna Group attracted much attention among evangelicals with a report proposing six reasons for the youth exodus. Table 10–2 shows the basis for this concern.

Table 10–2: Younger Americans Aren't Going to Church Regularly

	Under 30	30–49	50 and Over
% Attend weekly	24%	34%	43%

These data come from the highly reputable General Social Survey of American adults conducted annually by the National Opinion Research Center at the University of Chicago. Obviously, younger Americans *are* attending church less often than are older generations, and if this reflects the onset of a trend, American church attendance is going to drop substantially.

But the data in Table 10–2 were collected in 1980! And overall church attendance did not decline after that.

The truth is that similar results can be found in practically any national survey ever conducted. Younger people, especially those under thirty, have *always been*, and probably will continue to be, less likely than older Americans to attend church regularly. Why? Because they tend to be unmarried, to stay out late on Saturday night, and to prefer to sleep in on Sunday mornings. But, generation after generation, Americans have greatly increased their church attendance as they get married and have children. That doesn't stop each new generation of survey researchers from sounding false alarms that cause anxious responses from the pulpits.

Church attendance continues to decline! Whether reported gleefully or with grave concern, this is a constant refrain. It is typically published without any evidence, presumably because the decline is so well known. But the claim isn't true.

Table 10–3 shows that church attendance in the United States has held steady for forty years; variations from year to year are entirely within the range of random variation that applies to all surveys. It is true that church attendance was a bit higher before the late 1960s. But the decline that occurred then was limited to Roman Catholics, many of whom, subsequent to the liberalizations introduced by Vatican II, ceased to scrupulously attend every week and began to attend only most Sundays.

Table 10–3: Percentage Who Attend Church Weekly*

1974	36%
1978	35%
1980	35%
1984	37%
1988	34%
1990	34%
1994	32%
1996	29%
1998	32%
2000	34%
2004	33%
2007	36%
2010	37%
2011	33%
2014	34%

* Combined: more than once a week, once a week, about weekly

Sources: General Social Surveys, 1974–2004; Baylor Religion Survey, 2007, 2010, 2014; World Values Survey, 2011

The number of Americans who say they have no religion is rising rapidly! The Pew Research Center caused a stir when it reported this finding in 2015. The news was greeted with glee by the antireligious sector of the media and with gloom by most religious commentators: "Christianity in Widespread Decline as Americans Become Less Affiliated," headlined the *Washington Post* on May 12, 2015. "America Is Getting Less Christian and Less Religious," declared the *Huffington Post* the same day.

The findings would seem to be clear: the number of Americans who say their religious affiliation is "none" has increased from about 8 percent in 1990 to about 22 percent in 2014. But what this means is not so obvious, for, during this same period, church attendance did not decline and the number of atheists did not increase. Indeed, the percentage of atheists in America has stayed steady at about 4 percent since a question about belief in God was first asked in 1944. In addition, except for atheists, most of the other "nones" are religious in the sense that they pray (some pray very often) and believe in angels, in heaven, and even in ghosts. Some are also rather deeply involved in "New Age" mysticisms.[8]

So who are these "nones," and why is their number increasing— if it is? Back in 1990 most Americans who seldom or never attended church still claimed a religious affiliation when asked to do so. Today, when asked their religious preference, instead of saying Methodist or Catholic, now a larger proportion of nonattenders say "none," by which most seem to mean "no actual membership." *The entire change has taken place within the nonattending group*, and the nonattending group has *not* grown.

In other words, this change marks a decrease only in nominal affiliation, not an increase in irreligion. So whatever else it may reflect, the change does not support claims for increased secularization, let alone a decrease in the number of Christians. It may not even reflect an increase in those who say they are "nones." The reason has to do with response rates and the accuracy of surveys.

A survey's "completion rate" refers to the percentage of people from the original sample with whom interviews are successfully conducted. As the completion rate falls, surveys become less accurate portraits of the population sampled. That is because those who refuse to take part in a survey or who cannot be reached are known to differ in many important ways (such as income, education, race, and age) from those who do take part. When I was a young sociologist at the University of California, Berkeley, Survey Research Center, any survey that failed to interview at least 85 percent of those persons originally drawn into the sample was not to be trusted. The Pew survey of 2012 had a completion rate of only *9 percent*. The 2014 survey was based on samples of phone numbers and had a completion rate of 11.1 percent for the landline sample and 10.2 percent for the cell phone sample. The probable inaccuracy of such surveys is huge.

Pew's completion rates are much lower now than they were in earlier decades. The question arises: what has been changing, the extent of response rate bias or the actual percentage of Americans whose religious affiliation is none? It is impossible to say. But as response rates have fallen, those willing to take part in surveys increasingly are the less educated and less affluent. And, contrary to the common wisdom, those are precisely the people who are least likely to belong to a church.

Young evangelicals are becoming liberal, especially about sex! The media responded joyfully to the news that, compared with their elders, "young evangelicals are more likely to have more liberal attitudes on same-sex marriage, premarital sex, cohabiting, and pornography."[9] There have been many reports that younger people are abandoning evangelical denominations because they have taken the liberal side in the ongoing culture war.

Nonsense! In 2010 my Baylor associates Buster Smith and Byron Johnson presented solid national data that, aside from being slightly more likely than their elders to think more should be done to protect the environment, young evangelicals were as conservative, and sometimes more so, on major social issues.[10] Although published in a good journal (as well as in *First Things*), these results have been ignored by the media. More recently, Mark Regnerus of the University of Texas presented data from a huge survey involving 15,378 Americans. These results also showed no drift toward liberalism by young evangelicals. For example, only 11 percent of young evangelicals supported same-sex marriage, and only 5 percent thought cohabitation acceptable.[11]

There are many more such false alarms, but these should suffice to make the point. I now turn to a major factor concerning the continuing good health of American churches, one that is far too often overlooked: religious pluralism.

PLURALISM AND RENEWAL

Not so many years ago, a select set of American denominations was always referred to as the Protestant "Mainline": Congregationalists, Episcopalians, Presbyterians, Methodists, American Baptists, Christian Church (Disciples of Christ), and, more recently, the Evangelical Lutherans.[12] As the name "Mainline" suggests, these denominations had such social cachet that when Americans rose to prominence they often shed their old religious affiliation and joined one of these bodies. Today that designation, though still commonly used, is out of date; the old Mainline has rapidly faded to the religious periphery, a trend that first was noticed more than forty years ago.

In 1972 Dean M. Kelley, a Methodist clergyman and an executive of the National Council of Churches, provoked a storm of criticism by pointing out a most unwelcome fact: "In the latter years of the 1960s something remarkable happened in the United States: for the first time in the nation's history most of the major church groups stopped growing and began to shrink."[13] Kelley was being diplomatic when he referred to "most of the major church groups," because the decline was limited to the Protestant Mainline bodies.

Kelley's book stirred up angry and bitter denials. Writing in the *Christian Century*, Carl Bangs accused him of using deceptive statistics,[14] even though Kelley had relied entirely on the official statistics reported by each denomination. Everett L. Perry, research director of the Presbyterian Church, called Kelley an ideologue who "marshaled data…to support his point of view."[15] The prominent religious scholar Martin E. Marty dismissed the declines as but a momentary reflection of the "cultural crisis" of the 1960s.[16] If so, then the declines should have been momentary as well. In fact, the declines accelerated, as Table 10–4 shows.

Table 10–4: The Declining "Mainline"

U.S. Members per 1,000 U.S. Population				
Denomination	1960	1970	2000	2010
United Church of Christ (formerly Congregationalist)	12.4	9.6	4.9	3.2
Episcopal	18.1	16.1	8.2	6.1
Presbyterian USA	23.0	19.8	12.7	8.7
United Methodist	54.7	51.6	29.7	24.9
American Baptist USA	8.6	7.7	5.2	4.2
Christian Church (Disciples of Christ)	6.2	6.1	3.8	2.0
Evangelical Lutheran Church in America	29.3	27.7	18.2	13.6

Sources: Yearbook of the American and Canadian Churches, appropriate editions

To eliminate the effects of population growth, Table 10–4 presents denominational size as the number of members per 1,000 Americans, which can be interpreted as each denomination's market share. As can be seen, each of these seven denominations has suffered catastrophic declines: most have lost more than half of their 1960 market share, some of them far more. To make matters worse, all these denominations have elderly congregations, presaging an even more rapid decline.

Some have dismissed these declines as merely reflecting a more general decline in the nation's religiousness, claiming that America finally has begun to follow Europe along the road to irreligion. Not so. As we have seen, church attendance has not declined, and more Americans now belong to a local church than ever before.[17] Others have said the declines show a drop only in the *relative* number of Protestants after high rates of Catholic immigration. But that excuse fails, because the Catholic market share has *declined* slightly since 1960.

If the data in Table 10–4 were all we had to go on, the debate as to why these declines occurred might be irresolvable. But Kelley did not merely claim that the Mainline was declining; he also pointed out that conservative churches were more than taking up the slack. In fact, Kelley headlined this contrast in the title of his book: *Why Conservative Churches Are Growing*. That was what really riled academics and Mainline clergy.

Some dismissed conservative growth, saying the statistics were fraudulent. Others admitted that the membership rolls kept by the conservative churches were honest, but they claimed that the numbers were greatly inflated because so many members hopped from church to church and got counted two or three times.[18] Several have argued that the growth of conservative churches results primarily from higher levels of fertility among their members.[19] But the difference in fertility levels mostly reflects the fact that the Mainline congregations grew old. Indeed, most who join conservative churches as adults grew up in Mainline churches.[20] In other words, the sons and daughters of the remaining Mainline members defected and took their fertility with them. Still others have suggested that the growth of conservative Protestant denominations reflects the growth of the South.[21] But the declines in Mainline churches have occurred in every region.

Many liberals have attempted to make a virtue of the Mainline decline, claiming that the contrasting trends reflect the superior moral worth of the Mainline. According to this view, if the conservative churches are growing it is because they are "herding insecure and frightened masses together into a superficial conformity," whereas the Mainline churches remain as a "faithful remnant of God's people whose prophetic courage and lifestyle truly point the way."[22] Meanwhile, the Mainline shrinks, and conservative churches grow.

As shown in Table 10–5, since 1960 many conservative religious groups have been gaining members at a rapid rate; many have trebled in size. As a result, the Assemblies of God is now larger than the combined total of Congregationalists and American Baptists, more than four times as large as the Christian Church, larger than the Episcopalians, and as large as the Presbyterians (USA). The Pentecostal Assemblies of the World has surpassed the Congregationalists, the American Baptists, and the Christian Church. There are more Mormons than Evangelical Lutherans, and the Church of God in Christ outnumbers all the old mainline bodies except the Methodists and is likely to pass them soon as well. There are as many Jehovah's Witnesses as there are Congregationalists.

Nevertheless, the growth of all of these conservative bodies is dwarfed by the number of Americans who have joined nondenominational, evangelical, Protestant congregations—people who often give their religious affiliation as "Christian." In 1960 there were very few such congregations. Today these nondenominational congregations enroll more members than do the Methodists and more than half as many as do the Southern Baptists. In fact, the growth of the nondenominational evangelical churches accounts for the slight recent decline in the Southern Baptist market share (from 53.8 members per 1,000 population in 1960 to 52.6 per 1,000 in 2010).

Table 10–5: Some Growing Denominations

U.S. Members per 1,000 U.S. Population		
Denomination	1960	2010
Latter-Day Saints (Mormons)	8.2	20.0
Church of God in Christ	2.2	17.9
Assemblies of God	2.8	9.7
Pentecostal Assemblies of the World	0.2	5.8
Jehovah's Witnesses	1.3	3.8
Seventh-day Adventists	1.8	3.6
Church of God (Cleveland, TN)	0.9	3.6
United Pentecostal Church International	0.7	2.5
Nondenom. Evangelical Protestant Congregations	—	34.8*

Pew Forum Survey, 2007

Sources: *Yearbook of the American and Canadian Churches*, appropriate editions

Why have millions of Americans left the denominations in which they were raised for a more conservative church? The answer has to do with the influence of secularization among intellectuals—including seminary professors and clergy.

Some religious institutions—but not all—fail to keep the faith. In an unconstrained religious marketplace, secularization is a self-limiting process: as some churches become secularized and decline, they are replaced by churches that continue to offer a vigorous religious message. In effect, the old Protestant Mainline denominations drove millions of their members into the more conservative denominations. As Jeffrey K. Hadden pointed out in his prophetic 1969 book, *The Gathering Storm in the Churches*, by the 1950s a huge gap had opened between the Mainline clergy and the people in their pews. The gap had two primary features: clergy disbelief in the essentials of Christianity, and their faith in radical politics.

THEOLOGIES OF DOUBT AND DENIAL

The wreckage of the former Mainline denominations is strewn upon the shoal of a modernist theology that began to dominate the Mainline seminaries early in the nineteenth century. This theology presumed that advances in human knowledge had made faith outmoded. If religion were to survive, it must become "modern and progressive and...the meaning of Christianity should be interpreted from the standpoint of modern knowledge and experience" (as the theologian Gary Dorrien puts it).[23] From this starting point, science soon took precedence over revelation, and the spiritual realm faded into psychology. Eventually, Mainline theologians discarded nearly every doctrinal aspect of traditional Christianity.

One of the first leaders in this shift toward theologies of doubt and denial was William Ellery Channing (1780–1842), a Harvard graduate and Boston minister who became the most celebrated preacher of his era. Channing taught that most traditional Christian beliefs were "suited perhaps to darker ages" and "should pass away." He added, "Christianity should now be disencumbered and set free from unintelligible and traditional doctrines, and the uncouth and idolatrous forms and ceremonies, which terror, superstition, vanity, priestcraft and ambition have laboured to identify with it."[24]

A long line of celebrated theologians followed Channing, all echoing his message. Most significantly, Paul Tillich (1886–1965) took up this argument. To look up Tillich online is to confront hundreds of entries, nearly all of them hailing him as the leading theologian of the twentieth century. Tillich has had more lasting impact on the beliefs of contemporary Mainline clergy than anyone else—this despite the fact that his theology, and especially his definition of God, is fundamentally incomprehensible.

The logical inadequacy of Tillich's theology would seem obvious to an unbiased reader.[25] But few read him without first having been assured that they are encountering a profound thinker and thus they suppose that something deeply meaningful must underlie passages such as this one: "Faith is a total and centered act of the personal self, the act of unconditional, infinite, and ultimate concern.... The unconditional concern which is faith is the concern about the unconditional. The infinite passion, as faith has been described, is the passion for the infinite. Or, to use our first term, the ultimate concern is concern about what is experienced as ultimate."[26] These are empty tautologies. Herein lies the secret of the immense prestige and influence of Tillich and other liberal theologians. Their convoluted prose earned them a reputation for profundity while obscuring their lack of Christian faith.

Tillich devoted hundreds of pages to asserting his belief in God. But what did he mean by the word *God*? Surely not God the father almighty, maker of heaven and earth. He condemned that God as an

> invincible tyrant, the being in contrast with whom all other beings are without freedom.... He is equated with recent tyrants who with the help of terror try to transform everything into...a cog in the machine they control.... This is the God Nietzsche said had to be killed because nobody can tolerate being made into a mere object of absolute knowledge and absolute control. This is the deepest root of atheism. It is an atheism which is justified as the reaction against theological theism and its disturbing implications.[27]

Thus, in Tillich's view, God is not a being, and to claim otherwise is to "relapse into monarchic monotheism."[28] Indeed, "God does not exist. He is being itself beyond essence and existence."[29] God is "the ground of being."[30] What does this phrase mean? "God as being-itself is the ground of the ontological structure of being without being subject to this structure himself.... Therefore, if anything beyond this base assertion is said about God, it no longer is a direct and proper statement, no longer a concept. It is indirect, and it points to something beyond itself. In a word, it is symbolic."[31] If God is strictly defined as being-itself, and being-itself has only symbolic meaning, then Tillich's God is merely symbolic.[32]

Tillich's God came to dominate Mainline seminaries in the twentieth century. How can clergy who reject a God who sees, hears, or cares in good conscience conduct a worship service? One could as effectively pray to any stone idol. Through the years many people in the pews glimpsed pastors' lack of belief in a personal God, and they recognized the pointlessness of worshipping the God imagined by Tillich and Mainline theologians.

Mainline liberals displayed contempt for any clergy who still believed in a personal God. In 1959 the president of the National Council of Churches complained about the "cultural crudities" of believing Christians and urged his colleagues to bring these people out of their "personal provincialism."[33] When Billy Graham led his very successful New York Crusade in 1957, the editors of the *Christian Century*, then as now the leading liberal Protestant periodical, were incensed by his "fundamentalism" and published a series of antagonistic editorials. When this failed to harm Graham, Martin E. Marty and his colleagues at the magazine attempted to find evidence that the evangelist was guilty of financial irregularities. They did not find any, so they sought other grounds to discredit him.[34] Ultimately, their efforts had little effect, though they clearly expressed the prevailing liberal mentality.

In contrast, the editors of the *Christian Century* have found no fault with clergy disbelief. When a survey study of local pastors conducted in 1968 revealed that a substantial proportion of Mainline clergy were unwilling to express certainty in the existence of God or the divinity of

Jesus, the editors ignored it.[35] So, too, did they ignore the fact that, while serving as an Episcopal bishop for several decades, John Shelby Spong was a prolific author of books that explicitly rejected the central tenets of Christianity. (Bishop Spong's "twelve theses" include the claims that "theism, as a way of defining God, is dead," that it is "nonsensical to seek to understand Jesus as the incarnation of the theistic deity," and that "the virgin birth, understood as literal biology, makes Christ's divinity, as traditionally understood, impossible.") Under Spong's leadership, his diocese in New Jersey lost more than 40 percent of its members, compared with a 16 percent decline in the Episcopal Church as a whole during these years.[36]

Even though so many have left, most of the people remaining in the former Mainline pews still regard the traditional tenets of Christianity as central to their faith. As a result, the exodus continues.

RADICAL POLITICS

Hand in hand with theologies of doubt and disbelief came certainty in the virtues of the socialist revolution. In 1934 a national survey asked nearly twenty thousand Mainline clergy, "Which economic system appears to you to be less antagonistic to and more consistent with the ideals and methods of Jesus and the noblest of the Hebrew prophets? Capitalism or a Cooperative Commonwealth?" In response, 5 percent opted for capitalism and 87 percent for a cooperative commonwealth, which everyone understood to mean socialism.[37]

This finding was consistent with the formal resolutions of the Federal Council of Churches (FCC), an association the Mainline churches had formed in 1908. (The FCC was the forerunner to the National Council of Churches.) The FCC's founding "creed" called for the reduction of the workday "to the lowest practicable point," for the "highest wage that each industry can afford," "for the abatement of poverty," "for the most equitable division of the products of industry that can ultimately be devised," and so on. The creed set a pattern for future FCC statements that nearly always involved "outspoken liberal advocacy," as Yale historian Sydney Ahlstrom put it.[38] For example, in its annual report for 1930, the FCC noted: "The Christian ideal calls for hearty support for a planned economic system in which maximum social values shall be brought. It demands that cooperation shall supplant competition as the fundamental method."[39] Again, everyone involved regarded this as a call for socialism.

Consider this astonishing example of the Mainline clergy's open commitment to socialism in this era: three days after France fell to the Nazi blitzkrieg in 1940, the editors of the *Christian Century* solemnly pondered whether Hitler would remain committed to "social revolution...of which he has been the prophet and leader in Germany." Will he continue to reject "Capitalist imperialism?" the editors asked.[40] Surely any open-minded observer would have rated this potential "failure" as the least of Hitler's sins.

Such uncritical left-wing commitment did not change when the FCC became the National Council of Churches in 1950. Although the National Council (and the Mainline clergy in general) has avoided open use of the term *socialism*, the commitment to a radical redistribution of wealth and antagonism toward capitalism has continued without pause. Frequent, too, are expressions of support for the Castro regime in Cuba. Attacks on Israel and commendations of the Palestinians are emitted with regularity. The National Council of Churches has claimed that the purpose of the American criminal justice system is not to lower crime but to repress dissent. The organization has condemned home-schooling and public Christmas displays. And on and on.

Aware that most members reject their radical political views, the Mainline clergy claim it is their right and duty to instruct the faithful in more sophisticated and enlightened religious and political views. So every year thousands of members claim their right to leave. And, of course, in the competitive American religious marketplace, there are many appealing alternatives available.

Has rapidly falling membership caused second thoughts among the prominent Mainline clergy, among faculty at the famous divinity schools, or in the headquarters of the National Council of Churches on Riverside Drive in Manhattan? Not for a minute. Instead, the gap Jeffrey Hadden noted in 1969 has widened and membership has continued to shrink; large, organized, dissenting groups have begun departing en masse. As the Protestant theologian and Duke Divinity School professor Stanley Hauerwas explained, "God is killing mainline Protestantism in America, and we goddam well deserve it."[41]

Note that he said *Mainline* Protestantism. Protestantism is as strong as ever in America—only the names have changed.

THE AMERICAN JEWISH REVIVAL

Until recently, secularization seemed to be overtaking American Judaism. It was widely agreed that Orthodox Judaism was hopelessly unsuited for modern times. And Reform Judaism, initiated in the nineteenth century to free Jews from the constraints of Orthodoxy, proved to be as ineffective as Mainline Protestantism. Generation after generation, synagogue membership and attendance declined, so by the 1960s stories began to appear in the media about the "vanishing American Jews."[42] The National Jewish Population Survey conducted in 1990 found that more than a third of Americans of Jewish parentage had left the faith—16 percent now declared themselves to be irreligious, and 19 percent had become Christians. Of those who continued to identify as Jewish, only a third had *ever* belonged to a synagogue and only 10 percent attended weekly.[43]

Nevertheless, these sad tidings failed to reflect the eruption of a Jewish revival, of a sudden and dramatic swing back to orthodoxy—even by the Reform synagogues. As recently as 1955 the policy committee of Reform rabbis had ruled that no traditional customs could be observed at bar mitzvah and wedding ceremonies, and in 1959 a leading rabbi had explained that he and his colleagues must resist any attempts to restore "a romanticized Jewish past." He added, "We cannot lead our people forward by stumbling backward."[44] Mainline Protestant leaders could not have said it better. But unlike the Mainline Protestants, who remain steadfast in their disdain for Christian orthodoxy, during the 1970s Reform Jewish leaders made a complete about-face, culminating in a statement issued in 1979 acknowledging that traditional customs could now be observed. Although Reform temples had long barred men from wearing yarmulkes or prayer shawls to Sabbath services, many men now began to do so. Some Reform temples even reinstated the mikveh bath ritual for women following menstruation.

The push for the revival of a more traditional Judaism in the Reform temples came from the increased religiousness of younger Jews. By 1990 the youngest members of American Reform temples were the most religiously observant, as Table 10–6 demonstrates.

Table 10–6: Age and Observance among American Reform Jews (1990)

	Age			
	18–29	30–39	40–49	Over 50
% who always or usually light Hanukkah candles	74%	71%	68%	53%
% who very often attend Seder	78%	72%	65%	65%
% who had a bar or bat mitzvah	67%	52%	55%	45%
% who fast on Yom Kippur	61%	50%	51%	44%
% who buy kosher meat	38%	37%	29%	24%

Source: 1990 National Jewish Population Survey

All these age effects were statistically significant. The findings suggested that members of Reform temples would become increasingly more traditional in their religious preferences. And that seems to be what has happened over the past quarter century.

Initially, the move toward traditionalism reversed the downward trend in Reform membership. Between 1980 and 1998, the number of households enrolled in a Reform temple increased by about 24 percent and the number of temples increased as well. But then growth leveled off, and since 2000 there has been a slight decline. Much of this decline has resulted from the very low fertility of Reform Jews. As the larger older generations die, they are not fully replaced by their offspring, meaning that substantial recruitment is necessary to offset mortality.

By contrast, the fertility rate for Orthodox and ultra-Orthodox Jews is far above replacement level. As a result, membership in these Jewish groups has overtaken that of the Reform temples: in 2013 both groups numbered about 670,000. If these differential fertility trends hold, soon most American Jews will be Orthodox and ultra-Orthodox. Consider that in New York City, where about a third of all the nation's Jews reside, "a startling 74 percent of Jewish children . . . can be identified as Orthodox," as *Jewish Ideas Daily* reported in 2012.[45] This was inevitable given that in modern times a total fertility rate (the number of children born to the average female in her lifetime) of 2.01 is needed to prevent a population from declining. At present secular Jews have a rate of 1.29, Reform Jews have a rate of 1.36, and Conservative Jews have a rate of 1.74. In contrast, Orthodox Jews have a rate of 3.39 and ultra-Orthodox Jews a rate of 6.72. In addition, intermarriage is a common cause of defection from Judaism, but not among the Orthodox and ultra-Orthodox, fewer than 6 percent of whom marry outside their group.

Two scholars have calculated a projection of the future of American Judaism.[46] They assumed that each of the five Jewish groups above have 100 members. On the basis of their fertility and their differential intermarriage rates alone, in four generations the group of 100 ultra-Orthodox Jews would number 3,401; the Orthodox Jews would number 434; Conservative Jews, 29; Reform Jews, 10; and secular Jews, 7.

That dramatic projection captures the driving forces behind the Jewish revival.

ENCHANTMENT

Recall that Charles Taylor claims America is secularized because modern Americans no longer experience the world as enchanted—as a place filled with "spirits, demons, and moral forces." Taylor was hardly the first to make this claim. The German sociologist Max Weber (1864–1920) is famous for the phrase "the disenchantment of the world," and he borrowed it from the poet and philosopher Friedrich Schiller (1759–1805).

But is this claim true?

At the start of the chapter I gave several examples showing that despite what we hear from many intellectuals—heirs to Weber and Schiller—most people, even in the West, do not find the world "disenchanted." I noted that 52 percent of Americans believe they have been protected by harm from a guardian angel. Table 10–7 pursues the issue of enchantment—and I think the results are definitive.

Table 10–7: Aspects of Enchantment

In your opinion, does each of the following exist:			
Angels	Absolutely: 61%	Probably: 21%	Total: 82%
Satan	Absolutely: 58%	Probably: 17%	Total: 75%
Demons	Absolutely: 46%	Probably: 22%	Total: 68%
Ghosts	Absolutely: 20%	Probably: 29%	Total: 49%
It is possible to be possessed by demons.			
	Agree: 63%	Undecided: 15%	Total: 78%
Dreams sometimes foretell the future or reveal hidden truths.			
	Agree: 55%	Undecided: 16%	Total: 71%
Places can be haunted.			
	Agree: 39%	Undecided: 15%	Total: 54%
It is possible to communicate with the dead.			
	Agree: 21%	Undecided: 19%	Total: 40%

Sources: Baylor Religion Surveys, 2005, 2007

Belief in angels is nearly universal. Three-fourths of Americans believe in Satan; two-thirds believe in demons; and about half believe in ghosts. Most Americans believe it is possible to be possessed by demons; most think dreams can reveal the future; more than a third agree that places can be haunted; and one out of five believes it is possible to communicate with the dead, while another 19 percent are undecided. Where are the grounds for claiming that people no longer experience the world as filled with spirits and demons? And who is so "enlightened" as to suppose that people consciously pray to an empty universe?

Conclusion

WHY FAITH ENDURES

hether or not it is so, the universe testifies to intelligent design. Even the militant atheist Richard Dawkins agrees that "living systems give the appearance of having been designed for a purpose."[1] Of course, Dawkins goes on to argue that this is a false appearance— that the whole universe is an accident without purpose or meaning. But the point stands that life, indeed the entire physical universe, seems so complex and yet so orderly that to regard it as a pointless accident seems absurd. Again, the truth of intelligent design is irrelevant to my purpose here. That design seems self-evident to most people is sufficient.

To assume intelligent design is, of course, to assume a creator, and this, in turn, supposes that there is a supernatural consciousness. Thus have humans repeatedly "discovered" the existence of a god or gods. And if people accept the existence of a supernatural consciousness, it is inevitable that they will seek its blessings, for the *supernatural is a plausible source of many things humans greatly desire, some of which are otherwise unobtainable.* Many of these desires are for tangible things such as good crops, protection against the elements or enemies, health, and fertility, and potentially tangible things such as life after death. People also desire intangibles, such as happiness or that there be meaning and purpose to life. In pursuit of all such rewards, people will attempt to enlist the aid of the supernatural, which raises the question: what does the supernatural desire? Sometimes this question is answered through reason (theology), sometimes through trial and error; and sometimes people experience what they perceive to be communications from the supernatural (revelations).[2] This is how religion arises and endures.

I have analyzed this process of the origin and evolution of religion at great length elsewhere.[3] Here it is sufficient to consider several basic issues. Perhaps the most important is the claim that religious faith is irrational, an assumption based in part on the additional premise that religion was originated by ignorant and irrational primitives and thus is rooted in crude superstition.

RELIGION AND RATIONALITY

There are two rather different claims involved in the charge that it is irrational to be religious. One is that religious beliefs are, in and of themselves, irrational because they are demonstrably untrue. The second is that people do not reason about their religious choices but simply take them for granted based on the culture into which they are born. Both claims are easily exposed as false.

Although endlessly proclaimed by professional atheists, the charge that religion is intrinsically irrational is based on the ignorant claim that scientific "laws" about the material world govern the immaterial realm postulated by religion. Carl Sagan frequently and smugly asserted that miracles can't happen because they violate laws of nature. For example, the Red Sea could not have parted to allow Moses and the Israelites to escape from Egypt because no physical principles involving tides or currents could have made it possible—as if that would come as shattering news to the religious believer. What Sagan could not grasp was that *nothing* qualifies as a miracle *unless* it violates laws of nature. The Old Testament does not claim that Moses chose the very moment of a rare tidal phenomenon to lead his people out of Egypt; it says that God worked a miracle and parted the sea just long enough for the Israelites to pass. It may be that this miracle didn't happen, but to say it could not have done so because it violates the laws of nature misses the point entirely.

More generally, the claim that science disproves religion is nonsensical. Science is limited to study of the natural, empirical world. It can say nothing about the existence or nature of a nonempirical realm. Of course, one is free to argue that there is no nonempirical world, but one may not cite "scientific proof" of that claim.

Secularists insist on portraying science and religion as being in opposition. But the truth is that modern science arose *because* of religion. Science began and flourished only in the West. Why? Because only Christians and Jews conceived of God as a rational creator and concluded that therefore the universe must run according to rational principles that could be discovered.[4] Elsewhere in the world it was assumed that the universe was an incomprehensible mystery, an object suitable for meditation only. The uniquely Judeo-Christian notion of a universe functioning according to rational principles inspired a group of learned figures—mostly very religious people—on to groundbreaking scientific discoveries. A study of the fifty-two most important scientists of the era known as the "Scientific Revolution" (1543–1680) demonstrated that thirty-one were extremely devout (many were clergy members, in fact), twenty were conventionally religious, and only one (Edmond Halley) was irreligious.[5]

As to whether or not people are rational about accepting and practicing their religion, consider that 44 percent of Americans have adopted a religious affiliation different from that of their parents.[6] Although a few American sons and daughters of religious parents choose to drop out of religion entirely, the majority of those raised in irreligious homes choose to become religious.[7] Moreover, even those who don't leave the religion in which they were raised choose whether to be active or inactive in pursuing their faith, and this is true around the world. *Choose* is the critical verb; it assumes rationality.

But to assume rationality is not to assume that human beings follow the path of pure reason in all ways at all times. No competent social scientists who begin their analysis of human behavior with the assumption of rationality believe our brains are little computers that always choose to gain the most at the least cost. Instead, everyone knows that humans are subject to many factors and forces that affect their decisions. It is more accurate to say: *Within the limits of their information and understanding, restricted by available options, guided by their preferences and tastes, humans attempt to make rational choices.*

The first part of this proposition—*within the limits of their information*—recognizes that we cannot select choices if we do not know about them, and that we cannot select the most beneficial choice if we have incorrect knowledge about the relative benefits of choices. The second part—*within the limits of their . . . understanding*—acknowledges that people must make choices based on a set of principles, beliefs, or theories they hold about how things work. Such baseline assumptions may be false, as the history of science demonstrates, but the rational person applies his or her principles because these are, for that moment, the most plausible assumptions. Finally, of course, people may select only from among *available options*, and the full range of choices actually available may not be evident to them.

If humans attempt to make rational choices, why is it that they do not always act alike? Why don't people reared in the same culture all seek the same rewards? Because their *choices are guided by their preferences and tastes*. This helps us understand not only why people do not all act alike but also why it is possible for them to engage in exchanges: to swap one reward for another—as a child I often traded my dessert to my sister in return for her second pork chop.

Of course, not all preferences and tastes are variable—clearly there are things that virtually everyone values regardless of their culture or upbringing: food, shelter, security, and affection among them. Obviously, too, culture in general, and socialization in particular, will have a substantial impact on preferences and tastes. It is neither random nor purely a matter of personal taste whether someone prays to Allah or Shiva, or, indeed, whether one prays at all. Still, the fact remains that within any culture, there is substantial variation in preferences and tastes. Some of this variation is at least partly the result of socialization differences—for example, we probably learn our preferences concerning highly liturgical services as children. But a great deal of variation is so idiosyncratic that people have no idea how they came to like or dislike certain things. As the old adage says, "There's no accounting for tastes."

Finally, as implied by the word *attempt* in the phrase "humans attempt to make rational choices," people don't always act in entirely rational ways. Sometimes we act impulsively—in haste, passion, boredom, or anger ("I really didn't stop to think about what I was doing"). Sometimes human also err because they are lazy, careless, or neurotic.

All that said, most of the time normal human beings will choose what they perceive to be the more reasonable option, and whenever they do so, their behavior is fully rational, even if they are mistaken. It follows that the religious choices people make are as rational as their other choices: religion offers things most people very much desire and does so with considerable *plausibility*.

Little of what people know about the world is the result of their own experience. For example, few have an experiential basis for knowing that the earth is round, let alone that the stars are distant suns. People "know" these things because they have been taught them by others in whom they have confidence. The same applies to religion: people are confident in a religion because others whom they respect express their confidence in it. People not only testify to their certainty in the truth of a religion but also often enumerate personal "proofs" that religion is true. Recall from chapter 10 that 55 percent of American adults believe they have been "protected from harm by a guardian angel." Twenty percent testify that they have heard "the voice of God speaking." In addition, 23 percent claim to have "witnessed a miraculous, physical healing," and 16 percent say that they themselves have "received a miraculous, physical healing."[8] This is not peculiar to Americans; in most other major religions in most of the rest of the world, similar testimonials abound. For most people, such proofs that religion is true are as convincing as claims by scientists that, for example, the universe came into being suddenly via the Big Bang—this, too, most people must accept on faith alone.

Critics such as Richard Dawkins would challenge this comparison by noting that, although laypeople must rely on testimony concerning the Big Bang, the scientists on whom they rely have firm empirical evidence for their claims. But many who offer testimonials as to the truth of religion believe they have firm empirical evidence, too: if you were sure you had been grabbed by invisible hands and saved from falling into traffic, might you tend to believe you had solid proof of the existence of angels?

In any event, it is hardly irrational for most people to believe in religion, even if they are wrong.

PRIMITIVE PHILOSOPHERS

All the early social scientists, including Herbert Spencer (1820–1903), Edward Burnett Tylor (1832–1917), and Emile Durkheim (1858–1917), agreed that the religion of primitive societies was crude to the point of being absurd. Spencer claimed that early humans were unable to distinguish their dreams from their experiences while awake, were "without curiosity," and even lacked any notion of cause and effect. Hence, their religious ideas were ignorant and "childlike."[9] Tylor agreed that primitive humans lived in a "childish" world, cluttered with spirits.[10] Durkheim even dismissed the idea that religion involves the worship of a god or gods, claiming that the actual object of religious worship is always society itself—even if the worshippers remain ignorant of this "fact."[11]

These early scholars went further. They held that what was true of primitive religion was also true for the religions of modern times—even if this was obscured by elaborate theologies. Moreover, they believed that the flaws of primitive religions were "a weapon which could be used...with deadly effect against Christianity."[12] As Charles Darwin put it in a letter to Tylor, upon having read his book *Primitive Society*, "It is wonderful how you trace [primitive religion] from the lower races up to the religious beliefs of the higher."[13]

Then came a shocking development. After studying a mountain of trustworthy reports from anthropological field studies of primitive tribes, Andrew Lang (1844–1912) revealed that most such tribes had a quasi-monotheistic religion based on high gods: "moral, all-seeing directors of things and men...eternal beings who made the world and watch over morality."[14] That is, rather than being crude and ignorant, the religions of even the most primitive groups reflected a clear concern to explain the meaning and purpose of life. In 1927 the distinguished anthropologist Paul Radin (1883–1959) published *Primitive Man as Philosopher*—a collection of interviews with members of preliterate societies (before any

contact with missionaries) on the great philosophical questions about the origin and meaning of life. A Greenland Eskimo explained: "Thou must not imagine that no Greenlander thinks about these things.... Certainly there must be some Being who made all these things."[15] Lang's and Radin's work caused a wholesale revision of anthropological claims about primitive religion—but it has been met with the counterclaim that *all* religious answers to existential questions are primitive and pointless.[16]

THE NEED FOR MEANING

Just as many of the secularization faithful continue mistakenly to believe that primitive people could not engage in "sophisticated" thought, these same academics generally assume that few people around the world today ever think about the "big" philosophical questions such as the meaning and purpose of life. It is widely claimed that most people simply believe what they are told, accepting without further reflection the answers provided by the religious culture into which they were born.

But that's not so, as shown in Table C–1 (page 213). The overwhelming majority of people on earth do think about the meaning and purpose of life. China is lowest, but even there half the population say they think about the meaning and purpose of life. Nearly everywhere else, three-fourths or more do so. Regional variations are modest, ranging from 89 percent in Sub-Saharan Africa to 76 percent in Asia.

When people think about the meaning and purpose of life, what do they conclude? Do many end up agreeing with Richard Dawkins that life has "no design, no purpose, no evil and no good, nothing but blind, pitiless indifference"?[17] Whatever else one makes of this claim, it certainly is not a view that people will be eager to embrace; not even Dawkins's most dedicated readers will find this claim sets their hearts soaring. People want life to have some purpose. And hardly anyone agrees with Dawkins that life does not serve any purpose, as can be seen in Table C–2 (page 216).

Comparisons with Table 1–8 (page 32) show that the percentage of people who think life serves no purpose is comparable to (but even lower than) the percentage of atheists in a country. Around the world, nearly everyone thinks their life has an important purpose or meaning, as shown in Table C–3 (page 218). Only in Hong Kong (62 percent) and Taiwan (66 percent) do fewer than 70 percent of the people think their life has an important purpose and meaning. In only a few nations is the percentage below 80, and in a great many it is above 90 percent.

THE GLOBAL RELIGIOUS AWAKENING

Contrary to the constant predictions that religion is doomed, there is abundant evidence of an ongoing worldwide religious awakening. Never before have four out of five people on earth claimed to belong to one of the great world faiths.

Today there are millions of devout Protestants in Latin America; not so long ago there were none. Even so, Latin American Catholics are far more religious than ever before. Sub-Saharan Africa is now home to more churchgoing Christians than anywhere else on earth, and North Africa and the Middle East are ablaze with Muslim fervor. Hinduism has never been stronger, and India's transport systems are straining to meet the demands of pilgrims. The Chinese have rebuilt tens of thousands of temples destroyed by the Red Guards, and millions have converted to Christianity. Only in parts of Europe are the churches still rather empty, but this is not the reliable sign of secularization it has long been said to be; it is, rather, a sign of lazy clergy and unsuitable established religions. As has been said, Europe is a continent of "believing non-belongers."

The three tables presented at the end of this chapter help to reveal why religion endures. People want to know *why* the universe exists, not that it exists for no reason, and they don't want their lives to be pointless. Only religion provides credible and satisfactory answers to the great existential questions. The most ardent wishes of the secularization faithful will never change that.

Secularists have been predicting the imminent demise of religion for centuries. They have always been wrong—and their claims today are no different. It is their unshakeable faith in secularization that may be the most "irrational" of all beliefs.

Table C–1: "How often do you think about the meaning and purpose of life?"

	Percentage Who Say "Often" or "Sometimes"
United States	78%
Canada	82%
Western Europe	
Andorra	82%
Cyprus	89%
Finland	79%
France	79%
Germany	80%
Great Britain	74%
Italy	88%
Netherlands	71%
Norway	73%
Spain	65%
Sweden	69%
Switzerland	80%
Average	**77%**
Eastern Europe	
Belarus	75%
Bulgaria	70%
Georgia	92%
Hungary	71%
Moldova	90%
Poland	70%
Romania	83%
Russia	71%
Serbia & Montenegro	68%
Slovenia	74%
Ukraine	77%
Average	**77%**

Islamic Nations*	*Nations in which the population is more than 50 percent Muslim
Algeria	70%
Armenia	90%
Azerbaijan	87%
Burkina Faso	84%
Egypt	82%
Indonesia	90%
Iran	87%
Iraq	76%
Jordan	88%
Palestinian Terr.	88%
Kazakhstan	72%
Kuwait	76%
Kyrgyzstan	91%
Lebanon	63%
Libya	85%
Malaysia	93%
Mali	78%
Morocco	82%
Pakistan	83%
Qatar	89%
Tunisia	76%
Turkey	89%
Uzbekistan	93%
Yemen	76%
Average	**83%**
Sub-Saharan Africa	
Ethiopia	93%
Ghana	91%
Nigeria	92%
Rwanda	89%
South Africa	87%

Zambia	81%
Zimbabwe	88%
Average	**89%**
Latin America	
Argentina	72%
Brazil	83%
Chile	80%
Colombia	84%
Ecuador	87%
Guatemala	86%
Mexico	81%
Peru	73%
Trinidad	95%
Uruguay	71%
Average	**81%**
Asia	
China	50%
Hong Kong	62%
India	56%
Japan	79%
Nepal	76%
Philippines	92%
Singapore	77%
South Korea	90%
Taiwan	72%
Thailand	90%
Vietnam	89%
Average	**76%**
South Pacific	
Australia	78%
New Zealand	80%

Sources: World Values Surveys, 2005–9; 2010–14 (most recent for a given nation)

Table C–2: Percentage Who Agree That
Life Does Not Serve Any Purpose

United States	3%
Canada	4%
Europe	
Austria	7%
Bulgaria	4%
Cyprus	6%
Czech Republic	3%
Denmark	10%
France	6%
Germany	6%
Great Britain	6%
Hungary	3%
Ireland (including Northern Ireland)	4%
Italy	6%
Latvia	4%
Netherlands	5%
Norway	4%
Poland	8%
Portugal	13%
Russia	12%
Slovenia	4%
Slovakia	19%
Spain	8%
Sweden	10%
Switzerland	3%
Other	
Australia	5%
Chile	11%
Israel	11%

Japan	3%
New Zealand	4%
Philippines	14%

Source: International Social Survey Program, 2008

Table C–3: "Do you feel your life has an important purpose or meaning?"

	Percentage Who Say "Yes"
United States	94%
Canada	92%
Western Europe	
Austria	77%
Belgium	77%
Cyprus	95%
Denmark	85%
Finland	85%
France	80%
Germany	88%
Great Britain	82%
Greece	84%
Ireland	90%
Italy	89%
Netherlands	73%
Norway	88%
Portugal	95%
Spain	80%
Sweden	89%
Switzerland	84%
Average	**85%**
Eastern Europe	
Albania	93%
Armenia	93%
Belarus	78%
Bosnia-Herzegovina	85%
Bulgaria	81%
Croatia	86%
Czech Republic	76%

Estonia	80%
Georgia	90%
Hungary	89%
Latvia	82%
Lithuania	88%
Macedonia	92%
Montenegro	93%
Poland	84%
Romania	78%
Russia	85%
Serbia	86%
Slovakia	91%
Slovenia	67%
Ukraine	82%
Average	**85%**
Latin America	
Argentina	96%
Belize	97%
Bolivia	96%
Brazil	97%
Chile	93%
Colombia	98%
Costa Rica	98%
Cuba	97%
Dominican Republic	97%
Ecuador	98%
El Salvador	98%
Guatemala	96%
Guyana	98%
Haiti	82%
Honduras	98%
Jamaica	99%

Mexico	94%
Nicaragua	98%
Panama	99%
Paraguay	99%
Peru	96%
Puerto Rico	99%
Trinidad & Tobago	97%
Uruguay	94%
Venezuela	99%
Average	**97%**
Islamic Nations*	** Nations in which the population is more than 50 percent Muslim*
Afghanistan	91%
Azerbaijan	92%
Bangladesh	91%
Burkina Faso	97%
Chad	92%
Egypt	89%
Guinea	97%
Indonesia	98%
Iran	85%
Jordan	90%
Kazakhstan	92%
Kosovo	97%
Kuwait	98%
Kyrgyzstan	94%
Lebanon	88%
Malaysia	96%
Mali	99%
Mauritania	95%
Morocco	89%
Niger	98%

Pakistan	82%
Palestinian Territories	81%
Saudi Arabia	95%
Senegal	95%
Sierra Leone	98%
Tajikistan	95%
Turkey	85%
Turkmenistan	97%
United Arab Emirates	97%
Uzbekistan	97%
Yemen	91%
Average	**93%**
Sub-Saharan Africa	
Angola	89%
Benin	97%
Botswana	93%
Cameroon	96%
Central African Republic	97%
Ghana	99%
Ivory Coast	99%
Kenya	98%
Liberia	99%
Madagascar	96%
Malawi	98%
Mozambique	97%
Namibia	98%
Nigeria	98%
Rwanda	89%
South Africa	97%
Tanzania	94%
Togo	99%

Uganda	97%
Zambia	96%
Zimbabwe	93%
Average	**96%**
Asia	
Cambodia	86%
Hong Kong	62%
India	91%
Japan	77%
Laos	99%
Mongolia	98%
Myanmar (Burma)	90%
Nepal	92%
Philippines	97%
Singapore	90%
South Korea	81%
Sri Lanka	95%
Taiwan	66%
Thailand	95%
Vietnam	98%
Average	**88%**
Other	
Australia	88%
Israel	88%
New Zealand	88%
Average	**88%**

Source: Gallup World Poll

Notes

INTRODUCTION: CONFOUNDING THE SECULARIZATION FAITHFUL

1   Portions of this introduction appeared in Stark, 1999a.
2   Pulliam Bailey, 2015.
3   Stark, 2008.
4   Geertz, 1996.
5   Stark, 2014: 309–10.
6   Woolston, 1735.
7   Quoted in Redman, 1949: 26.
8   In Healy, 1984: 373.
9   Finke and Stark, 1992.
10 Paulson, 2014. This *New York Times* writer thought this demonstrated secularization!
11 Müller, 1880: 218.
12 Crawley, 1905: 8.
13 Mills, 1959.
14 Wallace, 1966.
15 Berger, 1968.
16 Berger, 1997.
17 Wilson, 1992: 210.
18 Bruce, 1992, 2004, 2011.
19 Norris and Inglehart, 2004: 25
20 1999 World Values Survey.
21 Tomasson, 1980.
22 Nickerson, 1999; Swatos and Gissurarson, 1997.
23 Tomasson, 1980.
24 Swatos and Gissurarson, 1997.
25 Stark, 2015.
26 For extended discussions, see: Stark and Bainbridge, [1987] 1996; Stark and Finke, 2000; Stark, 2007.

27 See Stark, 2004: ch. 6.
28 Froese, 2008.
29 Greeley, 1994.
30 World Values Surveys.
31 Berger, 1997.
32 Huntington, 1997.

CHAPTER 1: A GLOBAL PORTRAIT OF FAITH

1 An earlier version of this section appeared in Stark and Corcoran, 2014. Here, data on China have been included and another year of Gallup World Poll data has been added.
2 See Stark and Corcoran, 2014.
3 Huntington, 1997.
4 Eberstadt and Shah, 2011.
5 Ibid.
6 Pew Research Center, 2015.
7 Jenkins, 2002, 2006.
8 These data are from the World Values Survey of 2005. The survey done in 2013 reported an absurd claim that 55 percent of people in Hong Kong are atheists, about twice as high as the percentage for the second-highest nation and ten times higher than the number reported for Hong Kong in 2005. Changes of that magnitude in so few years on significant characteristics simply do not occur. This is similar to the error in the 2010 World Values Survey showing that 18 percent of Taiwanese are Jews and 22 percent belong to the Greek Orthodox Church.

CHAPTER 2: EUROPE: THE GRAND ILLUSIONS

1 Berger, 1997.
2 Cox, 2003: 201.
3 Norris and Inglehart, 2004.
4 Brown, 2003; Clark, 2012; Nash, 2004; Williams, 1999.
5 Brown, 1992; Stark and Iannaccone, 1994.
6 For a brilliant summary, see Clark, 2012.
7 Loane, [1906] 2012: 26. Brought to my attention by Williams, 1999: 1.
8 Williams, 1999: 2–3.
9 Portions of this section appeared previously in Stark, 2011.
10 For more on the myth of the Dark Ages, see, e.g., Stark, 2014: ch. 4.
11 Walzer, 1965: 4.
12 Murray, 1972: 92.
13 Ibid.
14 Murray, 1972: 93–94.
15 Quoted in Coulton, 1938: 193.
16 Quoted in Coulton, 1938: 188.
17 Murray, 1976 edition: 189.
18 In Thomas, 1971: 162.
19 Coulton, 1938: 194.

20 Strauss, 1975: 49.
21 Ibid.
22 Ibid.
23 Strauss, 1978: 278.
24 Strauss, 1978: 278–79.
25 Strauss, 1978: 283.
26 Thomas, 1971: 161–62.
27 Strauss, 1978: 284.
28 Strauss, 1975: 56–57.
29 Straus, 1978: 284.
30 Strauss, 1975: 59.
31 Strauss, 1978: 273.
32 Coulton, 1938: 189–90.
33 Farmer, 1991: 336; Hay, 1977: 64.
34 Morris, 1993: 232.
35 In Thomas, 1971: 164.
36 Stark, Hamberg, amd Miller, 2005.
37 Strauss, 1988: 211.
38 Davie, 1994.
39 Stark and Bainbridge, 1980, 1985; Stark, 1985, 1993.
40 Stark and Bainbridge, 1980, 1985.
41 Bainbridge and Stark, 1982.
42 Stark, 1993.
43 J. Gordon Melton, personal communication of unpublished data.
44 Nolan and Nolan, 1989; Nolan and Nolan, 1992.
45 This section in based on the contribution of Eva Hamberg to Stark, Hamberg, and Miller, 2005.
46 World Values Survey, 2006.
47 Granqvist and Hagekull, 2001: 527.
48 World Values Survey, 1999.
49 Bråkenhielm, 2001.
50 Höllinger and Smith, 2002.
51 Houtman and Mascini, 2002.
52 Sjödin, 2002: 84
53 Ibid.
54 World Values Surveys.
55 Janssen, 1999:59.
56 Ibid.
57 Janssen, 1999.
58 Janssen, 1999: 73.
59 Quoted in Janssen, 1999: 79.
60 Bruno Borchert, quoted in Janssen, 1999: 82.
61 Janssen, 1999: 82.
62 World Values Survey, 1999.
63 In *RIA Novosti*, November 1, 2010.
64 Stephens, 1997: 358.
65 International Social Survey Project, 2008.
66 Epstein, 1995; Menzel, 2007.

67   Stark, 2012.

68   Menzel, 2007: 1

69   Menzel, 2007: 2.

70   World Values Surveys.

71   Berger, Davie, and Fokas, 2008: 16.

72   Schmied, 1996.

73   Beckford, 1985: 286.

74   Lodberg, 1989.

75   Selthoffer, 1997.

76   Grim and Finke, 2006.

77   *Ude og Hjemme* 24: 2005

78   Alvarez, 2003.

79   Rydenfelt, 1985.

80   In Pettersson, 1990: 23.

81   Asberg, 1990: 18.

82   In Preus, 1987: 9

83   Berger, 1969:133–34.

84   Stark, 1983; Stark and Finke, 2000.

85   Ibid.; ibid.

86   Iannaccone, 1991.

87   Stark, 1992; 1998.

88   Ibid.; ibid.

89   Hamberg and Pettersson, 1994, 1997; Pettersson and Hamberg, 1997.

90   Stark, 1964.

91   Stark, 1965.

92   *ADL Global 100*, 18.

93   See Stark and Corcoran, 2014.

94   Eberstadt and Shah, 2012; Pew Research, 2011.

95   Frejka and Westoff, 2008.

CHAPTER 3: THE CHURCHING OF LATIN AMERICA

1   This chapter is based in part on Stark and Smith, 2010 and 2012. I thank Buster G. Smith for his valuable contributions.

2   Encarnación, 2013.

3   Stark, 1992.

4   Robinson, 1923.

5   Chesnut, 2003b: 61; Gill, 1998: 68; Martin, 1990: 57–58.

6   Gill, 1998: 86.

7   Chesnut, 1997, 2003a, 2003b; Gill, 1998; Freston, 2008; Martin, 1990; Stoll, 1990.

8   Chesnut, 2003a: 22.

9   Mecham, [1934] 1966: 38.

10   Chesnut, 2003a: 23

11   Klaiber, 1970; Montgomery, 1979.

12   Gill, 1998.

13   Nuñez and Taylor, 1989.

14   Gill, 1989: 82.

15 Stark and Finke, 2000: 153, table 8.
16 Stark, 2001; Siewert and Valdez, 1997.
17 Welliver and Northcutt, 2004: 32.
18 Stoll, 1990: 6.
19 Prior to 2007, the Gallup World Poll did not distinguish Protestants and Catholics, but classified both as "Christians."
20 Barrett, Kurian, and Johnson, 2001.
21 Jenkins, 2002: 64; Martin, 1990: 143.
22 Jenkins, 2002: 64.
23 Cox, 1995: 168.
24 A. Smith, [1776] 1981: 2.788–89.
25 Drogus, 1995: 465.
26 Rubenstein, 1985–86: 162.
27 Gill, 1998.
28 Gooren, 2002.
29 Burdick, 1993; Hewitt, 1991; Mariz, 1994.
30 Cavendish, 1994; Hewitt, 1991.
31 Gooren, 2002: 30.
32 Winfield, 2015.
33 Goldberg, 2014.
34 Brusco, 1993, 1995; Burdick, 1993; Chesnut, 2003a & b, 1997; Cox, 1995; Gill, 1998; Hallum, 2003; Martin, 1990, 2002; Stoll, 1993, 1990.
35 Martin, 2002: 3.
36 Niebuhr, 1929: 19.
37 Cohn, 1961: xiii.
38 Marx, [1845] 1998: 61.
39 The results are reported in detail in Stark and Smith, 2010.
40 Laurentin, 1977; Mansfield, 1992
41 Chesnut, 2003b: 61.
42 *Catholic Almanac*, 1961, 2014.
43 *Miami Herald*, October 16, 1992.
44 Glock and Stark, 1966.
45 Dolan, 1975, 1978; Finke and Stark, 1992.

CHAPTER 4: ISLAM INTENSIFIED

1   Stark and Corcoran, 2014.
2   Douglas, 1982.
3   Mutlu, 1996.
4   Sivan, 1985.
5   Nasr, 1992.
6   Niandou-Souley and Alzouma, 1996.
7   Morocco omitted because of an obvious coding error.
8   Lapidus, 1997: 448.
9   Roy, 1994.
10 World Values Survey, Wave 4: 2000–4.
11 World Values Survey, Wave 6: 2010–14.

12 di Giovanni and Gaffey, 2015.
13 BBC News, 2015.
14 Malsin, 2015; Edwards, 2015.
15 Hirst, 2007.
16 Lagnado, 2015.
17 Alster, 2014.
18 *Saudi Arabia's Curriculum of Intolerance*. Freedom House. May 2006: 24–25.
19 Watson, 2011.
20 World Values Survey, Wave 4: 2000–4.
21 *Policy Exchange*, 2007.
22 *State of Human Rights in Pakistan in 2012*. Islamabad, Pakistan, May 4, 2013.
23 Chesler, 2010.
24 See the excellent summary in "Islamophobia," *Wikipedia*.
25 Quoted in Ali, 2013.
26 See Stark, 2009.

CHAPTER 5: SUB-SAHARAN AFRICAN PIETY

1 Lloyd, 1973.
2 Headrick, 1981: 63.
3 Curtin, 1964: 483–87.
4 Headrick, 1981: 71.
5 Dennis, Beach, and Fahs, 1911.
6 Ibid.
7 Dorrien, 2001, 2003.
8 Hocking, 1932: 49
9 Hicking, 1932: 49–50.
10 Hocking, 1932: 53.
11 Hocking, 1932: 54.
12 Ahlstrom, 1972.
13 Hutchison, 1987: 147.
14 Ibid.
15 Barrett, 1968: 79.
16 "Christianity in Africa," *Wikipedia*.
17 Barrett, 1968: 267.
18 Simon Maimela, quoted in Anderson, 2001: 36.
19 Jenkins, 2006: 24.
20 Noll, 2000: 290.
21 The discussion of Shembe draws from Anderson, 2001; Hexham and Oosthuizen, 1996; Sundkler, 1961; Sundkler and Steed, 2000.
22 Anderson, 2001: 107. These variations have led some to question whether the Nazareth Baptist Church is a legitimate Christian faith. See, e.g., Oosthuizen, 1968. Given the substantial differences among Western Christian denominations, I am inclined to the position that groups that claim to be Christian are. To deem otherwise is to venture into the dangerous precincts of heresy hunting.
23 The discussion of Harris draws from Anderson, 2001; Haliburton, 1973; Shank, 1994; Sundkler and Steed, 2000.

24 The discussion of Braide draws from Anderson, 2001; Tasie, 1982; Sundkler and Steed, 2000.

25 Moses Oludele Idowu, "An Instrument of Revival: The Story of Joseph Ayo Babalola, the first Apostle and General Evangelist of the Christ Apostolic Church," paper presented to an international religious conference organized by the Centre for World Christianity et al., August 2012, http://www.academia.edu/8300892/An_Instrument _of_Revival_The_Challenge_of_Joseph_Ayo_Babalola.

26 The discussion of Kimbangu draws from Anderson, 2001:125–27; Sundkler and Steed, 2000.

27 Anderson, 2001:254.

28 Ali and Matthews, 1999; Williams. 2011.

29 *Catholic Almanac*, 1961, 2014.

CHAPTER 6: THE "UNCHURCHED" JAPANESE

1 Miller, 1992.

2 World Values Survey, 2010.

3 Eades, et al, 1986; Fututake, 1981; Ikado, 1972; Wilson, 1977.

4 Inoue, 2003.

5 Breen and Teeuwen, 2010.

6 Bowker, 1997.

7 Lester, 1993.

8 McFarland, 1967.

9 McFarland, 1967; Moroto, 1976.

10 McFarland, 1967: 4

11 Moroto, 1976: 1.

12 Victoria, 2001: 78.

13 McFarland, 1967; White, 1970.

14 Dennis, Beach, and Fahs, 1911.

15 Snead, 1950.

16 *Yearbook of the Jehovah's Witnesses*, 1981, 2014.

17 *Deseret News Church Almanac*, 2014.

18 This section is based on the contribution of the late Alan Miller to Stark, Hamberg, and Miller, 2005. For statistics on those who are active "in a church," see World Values Survey, 2010.

19 Miller, 1992.

20 Nelson, 1992; *Wall Street Journal*, September 12, 2014: A1, A4.

21 This section is based on Stark, 2001; 2004: ch.7, but uses more recent data.

22 Smith, 1889: 53.

23 Durkheim, [1886] 1994: 21.

24 Malinowski, 1935: viii.

25 Tylor, [1871] 1958: 446.

26 Benedict, 1938: 633.

27 Douglas, 1975: 77.

28 For a recent, worldwide demonstration, see Stark, 2001; 2004, ch.7.

29 Clough, 1997: 57.

30 World Health Organization, 2012.

31   Naito, 2007; Ozawa-de Silva, 2010.
32   Nakagawa, 2011.
33   Haworth, 2013.
34   Wiseman, 2004.

Chapter 7: Converting China

1   This chapter draws upon Stark and Liu, 2011, and Stark and Wang, 2014, 2015.
2   In *Roughing It*, 1872.
3   Fried, 1987.
4   Fairbank, 1974: 1.
5   Overmyer, 2003: 1.
6   Lambert, 2006: 9.
7   Stark, 2007.
8   Sun, 2005.
9   Dean, 2003: 32–33.
10   Zürcher, 1959: 419.
11   Gladney, 2003.
12   Wang and Yang, 2006; Yang, 1998.
13   Lin-Liu, 2005.
14   Goossaert and Palmer, 2012: 302.
15   Yang, 2005.
16   Lyall, 1973: 139.
17   Glock, 1964.
18   Lenski, 1953; Lazerwitz, 1962; Stark, 1964, 1971; Glock and Stark, 1965.
19   Lester, 1993: 867.
20   Stark, 2007.
21   In Burkert, 1985: 296.
22   Lang, 1983.
23   Baumgarten, 1997.
24   Ramsay, 1893: 57; also Judge, 1960; Stark, 2011.
25   Costen, 1997: 70.
26   Lambert, 1992.
27   Parker, 1992: 45.
28   Stark, 2003.
29   Fogel, 2000: 2.
30   In Aikman, 2003: 5.
31   See Huilin and Yeung, 2006.
32   See Stark and Wang, 2015: ch. 5.

Chapter 8: Faith in the "Four Asian Tigers"

1   As calculated by the International Monetary Fund, 2013.
2   The World Values survey for 2010 obviously is badly miscoded—it claims that 18 percent of Taiwanese are Jewish and 22 percent belong to the Greek Orthodox Church!
3   Clark, 1986.

CHAPTER 9: THE HINDU REVIVAL

1   Malik and Vajpeyi, 1989.
2   Allen, 2003.
3   For a summary, see Lorenzen, 1999.
4   Smith, [1962] 1991: 144.
5   Ernst, 1992.
6   Lorenzen, 1999: 635.
7   Monier-Williams, [1919] 1993; Gonda, 1987.
8   Gonda, 1987.
9   Mahony, 1987.
10 Nanda, 2011: xv.
11 Nanda, 2011: 119.
12 "Amarnath Temple," *Wikipedia*.
13 Nanda, 2011: 71.
14 Nanda, 2001: 70–71.
15 Dalmia, 2014.
16 Nanda, 2011; Dalmia, 2014.
17 Nanda, 2011: xxviii.
18 Dennis, Beach, and Fahs, 1911.
19 For this calculation, Pakistan and Bangladesh were excluded from the population base to make it comparable with India today—there were almost no Christians in those Muslim areas then, or now.
20 Singh Kalsi, 2007: 24.

CHAPTER 10: RELIGIOUS AMERICA

1   Melton, 2009.
2   Baylor religion surveys, 2005, 2007.
3   Taylor, 2007: 25–26.
4   Taylor, 2007: 28.
5   Wilson, 1966: 166.
6   Wallis, 1986b.
7   Stark, 1997.
8   Based on recent Baylor National Religious Surveys and on the General Social Surveys.
9   Farrell, 2011: 517.
10 Smith and Johnson, 2010.
11 Regnerus, 2014.
12 This section is a revision of material originally published in Stark, 2012: ch. 1.
13 Kelley, 1972.
14 Bangs, 1972.
15 Perry, 1973: 198.
16 Marty, 1976: 71.
17 Stark, 2008.
18 Bibby and Brinkerhoff, 1973, 1983.
19 Hoge and Roozen, 1979; Roof and McKinney, 1987.
20 Perrin, Kennedy, and Miller, 1997.

21   Egerton, 1974; Shibley, 1991.
22   Miller, 1978: 257.
23   Dorrien, 2001: xiii.
24   Ahlstrom, 1967: 208.
25   Edwards, 1965; Rowe, 1962.
26   Tillich, [1957] 2009: 10–11.
27   Tillich, 1952: 185.
28   Tillich, 1951: 236.
29   Tillich, 1951: 205.
30   Tillich, 1951: 235.
31   Tillich, 1951: 239.
32   Edwards, 1965; Hammond, 1964; Rowe, 1962; Wainwright, 1971.
33   Finke and Stark, 1992: 199.
34   See the wonderful book by Elesha J. Coffman, 2013.
35   Stark, et al., 1971.
36   Stark and Finke, 2000: 261.
37   *World Tomorrow*, May 10, 1934.
38   Ahlstrom, 1972: 803.
39   *Annual Report of the Federal Council of Churches*, 1930: 64.
40   *Christian Century*, June 26, 1940: 814–16.
41   Quoted in Woodward, 1993: 47.
42   Wertheimer, 1993.
43   Kosmin et al., 1991.
44   Quote in Wertheimer, 1993: 11.
45   Moffic, 2012.
46   Gordon and Horowitz, 1996.

CONCLUSION: WHY FAITH ENDURES

1   Dawkins, 1986: 1.
2   Stark, 1999a.
3   Stark, 1999b, 2007.
4   For an extensive discussion of religion and science, see Stark, 2014: ch. 15.
5   Stark, 2014: ch. 15.
6   Pew Forum, Religious Landscape Survey, 2007.
7   Stark, 2008.
8   Stark, 2008: 57.
9   Spencer, [1876] 1896.
10   Tylor, [1871] 1958.
11   Durkheim, [1912] 1995.
12   Evans-Pritchard, 1965: 15.
13   In Street, 1981: 808.
14   Lang, 1898: 190–91.
15   Quoted in Lang, 1898: 184.
16   For a fuller discussion of this topic, see Stark, 2007.
17   Dawkins, 1995: 133.

Bibliography

Ahlstrom, Sydney E. 1972. *A Religious History of the American People*. New Haven: Yale University Press.

———. 1967. *Theology in America: The Major Protestant Voices from Puritanism to Neo-Orthodoxy*. Indianapolis: Bobbs-Merrill.

Aikman, David. 2003. *Jesus in Beijing: How Christianity Is Transforming China and Changing the Global Balance of Power*. Washington, DC: Regnery.

Ali, Ayaan Hirsi. 2013. "The Problems of Muslim Leadership." *The Wall Street Journal*, May 27.

Ali, Taisier M., and Robert O. Matthews, eds. 2011. *Civil Wars in Africa*. Montreal: McGill-Queen's University Press.

Allen, Charles. 2003. *The Search for Buddah: The Men Who Discovered India's Lost Religion*. New York: Carroll and Graf.

Alster, Paul. 2014. "Terror TV for Tots: Hama Show Has Child Vowing to 'Shoot the Jews.'" Fox News.com, May 9.

Alvarez, Lizette. 2003. "Tarbaek Journal: Fury, God, and the Pastor's Disbelief." *New York Times*, World Section, July 8.

Anderson, Allan. 2001. *African Reformation: African Initiated Christianity in the 20th Century*. Trenton, NJ: Africa World Press.

Asberg, Christer. 1990. "The Swedish Bible Commission and Project NT 81. In Gunnar Hanson, ed., *Bible Reading in Sweden*, 15–22. Uppsala, Sweden: University of Uppsala.

Ballard, Martin. 2008. *White Men's God: The Extraordinary Story of Missionaries in Africa*. Oxford: Greenwood World Publishing.

Bainbridge, W. S., and Rodney Stark. 1982. "Church and Cult in Canada." *Canadian Journal of Sociology* 7: 351–66.

———. 1980. "Client and Audience Cults in America." *Sociological Analysis* 41: 199–214.

Bangs, Carl. 1972. "Deceptive Statistics." *Christian Century* 89: 852–53.

Barrett, David B. 1982. *World Christian Encyclopedia*. Oxford: Oxford University Press.

———. 1968. *Schism and Renewal in Africa: An Analysis of Six Thousand Contemporary Religious Movements*. Nairobi: Oxford University Press.

Barrett, David B., George T. Kurian, and Todd M. Johnson. 2001. *World Christian Encyclopedia*. 2nd ed. Oxford: Oxford University Press.

Baumgarten, Albert I. 1997. *The Flowering of Jewish Sects in the Maccabean Era*. Leiden: Brill.

BBC News. 2015. "Syria's Beleaguered Christians," February 25.

Beckford, James A. 1985. *Cult Controversies: The Societal Response to New Religions*. London: Tavistock Publications.

Bediako, Kwame. 1995. *Christianity in Africa: The Renewal of a Non-Western Religion*. Edinburgh: Edinburgh University Press.

Benedict, Ruth. 1938. "Religion." In Franz Boas, ed., *General Anthropology*, 627–65. New York: C. D. Heath.

Berger, Peter. 1997. "Epistomological Modesty: An Interview with Peter Berger." *Christian Century* 114 (October 29): 972–75, 978.

———. 1968. "A Bleak Outlook Is Seen for Religion." *New York Times*, April 25, 3.

Berger, Peter, Grace Davie, and Effie Fokas. 2008. *Religious America, Secular Europe?* Burlington, VT: Ashgate.

Berryman, Phillip. 1987. *Liberation Theology*. Philadelphia: Temple University Press.

Bibby, Reginald W., and Merlin B. Brinkerhoff. 1973. "The Circulation of the Saints." *Journal for the Scientific Study of Religion* 12: 273–83.

Bowker, John. 1997. *The Oxford Dictionary of World Religions*. Oxford: Oxford University Press.

Bråkenhielm, Carl Reinhold. 2001. *Världbildbild och mening: En empirisk studie av livsådningar i dagens Sverige*. Nora, Sweden: Nya Doxa.

Breen, John, and Mark Teeuwen. 2010. *A New History of Shinto*. Oxford: Blackwell.

Brown, Callum. 2003. "The Secularization Decade: What the 1960s Have Done to the Study of Religious History." In Hugh McLeod and Werner Ustorf, eds., *The Decline of Christendom in Western Europe 1750–2000*, 29–46. Cambridge: Cambridge University Press.

———. 1992. "A Revisionist Approach to Religious Change." In Steve Bruce, ed., *Religion and Modernization*. Oxford: Clarendon Press: 31–58.

———. 1988. "Did Urbanization Secularize Britain?" *Urban History Yearbook 1988*: 1–14.

Bruce, Steve. 2011. *Secularization: In Defence of an Unfashionable Theory*. Oxford: Oxford University Press.

———. 2004. *God Is Dead: Secularization in the West*. Oxford: Blackwell.

———. 1992. *Religion and Modernization*. Oxford: Clarendon Press.

Brusco, Elizabeth. 1995. *The Reformation of Machismo: Evangelical Conversion and Gender in Columbia*. Austin: University of Texas Press.

———. 1993. "The Reformation of Machismo: Asceticism and Masculinity among Colombian Evangelicals." In Virginia Garrard-Burnett and David Stoll, eds., *Rethinking Protestantism in Latin America*, 143–58. Philadelphia: Temple University Press.

Burdick, John. 1993. *Looking for God in Brazil*. Berkeley: University of California Press.

Burkert, Walter. 1985. *Greek Religion*. Cambridge: Harvard University Press.

Cavendish, James. C. 1994. "Christian Base Communities and the Building of Democracy: Brazil and Chile." *Sociology of Religion* 55: 179–95.

Chaves, Mark. 1994. "Secularization as Declining Religious Authority." *Social Forces* 72: 749–74.

Chernysh, Mikhail. 1999. "Alternative Creeds Among Russian Youth." In Luigi Tomasi, ed., *Alternative Religions among European Youth*, 147–156. Aldershot, UK: Ashgate.

Chesler, Phyllis. 2010. "Worldwide Trends in Honor Killings." *The Middle East Quarterly.* (Spring): 3–11.

Chesnut, R. Andrew. 2003a. *Competitive Spirits: Latin America's New Religious Economy.* Oxford: Oxford University Press.

———. 2003b. "A Preferential Option for the Spirit: The Catholic Charismatic Renewal in Latin America's New Religious Economy." *Latin American Politics and Society* 45: 55–85.

———. 1997. *Born Again in Brazil.* New Brunswick, NJ: Rutgers University Press.

Clark, Donald N. 1986. *Christianity in Modern Korea.* Lanham, MD: University Press of America.

Clark, J. C. D. 2012. "Secularization and Modernization: The Failure of the 'Grand Narrative.'" *The Historical Journal* 55: 161–94.

Clough, Bradley S. 1997. "Buddhism." In Jacob Neusner, ed., *God,* 56–84. Cleveland: Pilgrim Press.

Coffman, Elesha J. 2013. *The Christian Century and the Rise of the Protestant Mainline.* New York: Oxford University Press.

Cohn, Norman. 1961. *The Pursuit of the Millennium.* 2nd ed. New York: Harper Torchbooks.

Costen, Michael. 1997. *The Cathars and the Albigensian Crusade.* Manchester, UK: Manchester University Press.

Coulton, G. G. 1938. *Medieval Panorama.* New York: Macmillan.

Cox, Harvey. 1995. *Fire From Heaven: The Rise of Pentecostal Spirituality and the Reshaping of Religion in the Twenty-First Century.* Cambridge, MA: Da Capo Press.

Cox, Jeffrey. 2003. "Master Narratives of Long-Term Religious Change." In Hugh McLeod and Werner Ustorf, eds., *The Decline of Christendom in Western Europe 1750–2000,* 201–17. Cambridge: Cambridge University Press:.

Coyne, Jerry A. 2012. "Religious 'Nones' Increase in America." whyevolutionistrue.wordpress.com, July 25.

———. 1982. *The English Churches in Secular Society: Lambeth, 1870–1930.* Oxford: Oxford University Press.

Crawley, A. E. 1905. *The Tree of Life: A Study of Religion.* London: Hutchinson.

Curtin, Philip D. 1964. *The Image of Africa: British Ideas and Action, 1780–1850.* Madison: University of Wisconsin Press.

Dalmia, Shikha. 2014. "Gold and Gods in Modern India." *Reason.com,* July 9.

Davie, Grace. 1994. *Religion in Britain since 1945.* Oxford: Blackwell.

Dawkins, Richard. 1995. *River Out of Eden.* New York: Basic Books.

———. 1986 *The Blind Watchmaker.* New York: Norton.

Dean, Kenneth. 2003. "Local Communal Religion in Contemporary South-east China." In Daniel L. Overmyer, ed., *Religion in China Today,* 32–52. Cambridge: Cambridge University Press.

Dennis, James S., Harlan P. Beach, and Charles H. Fahs. 1911. *World Atlas of Christian Missions.* New York: Student Volunteer Movement for Foreign Missions.

Di Giovanni, Janine, and Conor Gaffey. 2015. "The New Exodus: Christians Flee ISIS in the Middle East." *Newsweek,* March 26.

Doktór, Tadeusz. 1999. "New Religious Phenomena in Eastern Europe." In Luigi Tomasi, ed., *Alternative Religions Among European Youth,* 125–45. Aldershot, UK: Ashgate.

Dolan, Jay P. 1978. *Catholic Revivalism: The American Experience, 1830–1900.* Notre Dame: University of Notre Dame Press.

———. 1975. *The Immigrant Church: New York's Irish and German Catholics, 1815–1865.* Baltimore: Johns Hopkins University Press.

Dorrien, Gary. 2003. *The Making of American Liberal Theology: Idealism, Realism, Modernity, 1990–1950.* Louisville: Westminster John Knox Press.

———. 2001. *The Making of American Liberal Theology: Imagining Progressive Religion, 1805–1900.* Louisville: Westminster John Knox Press.

Douglas, Mary. 1982. "The Effects of Modernization on Religious Change." In Mary Douglas and Steven M. Tipton, eds., *Religion and America: Spirituality in a Secular Age*, 25–43. Boston: Beacon Press.

———. 1975. *Implicit Meanings: Essays in Anthropology.* London: Routledge and Kegan Paul.

Drogus, Carol Ann. 1995. "Review: The Rise and Decline of Liberation Theology: Churches, Faith, and Political Change in Latin America." *Comparative Politics* 27: 465–77.

Durkheim, Emile. [1912] 1995. *The Elementary Forms of the Religious Life.* New York: The Free Press.

———. [1886] 1994. "Review of Part VI of the *Principles of Sociology* by Herbert Spencer." *Revue Philosophique de la France et de l'Etranger* 21: 61–69. In W. S. F. Pickering, trans., *Durkheim on Religion*, 13–23. Atlanta: Scholars Press.

Eades, Carla, Jerry Eades, Yuriko Nishiyama, and Hiroko Yanase. 1986. "Houses of Everlasting Bliss." In J. Eades, Tom Gill, and Harumi Befu, eds., *Globalization and Social Change in Contemporary Japan*, 159–79. Melbourne: Transpacific.

Eberstadt, Nicholas and Apoorva Shah. 2012. "Fertility Decline in the Muslim World." *Policy Review* 173 (June 1).

———. 2011. "Fertility Decline in the Muslim World: A Veritable Sea-Change, Still Curiously Unnoticed." American Enterprise Institute Working Paper, Dec. 7.

Edwards, Steven. 2015. " 'You Are a Target': Muslim Extremists Terrorize Egypt's Coptic Christians." FoxNews.com, May 5.

Edwards, Paul. 1965. "Professor Tillich's Confusions." *Mind.* 74: 192–214.

Egerton, John. 1974. *The Americanization of Dixie: The Southernization of America.* New York: Harper and Row.

Encarnatión, Omar. 2013. "The Catholic Crisis in Latin America: Even an Argentine Pope Can't Save the Church." *Foreign Affairs* (March 19).

Epstein, Mikhail. 1995. *On the Borders of Cultures: Russia-America-Soviet.* New York: Slovo/Word.

Ernst, Carl. 1992. *Eternal Garden.* Albany: State University of New York Press.

Evans-Pritchard, E. E. 1965. *Theories of Primitive Religion.* Oxford: Oxford University Press.

Fairbank, John K., ed. 1974. *The Missionary Experience in China and America.* Cambridge: Harvard University Press.

Farmer, David L. 1991. "Marketing the Produce of the Countryside, 1200–1500." In Edward Miller, ed., *The Agrarian History of England and Wales: Vol. 3, 1348–1500*, 324–58. Cambridge: Cambridge University Press.

Farrell, Justin. 2011. "The Young and the Restless? The Liberalization of Young Evangelicals." *Journal for the Scientific Study of Religion* 50: 17–532.

Finke, Roger, and Rodney Stark. 1992. *The Churching of America, 1776–1990: Winners and Losers in Our Religious Economy.* New Brunswick, NJ: Rutgers University Press.

Fogel, Robert William. 2000. *The Fourth Great Awakening and the Future of Egalitarianism.* Chicago: University of Chicago Press.

Foy, Felician A. 1965. *1965 National Catholic Almanac.* Garden City, NY: Doubleday.

Foy, Felician A., and Rose M. Avato. 1987. *1987 Catholic Almanac*. Huntington, IN: Our Sunday Visitor.

Frejka, Tomas, and Charles F. Westoff. 2008. "Religion, Religiousness, and Fertility in the US and in Europe." *European Journal of Population* 24: 5–31.

Freston, Paul. 2008. *Evangelical Christianity and Democracy in Latin America*. Oxford: Oxford University Press.

Froese, Paul. 2008. *The Plot to Kill God: Findings from the Soviet Experiment in Secularization*. Berkeley: University of California Press.

Froese, Paul, and Steven Pfaff. 2005. "Explaining a Religious Anomaly: A Historical Analysis of Secularization in Eastern Germany." *Journal for the Scientific Study of Religion* 44: 397–422.

Fried, Morton H. 1987. "Reflections on Christianity in China." *American Ethnologist* 14: 94–106.

Fukutake, Tadashi. 1981. *Japanese Society Today*. Tokyo: University of Tokyo Press.

Geertz, Clifford. 1966. "Religion as a Cultural System." In Michael Banton, ed., *Anthropological Approaches to the Study of Religion*, 1–46. London: Tavistock Publications.

Gill, Anthony. 1998. *Rendering Unto Caesar: The Catholic Church and the State in Latin America*. Chicago: University of Chicago Press.

Gladney, Dru C. 2003. "Islam in China: Accommodation or Separatism?" In Daniel L. Overmyer, ed., *Religion in China Today*. Cambridge: Cambridge University Press: 145–61.

Global 100: An Index of Anti-Semitism. 2015. New York: Anti-Defamation League.

Glock, Charles Y. 1964. "The Role of Deprivation in the Origin and Evolution of Religious Groups." In Robert Lee and Martin E. Marty, eds., *Religion and Social Conflict*, 24–26. New York: Oxford University Press.

Glock, Charles Y., and Rodney Stark. 1966. *Christian Beliefs and Anti-Semitism*. New York: Harper and Row.

Gooren, Henri. 2002. "Catholic and Non-Catholic Theologies of Liberation: Poverty, Self-Improvement, and Ethics among Small-Scale Entrepreneurs in a Guatemala City." *Journal for the Scientific Study of Religion* 41: 29–45.

Goossaert, Vincent, and David A. Palmer. 2012. *The Religious Question in Modern China*. Chicago: University of Chicago Press.

Goldberg, Jonah. 2014. "Mr. Piketty's Big Book of Marxiness." *Commentary* (July).

Gonda, Jan. 1987. "Indian Religions: An Overview." In Mircea Eliade, ed., *The Encyclopedia of Religion*. New York: Macmillan.

Gordon, Antony, and Richard Horowitz. 1996. "Will Your Grandchildren Be Jews?" *Jewish Spectator* (Fall): 36–38.

Granqvist, Pehr, and Berit Hagekull. 2001. "Seeking Security in the New Age: On Attachment and Emotional Compensation." *Journal for the Scientific Study of Religion* 40: 527–45.

Greeley, Andrew. 1994. "A Religious Revival in Russia?" *Journal for the Scientific Study of Religion* 33: 253–72.

Grim, Brian J., and Roger Finke. 2006. "International Religion Indexes." *Interdisciplinary Journal for Research on Religion* 2, no. 1: 1–40.

Haliburton, Gordon MacKay. 1973. *The Prophet Harris*. New York: Oxford University Press.

Hallum, Anne Motley. 2003. "Taking Stock and Building Bridges: Feminism, Women's Movements, and Pentecostalism in Latin America." *Latin American Research Review* 38: 169–86.

Hamberg, Eva M., and Thorleif Pettersson. 1994. "The Religious Market: Denominational Competition and Religious Participation in Contemporary Sweden." *Journal for the Scientific Study of Religion* 33: 205–16.

―――. 1997. "Short-Term Changes in Religious Supply and Church Attendance in Contemporary Sweden." *Research in the Scientific Study of Religion* 8:3 5–51.

Hammond, Guy B. 1964. "Tillich on the Personal God." *Journal of Religion*. 44: 289–93.

Haworth, Abigail. 2013. "Why Have Young People in Japan Stopped Having Sex?" *The Guardian*, October 20.

Hay, Denys. 1977. *The Church in Italy in the Fifteenth Century*. Cambridge: Cambridge University Press.

Headrick, Daniel R. 1981. *The Tools of Empire*. New York: Oxford University Press.

Hexham, Irving, and C. G. Oosthuizen, eds. 1996. *The Story of Isaiah Shembe*. 2 vols. Lewisyom, NY: Edwin Melon Press.

Hewitt, W. E. 1991. *Base Communities and Social Change in Brazil*. Lincoln: University of Nebraska Press.

Hirst, Michael. 2007. "Rise in Radical Islam Last Straw for Lebanon's Christians." *The Telegraph* (UK), April 1.

Hocking, William. 1932. *Re-thinking Missions*. New York: Harper and Brothers.

Hoge, Dean, and David Roozen, eds. 1979. *Understanding Church Growth and Decline*. New York: Pilgrim Press.

Höllinger, Franz, and Timothy B. Smith. 2002. "Religion and Esotericism among Students: A Cross-Cultural Comparative Study." *Journal of Contemporary Religion* 17: 229–49.

Houtman, Dick, and Peter Mascini. 2002. "Why Do Churches Become Empty, While New Age Grows? Secularization and Religious Change in the Netherlands." *Journal for the Scientific Study of Religion* 41: 455–73.

Huilin, Yang, and Daniel H. N. Yeung, eds. 2006. *Sino-Christian Studies in China*. Newcastle, UK: Cambridge Scholars Press.

Huntington, Samuel P. 1997. *The Clash of Civilizations and the Remaking of the World Order*. New York: Touchstone Books.

Hutchison, William R. 1987. *Errand to the World: American Protestant Thought and Foreign Missions*. Chicago: University of Chicago Press.

Iannaccone, Laurence R. 1991. "The Consequences of Religious Market Structure." *Rationality and Society* 3: 156–77.

Ikado, Fujio, 1972. *Szoku shakai no Sukyo* (Religion in Secular Society). Tokyo: Nihon Kikan Kyodan.

Inoue, Nobutaka. 2003. *Shinto: A Short History*. New York: Routledge.

Introvigne, Massimo, and Rodney Stark. 2005. "Religious Competition and Revival in Italy: Exploring European Exceptionalism." *Interdisciplinary Journal of Research on Religion* 1, article 5, www.religjournal.com.

Isichi, Elizabeth. 1995. *A History of Christianity in Africa*. Grand Rapids, MI: William B. Eerdmans.

Janssen, Jacques. 1999. "The Abstract Image of God: The Case of Dutch Youth." In Luigi Tomasi, ed., *Alternative Religions among European Youth*, 57–90. Aldershot, UK: Ashgate.

Jenkins, Philip. 2006. *The New Faces of Christianity*. New York: Oxford Univesity Press.

―――. 2002. *The Next Christendom: The Coming of Global Christianity*. New York: Oxford University Press.

Judge, E. A. 1960. *The Social Pattern of Christian Groups in the First Century*. London: Tyndale.

Kelley, Dean. 1972. *Why Conservative Churches Are Growing*. New York: Harper and Row.

Klaiber, Jeffrey L. 1970. "Pentecostal Breakthrough." *America* 122 (4): 99–102.

Kosmin, Barry, et al. 1991. *Highlights of the CJF 1990 National Jewish Population Survey*. New York: Council of Jewish Federations.

Lagnado, Lucette. 2015. "The Last of the Arab Jews." *Wall Street Journal*, Feb. 14.

Lambert, Malcolm. 1992. *Medieval Heresy: Popular Movements from the Gregorian Reform to the Reformation*. 2nd ed. Oxford: Basil Blackwell.

Lambert, Tony. 2006. *China's Christian Millions*. Oxford: Monarch Books.

Lang, Andrew. 1898. *The Making of Religion*. London: Longmans, Green, and Co.

Lang, Bernard. 1983. *Monotheism and the Prophetic Majority*. Sheffield, UK: Almond.

Lapidus, Ira M. 1997. "Islamic Revival and Modernity: The Contemporary Movements and the Historical Paradigms." *Journal of Economic and Social History of the Orient* 40: 444–60.

Laurentin, Rene. 1977. *Catholic Pentecostalism*. Garden City, NY: Doubleday.

Lazerwitz, Bernard. 1962. "Membership in Voluntary Associations and Frequency of Church Attendance." *Journal for the Scientific Study of Religion* 2 (October): 74–84.

Lee, Samuel. 2014. *The Japanese and Christianity*. Amsterdam: Foundation University Press.

Lenski, Gerhard. 1953. "Social Correlates of Religious Interest." *American Sociological Review* 18: 533–44.

Lester, Robert C. 1993. "Buddhism: The Path to Nirvana." In H. Byron Earhart, ed., *Religious Traditions of the World*, 849–971. San Francisco: HarperSanFrancisco.

Lin-Liu, Jen. 2005. "At Chinese Universities, Whispers of Jesus." *Chronicle of Higher Education* (June10): 40.

Loane, M. [1906] 2012. *The Queen's Poor: Life as They Find It in Town and Country*. Ulan Press (location unknown).

Lodberg, Peter. 1989. "The Churches in Denmark." In Peter Brierly, ed., *Danish Christian Handbook*, 6–9. London: MARC Europe.

Lorenzen, David N. "Who Invented Hinduism?" *Comparative Studies in Society and History* 41: 630–59.

Lloyd, Christopher. 1973. *The Search for the Niger*. London: Collins.

Lyall, Leslie T. 1973. *China's Three Mighty Men*. London: Overseas Missionary Fellowship.

Mahony, William K. 1987. "Upaniṣads." In Mircea Eliade, ed., *The Encyclopedia of Religion*. New York: Macmillan.

Malik, Yogendra K., and Dhirendra K. Vajpeyi. 1989. "The Rise of Hindu Miitancy: India's Secula Democracy at Risk." *Asian Survey* 29: 308–25.

Malinowski, Bronislaw. 1935. *The Foundation of Faith and Morals*. Oxford: Oxford University Press.

Malsin, Jared. 2015. "Christians Mourn Their Relatives Beheaded by ISIS." *Time*, Feb. 23.

Mansfield, Patti Gallagher. 1992. *As by a New Pentecost: The Dramatic Beginning of the Catholic Charismatic Renewal*. Lancashire, UK: Proclaim! Publications.

Mariz, Cecilia. 1994. *Coping with Poverty: Pentecostal Churches and the Christina Base Communities in Brazil*. Philadelphia: Temple University Press.

Martin, David. 2002. *Pentecostalism: The World Their Parish*. Oxford: Blackwell.

———. 1990. *Tongues of Fire: The Explosion of Protestantism in Latin America*. Oxford: Basil Blackwell.

Marty, Martin E. 1976. *A Nation of Behavers*. Chicago: University of Chicago Press.

Marx, Karl. [1845] 1998. *The German Ideology*. Amherst: Prometheus Books.

McFarland, Neill. 1967. *Rush Hour of the Gods*. New York: Macmillan.

Mecham, John Lloyd. [1934] 1966. *Church and State in Latin America*. Chapel Hill: University of North Carolina Press.

Melton, J. Gordon. 2009. *Melton's Encyclopedia of American Religions*. 8th ed. Detroit: Gale Centgage Leaning.

Menzel, Birgit. 2007. "The Occult Revival in Russia Today and Its Impact on Literature." *Harriman Review* 16: 1–14.

Metaxas, Eric. 2014. *Miracles*. New York: Dutton.

Miller, Alan S. 1992. "Conventional Religious Behavior in Modern Japan." *Journal for the Scientific Study of Religion* 34: 234–44.

Miller, Paul M. 1978. "Yes, Dean Kelly [sic], There Has Been Growth." *Gospel Herald*, March 28.

Mills, C. Wright. 1959. *The Sociological Imagination*. Oxford: Oxford University Press.

Moffic, Evan. 2012. "Can Reform Judaism Get Its Mojo Back?" *Jewish Ideas Daily*, Nov. 9, http://www.jewishideasdaily.com/5332/features/can-reform-judaism-get-its-mojo-back/.

Monier-Williams, Monier. [1919] 1993. *Hinduism: Hinduism and Its Sources*. New Delhi: Orientalist.

Montgomery, T. S. 1979. "Latin American Evangelicals: Oaxtepec and Beyond." In Daniel H. Levine, ed., *Churches and Politics in Latin America*, 87–107. Beverly Hills, CA: Sage.

Moroto, Aiko. 1976. "Conditions for Accepting a New Religious Belief." Master's thesis, University of Washington.

Morris, Jeremy. 2012. "Secularization and Religious Experience: Arguments in the Historiography of Modern British Religion." *Historical Journal*. 55: 195–219.

Müller, F. Max. 1880. *Lectures on the Origin and Growth of Religion as Illustrated by the Religions of India. Delivered in the Chapter House, Westminster Abbey, in April, May, and June, 1878*. London: Longmans Green.

Murray, Alexander. 1972. "Piety and Impiety in Thirteenth-Century Italy." *Studies in Church History* 8: 83–106.

Mutlu, Kayhan. 1998. "Examining Religious Beliefs Among University Students in Ankara." *British Journal of Sociology* 47: 353–59.

Naito, Ayumi. 2007. "Internet Suicide in Japan: Implications for Child and Adolescent Mental Health." *Clinical Child Psychology and Psychiatry* 12: 583–97.

Nakagawa, Ulara. 2011. "Marriage on the Rocks." CNN Travel, March 29, http://travel.cnn.com/tokyo/life/love-and-marriage-japan-176247

Nanda, Meera. 2011. *The God Market: How Globalization Is Making India More Hindu*. New York: Monthly Review Press.

Nash, David. 2004. "Reconnecting Religion with Social and Cultural History: Secularization's Failure as a Master Narrative." *Cultural and Social History* 1: 302–25.

Nasr, Seyyed Vali Reza. 1992. "Students, Islam, and Politics." *Middle East Journal* 46: 59–76.

Niebuhr, H. Richard. 1929. *The Social Sources of Denominationalism*. New York: Henry Holt.

Nelson, John. 1992. "Shinto Ritual: Managing Chaos in Contemporary Japan." *Ethnos* 57: 77–104.

Niandou-Souley, Abdoulaye, and Gado Alzouma. 1996. "Islamic Renewal in Niger: From Monolith to Plurality." *Social Compass* 43: 249–65.

Nickerson, Colin. 1999. "In Iceland, Spirits Are in the Material World." *Seattle Post-Intelligencer*, December 25, A12.

Nolan, Mary Lee, and S. Nolan. 1989. *Christian Pilgrimage in Modern Western Europe.* Chapel Hill: University of North Carolina Press.

———. 1992. "Religious Sites as Tourism Attractions in Europe." *Annals of Tourism Research* 19, no. 1: 68–78.

Noll, Mark. 2000. *Turning Points: Decisive Moments in Christian History.* Grand Rapids: Baker Academic.

Norris, Pippa, and Ronald Inglehart. 2004. *Sacred and Secular: Religion and Politics Worldwide.* New York: Cambridge University Press.

Nuñez, Emilio A., and William D. Taylor. 1989. *Crisis in Latin America: An Evangelical Perspective.* Chicago: Moody Press.

Oosthuizen, Gerhardus C. 1968. *Post Christianity in Africa.* London: Hurst.

Overmyer, Daniel L. 2003. "Introduction." In Daniel L. Overmyer, ed., *Religion in China Today,* 1–10. Cambridge: Cambridge University Press.

Ozawa-de Silva, Chikako. 2010. "Shared Death: Self, Sociality, and Internet Group Suicide in Japan." *Transcultural Psychiatry* 47: 392–418.

Parker, Geoffrey. 1992. "Success and Failure During the First Century of the Reformation." *Past and Present* 136: 43082.

Paulson, Michael. 2014. "Denominations Downsizing and Selling Assets in More Secular Era." *New York Times,* March 16, A16.

Perrin, Robin D., Paul Kennedy, and Donald E. Miller. 1997. "Examining the Sources of Conservative Church Growth." *Journal for the Scientific Study of Religion* 36: 71–80.

Perry, Everett L. 1973. "Review." *Review of Religious Research* 14: 198–200.

Pettersson, Thorlief. 1990. "The Holy Bible in Secularized Sweden." In Gunnar Hanson, ed., *Bible Reading in Sweden,* 23–45. Uppsala, Sweden: University of Uppsala.

Pettersson, Thorlief, and Eva M. Hamberg. 1997. "Denominational Pluralism and Church Membership in Contemporary Sweden: A Longitudinal Study of the Period 1974–1995." *Journal of Empirical Theology* 10: 61–78.

Pew Research Center. 2015. "The Future of World Religions: Population Growth Projections, 2010–2050," http://www.pewforum.org/2015/04/02/religiousprojections-2010-2050/. April 2.

Pew Research: Religion and Public Life Project. 2011. *The Future of the Global Muslim Population.* January 27.

Preus, J. Samuel. 1987. *Explaining Religion: Criticism and Theory from Bodin to Freud.* New Haven: Yale University Press.

Pulliam Bailey, Sarah. 2015. "Christianity Faces Sharp Decline as Americans Are Becoming Even Less Affiliated with Religion." *Washington Post,* May 12.

Ramsay, W. M. 1893. *The Church in the Roman Empire Before A.D. 170.* New York: Putnam's Sons.

Redman, Ben Ray. 1949. *The Portable Voltaire.* New York: Penguin Books.

Regnerus, Mark. 2014. "Sex in America: Sociological Trends in American Sexuality." Paper presented at Ethics and Religious Liberty Leadership Summit, Nashville, TN, April 22.

Robinson, Charles Henry. 1923. *History of Christian Missions.* New York: Charles Scribner's Sons.

Roof, Wade Clark, and William McKinney. 1987. *American Mainline Religion: Its Changing Shape and Future.* New Brunswick, NJ: Rutgers University Press.

Rowe, William L. "The Meaning of 'God' in Tillich's Theology." *Journal of Religion* 42: 274–86

Roy, Olivier. 1994. *The Failure of Political Islam*. Cambridge: Harvard University Press.

Rubenstein, Richard L. 1985–86. "The Political Significance of Latin American Liberation Theology." *World Affairs* 148: 159–67.

Rydenfelt, Sven. 1985. "Sweden and Its bishops." *Wall Street Journal*, Aug. 21, A25.

Schmied, Gerhard. 1996. "US-Televangelism on German TV." *Journal of Contemporary Religion* 11: 95–99.

Selthoffer, Steve. 1997. "German Government Harasses Charasmatic Christians." *Charisma* (June): 22–24.

Shank, David A. 1994. *Prophet Harris, the 'Black Elijah' of West Africa*. Leiden: Brill.

Shibley, Mark. 1991. "The Southernization of American Religion: Testing a Hypothesis." *Sociological Analysis* 52: 159–74.

Siewert, John A., and Edna G. Valdez. 1997. *Mission Handbook: USA and Canadian Christian Ministries Overseas*. 17th ed. Grand Rapids, MI: Zondervan.

Sing Kalsi, Sewa. 2007. *Sikhism*. London: Bravo Litd.

Sivan, Emmanuel. 1985. *Radical Islam: Medieval Theology and Modern Politics*. New Haven: Yale University Press.

Sjödin, Ulf. 2002. "The Swedes and the Paranormal." *Journal of Contemporary Religion* 17: 75–85.

Smith, Adam. [1776] 1981. *An Inquiry into the Nature and Causes of the Wealth of Nations*. 2 vols. Indianapolis: Liberty Fund.

Smith, Buster G., and Byron Johnson. 2010. "The Liberalization of Young Evangelicals: A Research Note." *Journal for the Scientific Study of Religion* 49: 351–60.

Smith, W. Robertson. 1889. *The Religion of the Semites*. Edinbugh: Adam and Charles Black.

Smith, Wilfred Cantwell. [1962] 1991. *The Meaning and End of Reliigion*. Minneapolis: Fortress Press.

Snead, Alfred C. 1950. *Missionary Atlas*. Harrisburg, PA: Christian Publications.

Spencer, Herbert. [1876] 1896. *The Principles of Sociology*, vol 1. New York: D. Appleton and Co.

Stark, Rodney. 2014. *How the West Won: The Neglected Story of the Triumph of Modernity*. Wilmington: ISI Books.

———. 2012. *America's Blessings: How Religion Benefits Everyone Including Atheists*. West Conshohocken, PA: Templeton Press.

———. 2011. *The Triumph of Christianity: How the Jesus Movement Became the World's Largest Religion*. San Francisco: HarperOne.

———. 2009. *God's Battalions: The Case For the Crusades*. San Francisco: HarperOne.

———. 2008. *What Americans Really Believe*. Waco: Baylor University Press.

———. 2007. *Discovering God: The Origins of the Great Religions and the Evolution of Belief*. San Francisco: HarperOne.

———. 2004. *Exploring the Religious Life*. Baltimore: Johns Hopkins University Press.

———. 2003. *For the Glory of God: How Monotheism Led to Reformations, Science, Witch-Hunts and the End of Slavery*. Princeton, NJ: Princeton University Press.

———. 2001. *One True God: Historical Consequences of Monotheism*. Princeton, NJ: Princeton University Press.

———. 1999a. "Micro Foundations of Religion: A Revised Theory." *Sociological Theory* 17: 264–89.

———. 1999b. "A Theory of Revelations." *Journal for the Scientific Study of Religion* 38: 286–307.

———. 1998. "Catholic Contexts: Competition, Commitment, and Innovation." *Review of Religious Research* 39: 197–208.

———. 1997. "German and German-American Religion: Approximating a Crucial Experiment." *Journal for the Scientific Study of Religion* 36:182–93.

———. 1993. "Europe's Receptivity to New Religious Movements: Round Two." *Journal for the Scientific Study of Religion* 32: 389–97.

———. 1992. "Do Catholic Societies Really Exist?" *Rationality and Society* 4: 261–71.

———. 1985. "Europe's Receptivity to Religious Movements." In Rodney Stark, ed., *New Religious Movements: Genesis, Exodus, and Numbers*, 301–43. New York: Paragon.

———. 1983. "Religious Economies: A New Perspective." Paper delivered at a conference on New Directions in Religious Research, University of Lewthbridge.

———. 1971. "The Economics of Piety: Religion and Social Class." In Gerald W. Thielbar and Saul D. Feldman, eds., *Issues in Social Inequality*, 483–503. Boston: Little, Brown and Co.

———. 1965. "Religion and Radical Politics." In Charles Y. Glock and Rodney Stark, eds., *Religion and Society in Tension*, 201–226. Chicago: Rand McNally.

———. 1964. "Class, Radicalism, and Religious Involvement." *American Sociological Review*. 29: 698–706.

Stark, Rodney, and William Sims Bainbridge. [1987] 1996. *A Theory of Religion*. New Brunswick, NJ: Rutgers University Press.

———. 1985. *The Future of Religion: Secularization, Revival, and Cult Formation*. Berkeley: University of California Press.

———. 1980. "Secularization, Revival, and Cult Formation." *Annual Review of the Social Sciences of Religion*, 4: 85–119.

Stark, Rodney, and Katie E. Corcoran. 2014. *Religious Hostility: A Global Assessment of Hatred and Terror*. Waco: ISR Books.

Stark, Rodney, and Roger Finke. 2000. *Acts of Faith: Explaining the Human Side of Religion*. Berkeley: University of California Press.

Stark, Rodney, Eva Hamberg, and Alan S. Miller. 2005. "Exploring Spirituality and Unchurched Religions in America, Sweden, and Japan." *Journal of Contemporary Religion* 20: 1–21.

Stark, Rodney, and Laurence Iannaccone. 1994. "A Supply-Side Reinterpretation of the 'Secularization' of Europe." *Journal for the Scientific Study of Religion* 33: 230–52.

———. 1999. "Why Jehovah's Witnesses Grow So Rapidly." *Journal of Contemporary Religion* 12: 133–57.

Stark, Rodney, and Eric Y. Liu. 2011. "The Religious Awakening in China." *Review of Religious Research* 52: 282–89.

Stark, Rodney, and Buster G. Smith. 2012. "Pluralism and the Churching of Latin America." *Latin American Politics and Society* 54: 35–50.

———. 2010. "Conversion to Latin American Protestantism and the Case for Religious Motivation." *Interdisciplinary Journal of Research on Religion* 6, article 7, www.religjournal.com.

Stark, Rodney, and Xiuhua Wang. 2015. *A Star in the East: The Rise of Christianity in China*. West Conshohocken, PA: Templeton Press

———. 2014. "Christian Conversion and Cultural Incongruity in Asia." *Interdisciplinary Journal of Research on Religion* 10, article 2, www.religjournal.com.

Stephens, Holly DeNio. 1997. "The Occult in Russia Today." In Bernice Glatzer Rosenthal, ed., *The Occult in Russian and Soviet Culture*, 357–76. Ithica: Cornell University Press.

Stoll, David. 1993. "Introduction: Rethinking Protestantism in Latin America." In Virginia Garrard-Burnett and David Stoll, eds., *Rethinking Protestantism in Latin America*, 1–19. Philadelphia: Temple University Press.

———. 1990. *Is Latin America Turning Protestant?* Berkeley: University of California Press.

Strauss, Gerald. 1988. "The Reformation and Its Public in an Age of Orthodoxy." In *The German People and the Reformation*, 194–214. Ithaca, NY: Cornell University Press.

———. 1978. *Luther's House of Learning: Introducing the Young in the German Reformation*. Baltimore: Johns Hopkins University Press.

———. 1975. "Success and Failure in the German Reformation." *Past and Present* 67: 30–63.

Street, Brian Vincent. 1981. "Tylor, Sir Edward Burnett. In *Encyclopaedia Britannica*, 15th ed., 808. Chicago: University of Chicago Press.

Sun, Anna Xiao Dong. 2005. "The Fate of Confucianism as a Religion in Socialist China: Controversies and Paradoxes." In Fenggang Yang and Joseph B. Tamney, eds., *State, Market, and Religions in Chinese Societies*, 229–53. Leiden: Brill.

Sundkler, Bengt G. M. 1961. *Bantu Prophets in South Africa*. Oxford: Oxford University Press.

Sundkler, Bengt, and Christopher Steed. 2000. *A History of the Church in Africa*. Cambridge: Cambridge University Press.

Swatos, William H., Jr., and Loftur Reimar Gissurarson. 1997. *Icelandic Spiritualism: Mediumship and Modernity in Iceland*. New Brunswick, NJ: Transaction Publishers.

Tasie, G. O. M. 1982. "The Prophetic Calling: Garrick Sokarie Braide of Bahana." In Elizabeth Isichei, ed., *Varieties of Christian Experience in Nigeria*, 99–115. London: Macmillan.

Taylor, Charles. 2007. *A Secular Age*. Cambridge: Belknap Press.

Thomas, Keith. 1971. *Religion and the Decline of Magic*. New York: Charles Scribner's Sons.

Tillich, Paul. [1957] 2009. *Dynamics of Faith*. San Francisco: HarperOne.

———. 1952 *The Courage to Be*. New Haven: Yale University Press.

———. 1951. *Systematic Theology*, vol. 1. Chicago: University of Chicago Press.

Tomasson, Richard E. 1980. *Iceland*. Minneapolis: University of Minnesota Press.

Twain, Mark. *Roughing It*. San Francisco: American Publishing Company.

Tylor, Edward Burnett. [1871] 1958. *Religion in Primitive Culture*. New York: Harper.

Victoria, Brian Daizen. 2001. "Engaged Buddhism: A Skeleton in the Closet?" *Journal of Global Buddhism* 2: 72–91.

Voyé, Lillian, and Karel Dobbelaere. 1994. "Roman Catholicism: Universalism at Stake." In Roberto Cipriani, ed., *Religions sans frontièrs?*, 83–113. Rome: Dipartmento per l'informazione e editoria.

Wainwright, William J. 1971. "Paul Tillich and Arguments for the Existence of God." *Journal of the American Academy of Religion* 39: 171–85.

Wallace, Anthony F. C. 1966. *Religion: An Anthropological View*. New York: Random House.

Wallis, Roy. 1986a. "The Caplow—de Tocqueville Account of Contrasts in European and American Religion: Confounding Considerations." *Sociological Analysis* 47: 50–52.

———. 1986b. "Figuring Out Cult Receptivity." *Journal for the Scientific Study of Religion* 25: 494–503.

Walzer, Michael. 1965. *The Revolution of the Saints*. Cambridge: Harvard University Press.

Wang, Yuting, and Fenggang Yang. 2006. "More than Evangelical and Ethnic: The Ecological Factor in Chinese Conversion to Christianity in the United States." *Sociology of Religion* 67: 179–92.

Watson, Leon. 2011. "The Arabic School Textbooks Which Show Children How to Chop Off Hands and Feet under Sharia Law." *Daily Mail*, December 23.

Welliver, Dotsey, and Minnette Northcutt. 2004. *Mission Handbook, 2004–2006.* Wheaton, IL: Wheaton College.

Wertheimer, Jack. 1993. *A People Divided: Judaism in Contemporary Ameica.* New York; Basic Books.

White, James W. 1970. *The Sōkagakkai and Mass Society.* Stanford, CA: Stanford University Press.

Williams, Paul D. 2011. *War and Conflict in Africa.* Cambridge, UK: Polity Press.

Williams, Sarah. 1999. *Religious Belief and Popular Culture in Southwark, c.1880–1939.* Oxford: Oxford University Press.

Wilson, Bryan. 1992. "Reflections on a Many-Sided Controversy." In Steve Bruce, ed., *Religion and Modernization: Sociologists and Historians Debate the Secularization Thesis,* 195–210. Oxford: Oxford University Press.

———. 1977. "Aspects of Kinship and the Rise of Jehovah's Witnessess in Japan." *Social Compass* 24: 97–120.

———. 1966. *Religion in Secular Society.* London: C.A. Watts.

Winfield, Nicole. 2015. "Liberation Theology Founder to Speak at Vatican on Creating 'A Poor Church for the Poor.'" Associated Press, May 7.

Wiseman, Paul. 2004. "No Sex Please—We're Japanese." *USA Today,* June 2.

Woodward, Kenneth L. 1993. "Dead End for the Mainline?" *Newsweek,* Oct. 8.

Woolston, Thomas. 1735. *Works of Thomas Woolston.* London: J. Roberts.

World Health Organization. 2012. "Suicide Rates, Data by Country, 2012," http://apps.who.int/gho/data/node.main.MHSUICIDE?lang=en.

Yang, Fenggang. 2005. "Lost in the Market, Saved at McDonald's: Conversion to Christianity in Urban China." *Journal for the Scientific Study of Religion* 44: 423–41.

———. 1998. "Chinese Conversion to Evangelical Christianity: The Importance of Social and Cultural Contexts." *Sociology of Religion* 59: 237–57.

Zuckerman, Phil. 2008. *Society without God.* New York: New York University Press.

Zürcher, Erik. 1959. *The Buddhist Conquest of China.* Leiden: E.J. Brill.

Index

INTERCOLLEGIATE STUDIES INSTITUTE
Educating for Liberty

ISI Books is the publishing imprint of the **Intercollegiate Studies Institute**, whose mission is to inspire college students to discover, embrace, and advance the principles and virtues that make America free and prosperous.

Founded in 1953, ISI teaches future leaders the core ideas behind the free market, the American Founding, and Western civilization that are rarely taught in the classroom.

ISI is a nonprofit, nonpartisan, tax-exempt educational organization. The Institute relies on the financial support of the general public—individuals, foundations, and corporations—and receives no funding or any other aid from any level of the government.

www.isi.org

About the Author

R odney Stark is the author of *How the West Won, The Victory of Reason, The Rise of Christianity, God's Battalions*, and many other books. He serves as Distinguished Professor of the Social Sciences at Baylor University, where he is codirector of the Institute for Studies of Religion.

A Pulitzer Prize nominee, Stark has won three Distinguished Book Awards from the Society for the Scientific Study of Religion. He also served as president of that organization, and of the Association for the Sociology of Religion. His scholarship has so reshaped the social scientific study of religion that his work is widely acknowledged as the basis of a "new paradigm."

Before earning his PhD at the University of California, Berkeley, Stark was a staff writer for several major publications. Visit the author online at www.rodneystark.com.